Confessions
of a
Cineplex
Heckler

JOE QUEENAN

Confessions of a Cineplex Heckler

Celluloid
Tirades and
Escapades

HYPERION
New York

To Thomas Donahue

The essays in this book have previously appeared in *Movieline* magazine, with the exception of "It's All Greek to Me," "Big Wigs," "Toy Story," and "The Mirror Has Two Faces, One Worse Than the Other," which appeared in *The Guardian*; "Matinee Idle," which appeared in *GQ*; "That's Entertainment," which appeared in *The Washington Post*; and "Model Roles," which appeared in *Allure*.

Library of Congress Cataloging-in-Publication Data

Queenan, Joe.
    Confessions of a cineplex heckler / Joe Queenan.—1st ed.
      p. cm.
    1. Motion pictures—Humor. I. Title.
  ISBN 0-7868-8464-9
  PN1994.9.Q44   1999
  791.43'02'07—dc21   98-34695
                                      CIP

FIRST EDITION

10 9 8 7 6 5 4 3 2

The author offers profuse thanks to Virginia Campbell, Ed Margulies, Heidi Parker, and Ben Olins; heartfelt thanks to Marty Beiser, Kathy Rich, and Jodie Allen; genuine thanks to Josh Mooney, Tom Lantos, and Wolf Schneider; copious thanks to Jennifer Barth; and generic, but nonetheless sincere, thanks to Joe Vallely.

CONTENTS

INTRODUCTION

About five years ago, I founded the Antonio Banderas Research Institute, a nonprofit organization dedicated to scientifically determining if and when the swarthy Spaniard was ever going to become a bona fide movie star. I had set up the organization because I was sick and tired of hearing about how Banderas was going to be *the next big thing*, even though each vehicle that was supposed to make him a star turned out to be a bigger flop than the one before. Despite all those glossy magazine covers, despite all the gossip about his liaison with Melanie Griffith, despite all the hype, the buzz, the shilling, the blather, the public wasn't biting.

In order to scientifically determine precisely how great a distance separated Banderas from genuine stardom, I ventured into Times Square one blustery winter morning armed with a fistful of magazines emblazoned with the actor's face, and then asked ordinary people if they knew who the man was. (Naturally, I had covered over his name.) The results were deeply discouraging.

One person thought Banderas was Julio Iglesias. A couple of others exhumed the name "Fernando Lamas." One guy said the man looked a lot like a young Ricardo Montalban, another the young Engelbert Humperdinck. But not one person knew that the person adorning all those magazine covers was Antonio Banderas, anointed by the press as *the next big thing*. Not one. And even when I told my test subjects who Banderas was, and mentioned the films he had been in (*Philadelphia, Interview with the Vampire, The Mambo Kings*), very few of them could remember ever having heard his name before. Including people who had seen those films.

I mention this incident because of a seminal experience I had as a small boy. One day, our fourth grade teacher, who will here be referred to as Sister Regina Vulcan, summoned each of us to the front of the class and asked what we would like to be when we grew up. "A policeman," said many of the boys; "a nun," said many of the girls. Baseball players, jet pilots, mommies, and ballerinas were all well-represented in this informal poll. But when it came my turn to reveal my career objective, I sputtered, "I want to grow up to be the kind of person who goes into Times Square asking complete strangers if they can tell me the name of the swarthy Spanish actor depicted on the cover of seemingly every glossy magazine in America."

Sister Regina slugged me hard and she slugged me often, then wrote a strongly worded note to my parents encouraging them to break my arms until I'd learned that the correct response to her query was: "I want to be a policeman, a fireman, or a soldier of Christ." My parents were happy to oblige. But it was I who was to have the last laugh. It was I who was to grow up and earn my living by going into Times Square and asking complete strangers if they could tell me the name of the swarthy Spanish actor depicted on the cover of seemingly every glossy magazine in America. It was I who was to earn my living by trying to roll down two flights of stairs in a wheelchair the way Mel Gibson does in *Conspiracy Theory*. And it was I who was to earn my living by pretending to be blind and trying to walk across a crowded street in front of a fleet of taxis without getting hit the way Al Pacino does in *Scent of a Woman*.

Today, you hold in your hands the work of a starry-eyed young boy who refused to give up his dream of one day founding the Antonio Banderas Research Institute, who refused to give up his dream of one day asking Spike Lee if he would like to make a movie about Sammy Davis Jr., who refused to give up his dream of one day masquerading as an angel sent to earth by Almighty God to give complete cash refunds to anyone unlucky enough to have sat through a Joe Pesci and Danny Glover movie about doomed, Jersey-based fishermen.

I am not saying that these were good dreams, worthwhile dreams, entertaining dreams, or lucrative dreams. All things considered, I would probably have been better off becoming a fireman, a policeman, or a soldier of Christ. But every society needs one person courageous enough to stand up and say: "I really don't think Antonio Banderas is the world's greatest actor, and I really can't remember the last time the American people clasped a swarthy Spaniard to their bosom and turned him into a superstar. So basically, I don't think it's going to happen. If you don't believe me, check out *The 13th Warrior*."

I am that courageous, starry-eyed boy. And this is my courageous, starry-eyed work.

DON'T TRY THIS AT HOME, PART II (1993)

Two years ago, *Movieline* published an extremely controversial article ("Don't Try This at Home") in which I proved that movies bore no resemblance to reality as we know it. Specifically, the article demonstrated, through a series of meticulous reenactments of famous scenes from motion pictures, that almost no scam, gambit, stratagem, scheme, trick, or ploy that worked in the movies could be reproduced in real life. Scrutinizing scenes as varied as the concealed latchkey incident in *Dial M for Murder* and the moment where Woody Allen orders a thousand grilled cheese sandwiches in *Bananas*, the article proved, without the shadow of a doubt, that pranks and ploys that work to perfection in the movies cannot be duplicated in real life. The conclusion of the study was that ordinary people should try to organize their lives around time-honored principles they have learned from their parents, the Bible, or valuable self-help books, but not try to run their lives by imitating the movies. This could only lead to heartbreak, sorrow, and even madness.

The response to the article was overwhelming; the magazine

was literally deluged with mail from readers all over the planet. Numerous individuals expressed their gratitude that someone had actually gone out and proven—*scientifically*—that it was not possible to masquerade as a corporate raider and get a hooker to attend a formal dinner with a chief executive whose company you were planning to take over, and therefore the entire premise of *Pretty Woman* went right out the window. Others were relieved that someone had taken the time to prove that women cannot successfully fake orgasms in crowded restaurants the way Meg Ryan did in *When Harry Met Sally* . . . because real men can spot fake orgasms a mile away. Still others were pleased to have in their possession irrefutable scientific evidence that a layman suffering from severe amnesia could not land a job as the director of a famous psychiatric institution (where he would occasionally be called upon to practice brain surgery) without at least coming in first for a face-to-face interview, thus proving that the maverick hiring techniques immortalized in Alfred Hitchcock's *Spellbound* are a complete joke that bear no relation to reality.

For the most part, *Movieline* readers were thrilled with the data presented in "Don't Try This at Home," and edified that someone would have the time, motivation, energy, and money to sally forth and put various cinematic assumptions to the test. Nevertheless, a small but vocal minority found the article to be juvenile, methodologically suspect, and even stupid. One reader wondered why I had not attempted to canoe down a river in rural Georgia to see if it was possible to negotiate this arduous trek without getting sodomized by dysfunctional mountain men. Another thought I should have attempted to recreate the scene from *Butch Cassidy and the Sundance Kid* where Robert Redford and Paul Newman leap several hundred feet into a roaring torrent of water without suffering any lesions, cuts, contusions, or even bumps. Perhaps the most memorable response came from a man doing five years in a Massachusetts prison, who wrote, "If only I had read your article before robbing that bank I would have known that crimes that work in the movies won't work in real life."

Speaking personally, I was enormously gratified at the extraordinary response to the article I had written at such vast personal risk to life and limb. But one question that perplexed me after the article was published was whether the powers that be in the movie industry would respond to my research in any way. Now that the public realized that movies were a huge joke that propagated a fatally skewed, hopelessly unrealistic image of ordinary life, would Hollywood producers take steps to improve their products, to make sure that films more accurately reflected life as we know it? Or would they simply dismiss my findings as the addled ramblings of a disgruntled asshole?

To answer this question, I decided to go back out into the streets and update my experiment. Once again, I would select a handful of memorable scenes from recognizable and/or *important* movies and attempt to determine whether the incidents depicted could be reproduced in real life. But this time, instead of choosing scenes from movies spanning the past forty years, I would limit myself almost exclusively to films that had been released in the past couple of years—films that most movie lovers would have either seen or read about somewhere along the line. The results appear below.

White Men Can't Jump. Ron Shelton's highly entertaining 1992 release starts with an extremely suspect scene in which a pasty-faced Caucasian played by Woody Harrelson sidles onto a blacks-only basketball court at Venice Beach, and succeeds in humiliating a talented black playground legend played by Wesley Snipes. From the moment I saw this film, I had my doubts about this premise. Neither Woody Harrelson nor the Billy Hoyle character he plays looks sufficiently fast, muscular, or talented to sidle onto a blacks-only basketball court and humiliate a playground legend. Neither do I. I too am a pasty-faced Caucasian short on speed, talent, muscles, and guts, and although I play basketball twice a week, I never play very well and I never play against playground legends. Thus, I seemed like the perfect candidate to step into Woody's shoes and find out how plausible the opening scene from *White Men Can't Jump* actually is.

I showed up about 7 o'clock on a torrid summer evening at a basketball court located at Sixth Avenue and Houston Street in lower Manhattan. I immediately approached the tallest, blackest, most athletic man on the court and said, "I've got sixty-two dollars that says you can't beat me." (Sixty-two dollars is the amount that Woody Harrelson won from Wesley Snipes in the movie.) The expression on the young man's face suggested that it had been quite some time since any pasty-faced white person with a baseball cap twisted backwards around his skull had used this unconventional approach. But he was more than game, happy to have an opportunity to win the $62. We agreed to play a one-on-one game to seven points, with airballs and steals going straight up, but anything off the backboard or rim going back to the charity stripe. He shot a long jumper to see who would take the ball out first; he missed and I inbounded. I pumped twice, getting him to leave his feet, and shot an airball directly into the fence behind the backboard. I checked up and handed him the ball; he hit a no-rim jumper from 18 feet, then a no-rim jumper from 15 feet; then he blew past me for two reverse layups: 4–0.

"Bend your knees and guard him," said a paunchy black man from the side, but I ignored him. I had last bent my knees when Gerald Ford was in office. The third time my opponent drove to the basket I partially blocked his shot, causing him to miss his layup—though not by much—and I hurried back to the foul line, from which I promptly launched another airball. He inbounded and blew past me for two more layups. Point game. Then he got too cocky. The last two times he'd scored, I'd noticed that he would first bang the ball off the backboard, catch it in the air, and then lay it home. So this time, as he tried to go past me at 220 mph, I drifted back, waited till he released the ball, and blocked it off the board. It flew over to the far side, where I grabbed it, retreated to the foul line, lined up an easy 15-footer, and drilled it home.

"Nobody beats me seven-zip," I sneered as I prepared to drive to the hoop. I missed a jumper, he rebounded and whipped past me for another easy reverse, winning the game 7–1. Incidentally, the entire contest could not have taken more than two minutes and ten seconds, 2:17 at the outside.

Purists may complain that my study was rigged because I am about fifteen years older than Woody Harrelson, and because the character he plays in the movie is supposed to have played college ball. Also Wesley Snipes is short. To these criticisms, I say: Bullshit. The average white person watching *White Men Can't Jump* is going to see a somewhat clumsy-looking white guy about 6 feet tall who is not especially fleet of foot putting a whipping on a fast, talented, muscular black man *on his own court*. The entire point of my article was to warn white men who look like Woody Harrelson not to go out and try to beat muscular black men on their own court unless they are prepared to lose $62.

All white men look like Woody Harrelson.

I should point out two things: that when I handed the victor a pile of fives, tens, and singles that I thought totaled $62, he counted them, found that I had overpaid and said, "Hey, man, you gave me fourteen dollars too much." This illustrated something I have always suspected about this wonderful sport: that basketball is an essentially chivalrous activity, with its own iron-clad code of behavior, where nobody tries to cheat anybody else. The second thing I learned on the court was about talking trash. At no point during our *mano a mano* confrontation did I ever say anything like, "Your momma's so fat she fell over and broke a leg and gravy poured out" or "Your momma's so old she used to drive chariots to high school." If I'd said anything like that, I suspect my opponent would have really kicked my ass.

Body of Evidence. Hey, I like sadomasochism as much as the next person, but they should have cleared this flick with the Consumer Product Safety Commission before releasing it. As the four people who saw it during its theatrical run will recall, Willem Dafoe plays a well-meaning lawyer who's a bit slow on the uptake, and Madonna, in a piece of truly inspired casting, plays a kinky slut. (What will they think of next? Brad Pitt as a good-looking young guy? Melanie Griffith as a moron?) About halfway through the film, Madonna pinions Dafoe's arms behind his back, then lovingly drips scalding candle wax all over his chest, then douses the wax with champagne, and then licks it off. Dafoe reacts to her offbeat ministrations by whimpering mildly, perhaps wincing slightly as the wax is applied. But he doesn't do anything terrifically visceral or emotional, like, say, screaming bloody murder and begging her to stop.

Let me tell you a few things about candle wax. Candle wax burns like hell. Candle wax doesn't feel good when it's applied to any part of the human body. Candle wax *hurts*. I know, because I used to accidentally drop the stuff on my forearms and fingers when I was an altar boy, and because I spent about fifteen minutes this morning trying to reenact the candle wax session from *Body of Evidence*. My wife, who is constitutionally opposed to any sexual practices utilized in films by Madonna, Mickey Rourke, or Marlon Brando, begged off on the experiment, so I had to do the whole thing myself. First I dripped candle wax on my chest. Then, unlike Willem Dafoe, I screamed. I even tried to wait five seconds, just like Madonna does, before spilling the champagne onto the wax, but there was just no way. Candle wax, spilled onto the human chest, burns like hell. What's more, it dries quickly, so unless Madonna was using some special, upscale, slow-reacting, professional S&M wax she bought from one of her deviant entrepreneurial friends, I can't see any way she could get the champagne onto the wax without having it cake, making it difficult to lick or suck, even if you have an extraordinarily versatile tongue like Madonna's.

Let me tell you another thing. In *Body of Evidence*, Madonna drips candle wax onto Dafoe three separate times, and the third time, the viewer gets the idea that she's dripping it directly onto his cock. Dafoe winces. *Winces—like he already has calluses on his cock or something.* This is the one part of the experiment I deliberately chose not to reenact. I already knew how much the candle wax burned on my chest. I didn't need to try it on my favorite organ. This is where my experiment with *Body of Evidence* parts company with my experiences in *White Men Can't Jump.* If you are an ordinary white person and you try to go out on a black basketball player's home court and challenge him to a game, you're probably going to come away with a few bruises and a damaged ego. Try doing to yourself what Madonna does to Willem Dafoe in *Body of Evidence* and you can just put that cock of yours in the deep freeze for the next six weeks. That's why I cannot emphasize too emphatically: *Don't try this at home.*

Howards End. You'll recall that this Merchant-Ivory extravaganza achieves its powerful *denouement* when the dorky, self-effacing Leonard Bast staggers into a massive bookcase and suffers a heart attack after the bookcase comes tumbling down upon him. The huge bookcase is novelist E. M. Forster's none-too-subtle symbol for the overly educated British upper class, a bunch of snooty toffs who literally crush the lower classes beneath them with what Bob Dylan once referred to as their "pointless and useless knowledge." (Actually, Dylan was probably not talking about the British upper class at the time.)

Well, the bookcase may be a great symbol for the insensitivity of the British aristocracy, but as an engine of destruction it fails miserably. Annoyed by the absurd finale to *Howards End*, I spent several weeks visiting friends' homes and running headlong into their bookcases, trying to see if the collapsing structures could possibly kill a full-grown man. *No way, José.* It is aerodynamically impossible for a bookcase loaded with heavy objects to collapse onto a human being, and even if the bookcase did collapse, the human being would have plenty of time to get out of the way of the literary cascade. Leonard Bast's contrived demise is an embarrassment to E. M. Forster, an embarrassment to Ismail Merchant and James Ivory, and an embarrassment to that Indian woman with the long name who writes all their screenplays. They should have used an axe, a truncheon, or even a deadly asp. Bookcases do not kill.

Sliver. Remember the scene where Sharon Stone goes to a restaurant in Manhattan and takes off her panties during lunch to impress her date? I went to three different lunches in midtown Manhattan with three different female friends, had three different nice conversations, ordered the angel hair pasta with arugula, then asked them to take off their panties. Two refused outright, and one said she'd do it, but only at her apartment. *Now, what's the point of that, I ask?* Generally speaking, I'd say the odds of getting a woman to take off her panties in a crowded New York restaurant are about the same as getting a woman to fake an orgasm in a crowded New York diner.

On the other hand, the request would probably be gladly met in Los Angeles.

Alive. Hey, what's the big deal about eating human flesh, anyway? You're stranded in the Andes, you haven't had anything to eat for four days, you're cold, you're hungry, and you're probably going to die. And you honestly expect me to believe that you're going to have qualms of conscience about eating human flesh, just because your friends back home might hold it against you? Hey, get real.

To illustrate how ridiculous this whole premise is, I decided to go on a strict fast and see how long it would take me to succumb to the lure of human flesh. I didn't even make it through Day II. After suffering through an entire day without so much as a breadstick, I got to about four o'clock in the afternoon and decided that I'd had it. Luckily, I'd been playing basketball that afternoon and had scraped my knee on the concrete, so I had a little bit of flesh hanging off my knee. Before it had a chance to scab up, I cut off a little morsel with my nail clipper and popped it straight into my mouth. It went down nice and smooth. That was sixteen days ago, and I still have no qualms of conscience about it. Morally, I think I'm home free. I did what I had to do, and I know that if I'm ever trapped in the Andes—or any other mountain range—and there's nothing to eat but human flesh, I'm noshing anthropoid.

Sophists will object that eating your own flesh is different from eating other people's flesh, and that it's different from eating the flesh of dead humans. Baloney. The day I nibbled that morsel off my knee I would have been more than happy to eat another person's flesh. The problem was, there wasn't any available. If there had been, I would have washed it right down with a sassy San Pellegrino. As for qualms of conscience about eating dead human flesh; hey, get serious. A person who eats his own flesh simply to make a point in a magazine article isn't going to draw the line at eating dead human flesh to save his own life just because society deems such dining tendencies culinarily and ethically unacceptable. He's going to strap on the feed bag and dig right in. Cannibalism is only bad if you think it's bad.

Contes des Quatre Saisons. After the first installment of "Don't Try This at Home" appeared in 1991, *Movieline* was flooded with letters from European readers complaining that none of the films we investigated were of Continental origin. Determined not to make the same mistake twice, I rented the 1989 Eric Rohmer film *Conte de printemps (A Tale of Springtime)*, which was released in video in this country in 1993, and took copious notes. As is true of all Eric Rohmer movies, it is not immediately clear to the viewer what this movie is about; it seems to have something to do with a woman who doesn't like her boyfriend's apartment but can't move back into her own because she's sublet it to her actress cousin, who is visiting from Bordeaux, so she has to spend a few days with a ditzy, twentyish pianist she met at a party where neither of them actually liked the host. In short, it is not the French *Basic Instinct*.

Rohmer has always been praised for the incisive realism of his films, for his ability to portray life as it really and truly is. There is a scene in the film where the main character, a schoolteacher, sits down at a table with the pianist, the pianist's father, and the pianist's father's sexy girlfriend, who is all of twenty-five, and begins to discuss the influence of Immanuel Kant's *a posteriori* arguments on the schoolchildren she teaches in a working-class district of Paris. Throughout this ten-minute scene, which cleverly weaves together the theories of Kant and Husserl with the vastly overlooked importance of maieutic dialogue, the conversation never flags, as both the pianist's dad and his hot little girlfriend are literally mesmerized by the subject, and jump right into the discussion with their own thoughts on syllogisms, maieutic dialogue, and the validity of *a priori* arguments.

To see if this will work in real life, I had dinner with three of my most pretentious friends, all of whom have spent time in France, all of whom, I have reason to believe, adore Eric Rohmer. While they scanned the menu, I broached the subject of Kant's *a priori* and *a posteriori* arguments, pointed out how much I had been influenced by Kant's *Critique of Pure Reason*, and even threw in a few nice words about his *Prolegomena to Any Future Metaphysics*. I then sort of threw the floor open for a roundtable discussion.

They all looked at me like I was a complete asshole and went back to discussing how much they used to like the *New Yorker* before Tina Brown took over.

Indecent Proposal. It is no secret that Adrian Lyne's latest movie is flawed by an imbecilic premise: the fatuous notion that Woody Harrelson, having been offered $1 million to let his wife sleep with Robert Redford, would need more than eight nanoseconds to decide whether or not to let her do it. When I approached four of my friends about sleeping with their wives for $1 million, they responded:

1. $1 million was more than fair.

2. When could I do it?

3. Check or cash?

4. Did I need their American Banking Association routing number for direct deposit, or would the Insured Money Market Account number be sufficient?

I want to be perfectly honest here and admit that none of my friends' wives look like Demi Moore and thus none of them are worth $1 million for a single night. What's more, my friends know this. So eventually we got into a bit of dickering. One friend said that he wouldn't go any lower than $350,000 because that's how much he would need to buy a new house, which he reckoned was what he needed to salve his conscience for the awesome injustice he had done. But two other friends said in all seriousness that $10,000 would do the trick, and one told me, "Thirty-five hundred, and she's yours."

Here is another sampling of my friends' responses:

1. "Does *she* have to know about the money?"

2. "Can we do this off the books?"

3. "Will *Movieline* actually pay for this?"

4. "How do you report this kind of stuff on your 1040?"

5. "How much would *your* wife go for?"

The last question is the most pertinent of all, revealing how profoundly Adrian Lyne's depraved vision of marriage deviates from my own. For although my cash-strapped friends might be willing to whore out their wives for a few grand, this is anything but the case in my nest of conjugal bliss. My wife is not available for sex with lecherous strangers for $1 million, my wife is not available for sex with libidinous plutocrats for $2 million, my wife is not available for sex with a lascivious oligarch for all the gold in Fort Knox or for all the tea in China.

Me, on the other hand, you can have for fifty bucks, motel room included.

Scent of a Woman. Most of the movies that I investigated for this article proved to be hopelessly out of touch with reality, encouraging behavior that could lead to personal humiliation, catastrophic financial loss, or severe lesions on the penis. *Scent of a Woman* was the single exception, the single case in which an apparently idiotic action that takes place in the movie can actually be recreated in real life. The incident in question is the scene where the blind Al Pacino strolls directly into traffic on a busy New York street and somehow manages not to be run over. When I first saw this scene, I was appalled by its transparent falsity, by its refusal to depict New York the way it really is: a place where a blind man walking out into the street doesn't have a prayer in hell of getting to the other side, even if the light is green, even if he looks like Ray Charles.

Well, it just goes to show how wrong a person can be. Kitting myself out with sunglasses and a cane, and boldly strolling into traffic on a very busy, two-way street in Manhattan, I fully expected to be hurled fifty feet in the air by a rampaging, out-of-control taxi driven by somebody named Singh or Mahmud. Either that or leveled by an oncoming limousine carrying some burned-out rock star to a cable TV appearance far too late to stir the flickering embers in the dying hearth of his career.

Imagine my surprise when I repeatedly strode into traffic and was repeatedly given safe passage by the oncoming flotillas of vehicles. Not once, not twice, but three times I managed to walk back and forth across the street without being killed. Indeed, the only reason I did not continue the experiment until I was fatally injured was the two beat police officers standing on the corner eyeing me suspiciously. Imagine being arrested for impersonating Al Pacino. Well, that's still better than being arrested for impersonating Al Yankovic.

Conclusions: Despite the surprising finale to my study, which I believe should be written off as a fluke, the overwhelming evidence suggests that people who attempt to imitate the activities they see in motion pictures are doomed to humiliation, remorse, severe burns, and even death. Conversely, people seeking to kill themselves or others through the fatal intermediary of a large bookcase are merely wasting their time, and are well-advised to stick to AK-47s or hat pins jammed into the eardrum. Two years after the industry was exposed as an utter sham in "Don't Try This at Home," the same abuses continue. Hollywood continues to be a twisted dream factory, spoon-feeding the public a hopelessly skewed, transparently fake vision of reality. *Movieline* readers are thus cautioned, once again, to take everything they see in the movie house with a grain of salt, and to religiously avoid imitating the activities of actors and actresses appearing in movies produced or directed by anyone named Joel. Another thing: This is the last time I'm going to warn you. Candle wax burns.

CONFESSIONS OF A CINEPLEX HECKLER

The poignant film has reached an impossibly anguished moment. Marooned high in the Andes Mountains, as winter curls its icy mantle around them, the two dozen famished survivors of the 1975 airplane crash come face to face with the most horrifying nutritional dilemma a human being will ever confront. Completely out of food, the shivering group of seemingly doomed young rugby players must decide whether to eat the frozen flesh of their fallen comrades—or starve to death. The audience sits transfixed, literally bolted to their seats, as the emaciated young men gaze directly into the yawning abyss of cannibalism. Then, just when it seems that neither the actors on the screen nor the audience in the theater can survive another moment of primal human horror, a voice rings out from the back of the theater:

"Eat Vincent Spano first."

It is a horrible comment to make, a tasteless comment, and, in some ways, a stupid comment, since the character played by Vincent Spano is still very much alive, and since the other characters are merely contemplating eating the carcasses of friends who have already died, not butchering a particularly unpleasant survivor and preparing him in a piquant fricassee. Several movie patrons turn to look at the disruptive, albeit good-looking, fortyish man in the darkest recesses of the theater, murmuring comments such as "Shhh!" and "Asshole!" Sensing their pique, yet also sensing their confusion as to why he would even dare to suggest that the characters begin munching on a character who is still breathing, the boorish man cries out: "Eat Vincent Spano first. He's the only one who really deserves to die."

The patrons turn back to the screen, weary of such gauche, unsolicited comments. For the past hour, the garrulous churl in the last row of the theater has been taunting the characters on the screen, making it all but impossible for the two dozen patrons to concentrate on the ponderous moral and philosophical issues posed by the film. Twenty minutes earlier, when one of the characters began chugging down a bottle of red Chilean wine, the kibbitzer had guffawed, "I guess we're eating red meat tonight!" When Ethan Hawke, very convincingly cast as a college-aged Uruguayan rugger player, had announced his decision to go and look for the missing tail of the ruined airplane, the heckler had giggled, "Whose tail?" In between these tasteless comments, the maddening jerk-off had regaled the hapless audience with such remarks as "It takes a tough man to eat a tender human" and "Could somebody please pass the A-1 sauce?"

Now, as the sensitive, life-affirming film races toward its conclusion, Hawke and two friends at last find the missing airplane tail containing the all-important radio. But they also stumble upon something else.

Three frozen corpses.

"Great," cackles the heckler from the eerie bowels of the cinema. "Dessert!"

Finally, a patron can stand it no longer.

"You got some fuckin' attitude on you," the man opines, revealing a heavy Spanish accent. As he speaks, his wife and two teenaged sons turn to catch a glimpse of the heckler.

"*I* got some fuckin' attitude?" the heckler fires back. "You take your family to see a movie about cannibal rugby players and *I* got some fuckin' attitude?"

The man turns back to the motion picture.

"You got some fuckin' attitude," he reiterates.

He is right. I do.

As the savvy, prescient reader will have suspected from the very outset, it was indeed I who was sitting in the last row of the Hawthorne, New York, ten-plex, making all those tasteless, insensitive comments about cannibalism, the meaning of life, Frank Perdue, and Vincent Spano that glum Thursday evening last February. But I was not being a complete asshole merely for the fun of being a complete asshole. Far from it. I was being a complete asshole for lofty, professional, journalistic reasons. I had been sent out to the cinemas in my greater metropolitan region by *Movieline* magazine to find out what it is like to stand in the shoes—and sit in the seat—of the talkative moron who always seems to be two rows behind you in the movie theater, making an endless series of idiotic comments about a movie that you're trying to concentrate on, a movie that you're trying to enjoy.

My purpose in tackling this assignment was twofold: one, to find out how far movie audiences would allow themselves to be pushed before they complained to the usher, confronted the heckler, or drew a switchblade; and two, to find out whether being a complete asshole is any fun.

I will supply the answer to the second question right away. Generally speaking, it is not a whole lot of fun being the asshole who always seems to be sitting two rows behind every movie viewer who is trying to enjoy himself at the pictures. Tormenting helpless human beings is not really my idea of entertainment; with one or two exceptions, I would never do it just for the hell of it. I'd have to get paid.

On the other hand, I would be lying if I didn't admit that there were certain moments during my ten-film odyssey through the world of the remorseless heckler that were absolutely sublime. It's always fun to taunt people who have premeditatedly paid good money to see Vincent Spano movies. It's always fun to holler out, "If you're paying a million dollars, you're overpaying" when Robert Redford writes a check for that sum in exchange for the right to sleep with Demi Moore, who looks like she should come a lot cheaper. Finally, it's always fun—exhilarating, breathtaking fun— to torment French people when they're trying to concentrate on a pretentious art-house movie like *The Lover*. What kind of red-blooded Yank *wouldn't* accept a job where he gets to torment French people? This *is* the kind of stuff I would do for free.

Over a three-month period, I made life miserable for viewers at ten widely divergent motion pictures. The films, accompanied by genre description, were:

Indian Summer	Nostalgic, Ontario-based horseshit
The Lover	High-class kiddie porn
The Dark Half	The usual Stephen King crap
El Mariachi	The finest $7,000 Tex-Mex film *ever* made
Falling Down	Racist bullshit
Husbands and Wives	Interiors III: First Blood
The Crying Game	Formulaic Irish Republican Army cross-dresser melodrama

Alive	Triumph-of-the-human-spirit crap
To Proxenio Tis Annas	Typical, rollicking Greek fun
Indecent Proposal	Fresh slime from Adrian Lyne

The venues for the films ranged from generic, suburban multiplex human abattoirs to snooty, midtown Manhattan art houses such as the *Paris,* to the lower depths of the Museum of Modern Art, where you can always find plenty of empty seats at the Emerging West African Directors Film Festival or "Cine-Mythology: A Retrospective of Greek Film."

The most important thing that I learned while mercilessly tormenting my fellow audience members at these ten movies is that by and large the public seems fully prepared to take a huge load of shit from annoying people like me. I roughly estimate that during my experiment I must have colossally pissed off approximately a thousand people, yet on only one occasion was I ever thrown out of the movie theater, and on only one other occasion was I physically confronted by an audience member and told to shut up or I could expect to get my teeth kicked in. This was the most valuable lesson that I learned, and by far the most important lesson that I have to impart to my long-suffering readers. Based on my journey to the bottom of the cineplex, it's safe to say that the average person takes way too much unnecessary abuse from hecklers when he goes to see a movie, and really has to toughen up his attitude if he ever expects to enjoy a motion picture in a serene, tasteful environment.

The basic problem lies in the movie-going public's excessive dependence on the word *Shhh!* I'm six feet tall, I weigh 180 pounds, I exercise regularly, and I'm widely perceived to be a bit of a prick*. Although I *am*, in reality, the sort of person who can be fucked with, I do not look like the kind of person who can be fucked with, and I neither look like nor am the kind of person who can be fucked with by people who look like *they* can be fucked with. So if you're a short, thin French tourist and you think that hissing the word *Shhh!* at me after I've screeched "Child molester!!!" at the thirty-two-year-old Chinese playboy who seduces the fetching little French schoolgirl in *The Lover* is going to get me to shut up, think again. Screw you, frog-face.

The word *Shhh!* is also a completely useless form of cinematic retribution against a person determined to munch his way through a big, boisterous bag of potato chips while everyone else in the theater is trying to enjoy a vastly underrated 1972 Greek film directed by Pantelis Voulgaris (the name literally means unsophisticated trousers in Greek). Yes, before attending a screening of Mr. Voulgaris's unforgettable film at the Roy and Nuita Titus Theater at the Museum of Modern Art back in May, I deliberately went out and bought the noisiest bag of potato chips I could find—the ones with the really crinkly plastic bag—and also went out of my way to sit behind the dorkiest, puniest, lamest, most pretentious *cinephile* in the auditorium. It didn't take me long to find him. My prey not only had thick glasses and a lumberjack shirt just like Woody Allen, but he also had a copy of the 5th-century-B.C. Greek tragedian Aeschylus's *Oresteia* trilogy sticking out of his back pocket.

"Dead meat," I said to myself as I sat down directly behind him. Then, as soon as the Athenian skyline came into view during the opening credits of *To Proxenio Tis Annas*, I began to pry open the potato chip bag in the most excruciatingly annoying manner possible.

---

*Since this article appeared in August 1993, the author has beefed up to about 200 pounds. He remains a bit of a prick.

"Shhh!" a short, comparably dorky man seated a few seats ahead of me hissed. To no avail.

Crunch! came the first grating sound of potato chip against molar.

"There's no eating in this theater," snapped a woman a few yards to my left.

"Yes, there is," I countered. "Listen."

Crunch, came another collision of chip and canine, as I tortuously, methodically began to work my way through the bag. Periodically, other people in the theater would hiss "Shhh" or "Be quiet!" to which I would reply, "But I'm hungry." All the while, I noticed that the man sitting in front of me had not reacted in any way at all. While people in other parts of the darkened theater would intermittently express their verbal displeasure with my nettlesome gnawing, my actual target had no reaction whatsoever. This really pissed me off, so I gradually began to hunch forward, munching on my chips just a few inches from his ears. Still no reaction. Finally, the man who had originally cried "Shhh" turned around and said, "Nobody can hear."

"The movie's in Greek, pal," I reminded him. "Potato chips can't interfere with subtitles."

I went back to eating my chips and kept eating them until the bag was done. People continuously "shhh'ed" me, but the man sitting in front of me never said a word. Disgusted, I stormed out of the theater. It revolted me, it shook me to the very core of my being, to discover that it was possible for one boorish middle-aged man armed only with a bag of potato chips to make life miserable for a roomful of perhaps three hundred people. It made me believe for the first time in my life that we as a people have really gone soft, and are prepared to be browbeaten and mistreated by thugs, bounders, counter-jumpers, ruffians, ne'er-do-wells, and caitiffs. A people who would rather suffer in silence while a complete asshole munches an entire bag of potato chips while they're trying to watch a movie like *To Proxenio Tis Annas* probably don't deserve to have any civil rights. Or maybe they deserve to watch a lot more movies like *To Proxenio Tis Annas*.

The most awesome feeling of power that I experienced during my experiment was the afternoon I went to see the moose-honoring bomb *Indian Summer* at a midtown Manhattan theater. There was only one other person in the audience, a middle-aged woman, and she was sitting a dozen rows ahead of me, so in order to get out of the tiny theater she would have had to run the gauntlet right past me, and from her body language I could tell that she thought I had a hacksaw or a machete on my person. Wishing to avoid a confrontation, and hellbent on watching this hideously foolish movie, she chose to gut it out for almost two hours as I blistered her ears with withering, satirical remarks about this lame-brained eighteenth remake of *The Big Chill*.

"This movie is the eighteenth remake of *The Big Chill*," I would cackle. She pretended not to hear.

"This movie is the seventeenth remake of *Peter's Friends*," I hooted. Again, she pretended not to notice.

"This movie is the nineteenth remake of the *Return of the Secaucus Seven*." She still ignored me.

"This movie is the nineteenth remake of the *Return of the Secaucus Seven*, and Vincent Spano fucked up that one, too."

She changed seats, moving to the other side of the theater.

"What, does Vincent Spano act better on that side of the theater, lady?"

This went on for about two hours. Finally, as the credits came up, she gathered up her coat and whipped past me.

"Don't you have anything better to do with your time on a beautiful spring afternoon than to watch Vincent Spano movies, lady?" I inquired.

She said nothing, but I could see from the look in her eyes that she didn't.

On the other hand, neither did I.

•   •   •

Several movies that I attended were heckler-proof properties. For example, despite my best efforts to annoy my fellow audience members by making politically incorrect remarks at a midnight screening of Joel Schumacher's loathesome *Falling Down,* everyone in the audience was busy making racist comments of their own, or belly-laughing at Michael Douglas's *Revenge of the Nerds III* eyeglasses. I had a similar experience throughout most of *Indecent Proposal,* when my remark, "Hey, you can have my wife for thirty-five hundred, and I'll take singles," actually elicited guffaws from other people in the theater. And they hadn't even seen my wife.

Another thing that surprised me about my experiences in all these movie houses was the general indifference of the ushers to my disruptive behavior. One afternoon, I accosted an usher half-way through Woody Allen's interminable *Husbands and Wives* and said in a voice that was loud enough to piss off just about everyone in the theater: "Can I have your written guarantee that this film actually ends? I mean, I'm a little bit concerned that this is going to be one of these Luis Buñuel-type jobs and I'm never going to get out of this theater."

His response was positively laconic.

"No, it ends," he assured me. "There's another show at three twenty."

"You're sure?" I asked. "You're sure this movie doesn't go on forever?"

"No, it ends around two fifty-five."

Amazingly, I was ejected from only one theater. I'd gone to a 2:00 P.M. showing of Robert Rodriguez' seven-thousand-dollar, award-winning, el cheapo *chef d'oeuvre El Mariachi* and was regaling the sparse audience with remarks such as, "Boy, is this a cheap-looking film!" and "Jesus, it looks like the studio only spent around seven thousand dollars to make this movie!"

Finally, an unattractive, fiftyish woman sitting next to an un-attractive seventyish man wearing a pitiful Greek fisherman's cap turned around.

"It's Robert Rodriguez."

I wasn't quite sure what she was driving at. I puzzled over this enigma for several moments. Then my vast network of neural fibers processed the information.

"Oh! Oh, I get it! It's Robert Rodriguez! So it's allowed to look cheap, right?"

She didn't turn back to answer my question.

"Who the fuck is Robert Rodriguez, anyway?" I then asked no one in particular. There was no answer forthcoming, but at that very moment, I spotted a fresh pigeon sitting about four seats to my left in the row directly behind me. He was a fortyish Japanese gentleman, and he had *Affluent Tourist* written all over him. Leaning across, I said, "Excuse me, sir, but you're a foreigner, aren't you?"

He sort of winced, nervously.

"Could you tell me: In your own society back in the mysterious Orient, would a film such as this be considered a high-quality cinematic offering with impeccable production values? Because it looks like a piece of shit to me. . . ."

I badgered him with a few more questions such as this, none of which elicited any response. Suddenly, two ushers appeared at my side.

"You have to be quiet," said the taller one. "If you can't be quiet, you have to go."

"I spent more on my ticket than they spent on this film," I replied. The usher didn't care. He'd had enough. He indicated that my patronage was no longer desired at the establishment where he worked. He also looked like somebody I didn't want to fuck with, so I didn't fuck with him.

I never figured out who it was who ratted on me—the guy in the fisherman's cap? The fat lady with the packet of Gauloises in her oversized Channel 13 tote bag?—but their bold actions did restore in me a measure of faith in the movie-going public. Nobody should have to sit there and take a shitload of abuse from some heckler while they're trying to watch a grainy, $7,000 Tex-Mex film that looks worse than that Barbra Streisand lookalike porn flick that's been floating around all these years. It's hard enough to watch a film like *El Mariachi* under the best of circumstances, without having to suffer through a bunch of wisecracks from some dickhead in the next-to-last row. So whoever it was who called the ushers had made the right decision. Contact the proper authorities. Throw the bum out on his ass. Then the grateful audience can get back to concentrating on a really, really *important* film.

My faith in audiences was also bolstered somewhat by my experiences at *Indecent Proposal*. As previously noted, the audience was initially quite amused by most of my loud, sarcastic remarks, in part because a lot of them were making loud, sarcastic remarks of their own, most of which had to do with Woody Harrelson's dick. But toward the end of the film, as my nonstop ranting continued, I began to detect a certain *frisson*. Finally, someone took action. My undoing occurred right after the unforgettable scene where Harrelson, who is supposed to be a brilliant but unemployed architect, shows a brick to the kids in his architecture class and tells them: "Even a brick wants to be something."

"IT WANTS TO BE WOODY HARRELSON!!!" I bellowed at the top of my lungs.

No sooner were the words out of my mouth than I could feel a large, dark presence making its way toward me.

"Shut the fuck up, motherfucker," the unhappy moviegoer urged me. "Shut the fuck up or I'll break your motherfucking face."

"Fine," I replied. Now, *that* was the kind of reaction that I'd been looking for. This was precisely the kind of direct democracy that had been so sorely lacking in most of my other moviegoing experiences. Nobody had bothered to get right up in my face and say, "Shut the fuck up!" when I'd hollered, "It's a guy!" at the opening of *The Crying Game*. Nobody had bothered to get in my face and say, "Shut the fuck up!" when I'd screamed, "It's all Greek me to me!" during a particularly poignant moment in *To Proxenio Tis Annas*. Nobody had dared to holler, "Shut the fuck up!" during *Indian Summer*, when Vincent Spano asks the elderly camp director what his teenaged secret Indian name was, and I'd bellowed, "Man Who Runs With the Assholes!" Nobody had bothered to say, "Shut the fuck up!" when I'd screeched, "That's a woman!" the first time Forest Whitaker appeared on the screen in *The Crying Game*. Nobody had bothered to say, "Shut the fuck up!" when I'd jeered, "You'd better marinate him first!" halfway through *Alive*. Nobody had hollered, "Shut the fuck up!" when I'd hissed, "Remember Pearl Harbor!" halfway through *Okoge*, a sensitive, life-affirming foreign film about an unorthodox young Japanese woman who lets two gay men screw each other in her apartment while she listens downstairs. Nobody at any of these pictures had ever told me to shut the fuck up. So I never shut the fuck up.

What can we learn from all this? Sadly, the lessons are not as transparent as they might seem. While it is true that I did shut the fuck up after being instructed to shut the fuck up during the waning moments of *Indecent Proposal*, it is highly doubtful that I would have shut the fuck up had the request not been made by a man about five inches taller, forty pounds heavier, and fifteen years younger than me. My decision to shut the fuck up was motivated at least as much by the vigor with which he presented his case as by the fact that he bore a great deal more resemblance to Woody Harrelson than to Robert Redford, though to be perfectly honest about it, he actually looked a lot more like Woody Strode than Woody Harrelson. Which is probably the real reason that I shut the fuck up.

The upshot? The bottom line? The whole enchilada? The naked truth? The truth is: I would probably not have shut the fuck up for just anybody. For instance, if you were a spindly, dorky, bespectacled Smurf carrying a copy of Aeschylus's *Greatest Hits* in your back pocket at the Museum of Modern Art, or anywhere else for that matter, it is extremely unlikely that I would have shut the fuck up had you asked me. Ditto the lady with the Channel

13 tote bag, the Japanese tourist at *El Mariachi,* or any French person this side of Jean-Claude Van Damme, who's Belgian, anyway. The horrible truth that I have learned from my experiences is that unless you are a twenty-five-year-old, muscular, six-foot-five male with a very rugged demeanor, preferably wearing a black baseball cap with a large *X* sewn onto it, there is very little you can do about the asshole sitting two rows behind you in the movie theater.

Of course, there are always machine guns.

BLARNEY STONED

Nobody goes to Ireland to make a western, a sci-fi fantasy, an Adam Sandler movie, or a film about teetotalers. In the entire history of motion pictures, an average of fewer than one film per year has been made about the Emerald Isle, and judging by the results, that seems to be more than enough.

In recent years, though, there has been an explosion of films set in Ireland or involving the Irish, including such big-budget affairs as *Far and Away* and such well-received smaller films as *The Commitments* and *The Snapper*. Even for a proud Irish American such as myself, whose grandparents hail from County Cork, this is a development that must be viewed with a certain amount of apprehension.

Let me explain.

Almost without exception, motion pictures about Ireland— whether they are set in the North, the South, the twentieth century, or the nineteenth century—fall into one of two categories. Either they are searing portrayals of the struggles of the Irish Republican Army against the brutal heirs of Oliver Cromwell, or they are charming films filled with mirth and wit about wee, lovable, canny Irishfolk.

The first group of films, which includes everything from *Odd Man Out*, *Cal*, and *In the Name of the Father* to *Patriot Games*, *The Crying Game*, *Blown Away*, and *A Prayer for the Dying*, all carry the same messages: we're a pretty nasty lot, but it's the Brits' fault. The second group of films, which includes everything from *Ryan's Daughter*, *The Quiet Man*, and *The Secret of Roan Inish* to *Circle of Friends*, *The Field*, and *Far and Away*, are, like I said, wee and canny and full of wit and wisdom. They are charming and knowing and wise and innocent. They are both sweet and bittersweet. Collectively and individually, they constitute one of the biggest loads of horseshit that ever came down the pike. They are twaddle. They are balderdash. They are malarkey.

They are blarney.

Let's get one thing straight. Personally, it would be all right with me if people went on making IRA-versus-the-Brits films until the cows came home. Even though every movie about the IRA basically has the same plot—serious revolutionaries eventually become as remorseless as the people they are revolting against—I've found that most films of this sort are up to a pretty high standard. With two notable exceptions—*The Informer* and *A Prayer for the Dying*—these films try to steer clear of the maudlin, cry-in-your-beer, Who'll-save-the-Old-Sod? tradition that is such a cornerstone of Celtic culture. But the wee, canny, charming films about the lovable Irish are another matter entirely.

In the following pages, I would like to discuss a number of Irish-themed films in an effort to determine which Mick movie constitutes the biggest load of blarney available at the video store today. In doing so, I am trying to register my own horror, as an Irish American, at the proliferation of motion pictures that attempt in some way to advance the notion that Irish people are secretly leprechauns. I am aware that I am also inadvertently performing a public service for many of my Irish-American friends by making it that much easier for them to pick out films most suited to their mawkish needs come March 17. Not all Irish Americans are philosophically opposed to blarney. The sad truth is, a lot of my Irish-American friends secretly think they *are* leprechauns.

First, some history. Cinematic blarney of a high order first arose in the 1935 classic *The Informer*, which is basically an IRA-versus-the-Brits film, but instead of being gritty like other movies of the same genre, is a ghastly encyclopedia of Irish sentimentality. This is the film in which Victor McLaglen won an Academy Award by playing a cash-strapped simpleton who sells his best friend—an IRA gunman—down the river for twenty pounds, then attracts the attention of the entire Irish Republican Army by throwing a party for everyone in Dublin—pulling a sort of *GoodFellas Goes to Galway*. Based on a very fine novel by Liam O'Flaherty, the film is practically impossible to sit through today, largely because McLaglen is all too convincing as a complete idiot. With its weeping mothers, lugubrious wakes, flailing shillelaghs, boisterous pubs, drunken layabouts, ubiquitous crucifixes, gentle clerics, duplicitous Englishmen, angelic choirs, contrite stool pigeons, faithful sisters, lovable tarts, implacable IRA operatives, and piping pipes, *The Informer* is a masterpiece of celluloid blarney, a film that has towered over its competitors for more than half a century. And yes, the soundtrack does include a stirring rendition of the unofficial IRA anthem, "The Minstrel Boy." Faith and begorra, it's enough to make a grown man weep. I know. I wept.

The Informer concludes with a scene so replete with blarney that it has set the standard by which all subsequent Irish films must be judged. The mortally wounded McLaglen staggers into the church to beg his best friend's mother to forgive him. Being Catholic, she does. Why? Don't ask; it's a league rule. Overjoyed that Mrs. Flannery has absolved him of his heinous crime, McLaglen bellows: "Frankie, your mother forgives me!" Then he tumbles to the ground, slain by the IRA, in the shadow of a crucifix from which a bleary-eyed Christ looks on. You get the definite impression from the expression on Christ's face that this is not the first time He's seen one of these over-the-top performances. Though Judas, at least, held out for *thirty* pieces of silver.

For many, many years, *The Informer* reigned as the undisputed King of Blarney. In part, this is because not all that many films set in Ireland were made in the next thirty years. One of the few was *Odd Man Out,* a drama in which the leader of the Belfast branch of the IRA robs a bank as a bit of a fund-raiser for local women whose husbands are languishing in the calaboose. When the heist goes awry, James Mason inadvertently kills a bank guard, but is wounded so badly that he falls out of the getaway car, whereupon, in vintage Celtic style, his three accomplices start arguing about who's responsible for leaving him behind. Mason spends the rest of the film marooned on the wrong side (is there such a thing as a right side?) of Belfast. Yet, despite the presence of the faithful girlfriend, the loyal adjutant, the hated Brits, and the implacable IRA, *Odd Man Out* is curiously devoid of blarney. It is, in fact, one of the least blarney-laden films ever made.

In the fifties and sixties, the only serious challenger for sheer acreage of malarkey was *The Quiet Man*, which has more than its share of clerics, pubs, pipes, and canny locals. Many young Irish people of my acquaintance have singled out this film as an example of "paddywhackery"—an earnest attempt to portray the Irish as lovable nitwits—but because it is basically about John Wayne, an American who is playing an American, the potential for blarney is vastly diminished. I don't mean to suggest that *The Quiet Man* is not a huge load of crap. It was, after all, made by the same guy who made *The Informer*, John Ford. I am only saying that if *The Informer* registers a solid 9.9 on the Shamrock Scale, *The Quiet Man* is but a respectable 8.5.

For the next thirty years or so, movies made about the Irish were either overtly silly or merely strange. Disney honored the Emerald Isle twice—in *The Fighting Prince of Donegal*, a 1966 lightweight swashbuckler, and *Darby O'Gill and the Little People*, a piece of leprechaun-ridden fluff that was produced back in 1959. Both were aggressively charming films filled with wee, canny folk, but because of their essentially frivolous nature—they were Disney flicks—neither picture could seriously contend for the title of King of Blarney.

In 1970, David Lean made his own valentine to the land of his forebears. This epic tale (originally 206 minutes, but later cut to 176 after an appeal by the Vatican for mercy) of a schoolteacher's wife who enters into a doomed relationship with a British soldier is one of the flattest, least affecting movies ever made. Clearly designed to be a "big film," *Ryan's Daughter* is hamstrung by a meandering plot and a spectacularly miscast Robert Mitchum, who plays the cuckolded schoolteacher. (N.B.: A cuckold is someone whose wife sleeps with another man who is not himself a cuckold. As a general rule of thumb, an actor who used to make movies with Jane Russell cannot be effectively cast as a cuckold.) Though it comes with the full complement of wise old clerics, lovable village idiots, and canny locals, *Ryan's Daughter* never seriously emerged as a threat to *The Informer*'s position as the biggest load of Gaelic gibberish ever made. One big failing: It didn't have nearly enough pipes.

After *Ryan's Daughter* came and went, it looked like *The Informer* would reign as the Sultan of Celtic Schmaltz until the end of the millennium. But in the past ten years, *The Informer*'s stranglehold on the scepter of blarney has been seriously challenged on numerous occasions. First came *A Prayer for the Dying*, the Mickey Rourke vehicle about a penitent IRA gunman who decides on an immediate career change after he watches an IRA attack in which a bomb intended for the hated Brits blows up a bunch of Irish school kids instead. Sporting a brogue as thick as the mists wafting in from the Irish Sea, Mickey, not technically Irish, is the only actor in history who has ever given the oversized McLaglen a serious run for his money as the Bey of Blarney.

People familiar with my work will note that this is not the first time I have written about *A Prayer for the Dying*. First I featured it in a story focusing on ridiculous accents. Then I dissected it in a story in which I impersonated Mickey Rourke for a day. Then

I eviscerated it in a story about blind people. Then I included it in a story highlighting lovable psychopaths. And now I am examining it here. Cynical readers might be tempted to say that I am merely recycling my old material—that I have become a lazy old hack. This is terribly shortsighted. The reason I have written about *A Prayer for the Dying* so often is that, from the dyspeptic critic's point of view, it is the most useful film ever made. No matter what your subject, this is the movie you can always fall back on to get you out of a tight spot. It has bad accents, blind teenagers, lovable terrorists, overwrought crucifixion imagery, blustery priests, convivial whores, and Mickey Rourke. It is the one-size-fits-all bad movie. I love this movie more than life itself.

The next load of pure malarkey to challenge *The Informer* was the 1990 film *The Field*. A genuine Curse-of-the-Chieftains affair, this film *starts* with the pipes—the pipes, which, needless to say, are calling—then quickly gets worse. Richard Harris plays Bull ("The Bull") McCabe, an ornery farmer who is determined to buy a field he has been renting for many years from a local widow. Because the rented field was nothing but rock when he started working it, Harris feels that in a certain Paddy O' Mythical sense it belongs to him now. Alas, this is not the way the Hibernian real estate system works. The widow decides to put the field up for sale, whereupon Tom Berenger appears, an Ugly American who wants to buy the field, pave it over, and develop it. Talk about ethnic stereotyping.

Harris handles this situation in the traditional way, by killing Berenger, but when a wise local priest points the finger at him for the unsolved murder, he decides to throw a huge temper tantrum and drive all his cattle off a cliff, killing his son in the process. With its knowing clerics, love of the land, canny locals, village idiots, the pipes—the pipes that are constantly calling from glen to glen and down the mountainside—and lines such as, "You could do worse than lie with the tinker's daughter under the stars," *The Field* is a major work of blarney, and deserves to be honored as such. In fact, in Ireland itself the film is known as *Sean de Florette*. And yes, it is true that you could do worse than lie with the tinker's daughter. You could lie with the tinker's daughter and have to watch this film at the same time.

Despite its many charms, *The Field* cannot really hold a candle to the 1994 film *A Man of No Importance*. In this wee, charming affair, Albert Finney plays a lovable ticket taker on a Dublin bus who recites poetry to his passengers every morning. Surprisingly, they do not tear him limb from limb. The ticket taker, a bit of a swish, wants to stage Oscar Wilde's heathen play *Salome* at the local church—and hence the film is notable for being the first major Celtic coming-out picture. Towards the end of the movie, Finney, who has never actually been intimate with another man, gets dressed up like Oscar Wilde and visits a gay bar, where he is beaten and robbed by a bunch of gay, young Irish hustlers, which is what usually happens to senior citizens who get dressed up like Oscar Wilde, and not just in Dublin. He then tries to drown himself in about 18 inches of water, a scene lifted directly from *The Music Lovers*, which also deals with a tormented gay aesthete. However, in that film, the music was supplied by Tchaikovsky rather than the Chieftains.

What is this wee little motion picture trying to tell us? It is telling us that Finney is a rebel, a maverick, a man who goes his own way, a will-o'-the-wisp, and in a very real sense, a complete knucklehead. Indeed, the only thing that prevents the film from being one of the biggest loads of blarney of all time is that it has no pipes. For the life of me I can't figure out how they left *them* out.

The Secret of Roan Inish does have pipes. And it's got flutes. It's got drums. It's got superstition. It's got wee, canny locals running all over the place. And yes, like most of its predecessors, it has a village idiot. A charming tale of a wee tyke who makes a deal with a pack of seals to restore her kidnapped brother to his real family, *The Secret of Roan Inish* rates very high on the Blarney-o-meter. Malarkey of a very high quality is also evident in *Circle of Friends* (Catholic girls, abortion, the pipes, the pipes), *Into the West*,

The Snapper, *My Left Foot*, and *The Commitments* (also known as "Motown Go Bragh"). But in recent years, the biggest threats to *The Informer* have emerged from an utterly unexpected locale. Not as unexpected as Iraq, say, but still surprising. I'm talking about the good old U.S.A.

Yes, full-blown Blarney explodes into the mean streets of New York in the 1990 film *State of Grace*. With its opening shots of the pipes and drums at New York's Saint Patrick's Day parade, this saga of Irish thugs gradually surrendering their beloved Hell's Kitchen turf to Little Italy's encroaching, utterly charmless mafiosi, pushes most of the bragh-o-buttons. Particularly symbolic is the scene where Gary Oldman does one of his trademark meltdowns and finds himself in a local church, where he tries to stick a beer bottle into a statue's hands. With tons of good material about saloons, religion, angels, Mom, brothers-in-arms, cops, the old neighborhood, brawls, and what an incredible prick Dad was, not to mention a shootout that takes place on St. Paddy's Day, *State of Grace* pulsates with blarney of a truly spectacular nature. And doesn't Sean Penn speak for an awful lot of Irish-American criminals when he explains his lifestyle by saying, "We drink. We shoot people."? Yup, that about covers it.

On a parenthetical note, *State of Grace* includes an annoying subplot about Italian gangsters who don't think the Irish are showing them enough respect. Guys, guys, could we lighten up on this respect thing?

Thank you for your time.

Blarney goes to Beantown in the 1994 film *Blown Away*, where Jeff Bridges plays a Boston bomb expert who had innocently gotten involved with the IRA as a youth, something that is not that easy to do. Now, back home in Boston many years later, he has to match wits with the mad bomber mentor of his college days, a sadistic lunatic played with demonic glee by the ubiquitous Tommy Lee Jones, fast becoming the Yank Gerard Depardieu (*If I ain't in the picture, the picture don't get made*). With its daunting brogues, Gaelic subtitles, Beantown bars, characters named Liam, and the pipes, the pipes, *Blown Away* has an amazingly high quotient of blatherful blarney. A tip of the old Tam o' Shanter to all those involved.

I don't mean to harp on this, but I would like to point out that *Blown Away*, whose first scenes are set in Ireland, opens with a camera shot coming in over a body of water; that *Far and Away* opens with a camera shot coming in over the water; that *The Secret of Roan Inish* opens with a camera shot coming in over the water; and that *Ryan's Daughter* opens with a camera shot coming in over the water. I know that Ireland is an island, so I understand the logic here, but, seriously, the next time someone makes a movie about the Irish, couldn't they ask the cameraman to try something a little different?

Thank you for your time.

Students of blarney who have borne with me this far must naturally be assuming that I plan to wrap up this article by anointing either *Finian's Rainbow* or *Far and Away* as the biggest crock of Celtic crapola ever. Sadly, I must disappoint them. *Finian's Rainbow* is a 1968 motion picture about a leprechaun cavorting in the rural South. I don't want to talk about it. As for Ron Howard's 1992 miscue, yes, *Far and Away* is a hypnotically bad movie, covering all the bases with the pipes, the pipes, duplicitous brothers, canny locals, a redheaded vixen named Shannon, brawling boxers, craven landlords, courageous immigrants, the Chieftains, and more famine than you could shake the same old shillegah my father brought from Ireland at. Nevertheless, it is fatally flawed by the hopeless miscasting of Tom Cruise, who simply doesn't have his Celtic chops down right. Alternately cocky and just plain stupid, Cruise turns what could have been *A Few Good Irishmen* into a *Top o' the Mornin' Gun*, and does not even come close to matching the epic blarnifulness of Victor McLaglen.

But Ed Burns does. Yes, the surprise winner of the Golden Blarney Award is Ed Burns's small, charming, canny film *The Brothers McMullen*. Seeing that Burns claimed to have made the movie for about $37,500—yes, there's a bit of blarney in those numbers—*The Brothers McMullen* is a film laden with ethnic flap-doodle of such a bathetically radiant quality that St. Patrick must be turning in his grave. In what we assume was a calculated attempt to surpass *The Informer* for pure tonnage of Hibernian hooey, Burns seems to have made an exhaustive checklist of every cliché about people of Irish descent and then jammed everything on the list into his film and down his audience's throat.

Consider the evidence. The film opens with a funeral scene (classic blarney), then features a conversation where the main character's mother says she is going back to Ireland to marry the man she should have married thirty-five years earlier, having spent the past three and a half decades living with a drunken bum who beat his sons. In other words, in the very first minute of the film, Burns assaults his audience with blarney blasts of truly thermo-nuclear dimensions.

And it just keeps getting better. You want pipes? You got pipes. You want long-winded conversations about the Church's stand on abortion? You got long-winded conversations about the Church's stand on abortion. You want seductive, hot-blooded ethnics trying to seduce good Irish boys? Use of Catholicism as an excuse for every adult personality dysfunction? A soundtrack by a guy named Seamus? A loving mother? Guilt, guilt, guilt? You got 'em in spades. Well, clover. Not a single character in *The Brothers Mc-Mullen* can toast a piece of bread, turn on a light switch, or go to the bathroom without putting on a Notre Dame Fighting Irish sweatshirt and grabbing another bottle of Guinness. Watching this movie for almost two hours is like having the entire St. Patrick's Day Parade rumble through your medulla oblongata. Well, maybe not those Irish lesbians.

And so, when all is said and done, there can be no doubt that the biggest load of blarney of all time is Ed Burns's tale of mopey, self-pitying Irish-American losers out in some dump on Long Island. The one-stop shopping center for every bit of crap ever written or said about the Irish, *The Brothers McMullen* beats *The Informer* hands down.

In a way, it is sad that such a distinction should go to an American rather than by someone from the Old Sod, but in a sense this is what every Irish immigrant came here to achieve. Ireland is a wonderful country, a lovely country, a country filled with wee, canny folks with a touch of the poet in their hearts. But if you really want to be in the horseshit business, you have to go to Hollywood.

Note: Since this article appeared in 1996, Hollywood has released several fine Irish films, including The Devil's Own, *a pipe-laden affair in which Brad Pitt plays an absolutely peachy IRA assassin. Though Pitt is not wee, he is quite amazingly canny. The film was shot in Irvington, New York, two miles down the road from the town where I live. I could not be prouder.*

LEND ME YOUR EARS

In the opening sequence of 1994's blockbuster *Speed*, mad bomber Dennis Hopper forcefully inserts a small knife in the eardrum of a security guard who has confronted him in the basement of a skyscraper in downtown Los Angeles. In doing so, Hopper became, as far as I can determine, the first major star in the history of motion pictures to appear in *two* motion pictures in which he severs, mutilates, pierces, or otherwise inflicts irreparable damage on another human being's acoustical apparatus, having already chopped off a man's ear in *Blue Velvet*. Although it is in some ways disheartening that the man who once embodied the counter-cultural ethos in renegade films such as *Easy Rider* and *The Last Movie* now plies his trade by mutilating other actors' auditory equipment in mainstream summer films such as *Speed*, it should not come as a huge surprise to the viewing public that Hopper should be the man singled out by the industry as the first recidivist ear mutilator in the rich history of the art form. If somebody has to be a serial ear brutalizer, Dennis Hopper seems like the right man for the job.

The ear-piercing incident in *Speed*, following so closely upon the scene in which a hired gun blows a hole through Gary Busey's ear in *The Firm*, and preceding by scant months the scene where Woody Harrelson blows off part of Robert Downey Jr.'s ear in *Natural Born Killers*, is a watershed moment in the history of cinema, signifying that auscultatory trauma has now become a staple in motion pictures made in this country. In recent years, ears have been severed in films as varied as *Blue Velvet*, *Reservoir Dogs*, *The Last Temptation of Christ*, and *Vincent & Theo*, and ears have been bitten or gnawed upon in *The Godfather Part III* and *A Perfect World*. But none of these films was a huge hit like *The Firm* or *Speed*. *Godfather III* and *A Perfect World* were commercial disappointments at the box office; *Reservoir Dogs*, *Blue Velvet*, and *Vincent & Theo* are cult classics that have garnered far more fame than dollars; and *Last Temptation* was a modest hit, nothing more.

Now, however, with the awesome success of *Speed*, whose very first violent act involves the brutalization of the human ear, and *The Firm*, we may well have entered into a new era of cinema— the Ear era—where tympanic trauma will be accepted by the general public as an appropriate, and perhaps even desirable, component of the moviegoing experience. In years to come, ear-piercing, ear-chopping, ear-slicing, ear-filleting, ear-microwaving, and ear-masticating incidents may become so popular that they will replace head butts and kicks to the genitals as the single most popular cliché in the lexicon of popular cinema. Of course, as is often the case with my theories, I could be wrong about this.

The purpose of this essay is fourfold:

1. To discuss the history of auricular atrocity in motion pictures and pay homage to trailblazers in the idiom;

2. To draw attention to the different types of ear mutilation in

motion pictures and stress the diverse cinematic objectives for which the savagery is utilized;

3. To draw a crucial distinction between films in which acoustic abuse is a peripheral, secondary element and those films in which the mistreatment of the human ear becomes a centrifugal force so powerful that no one can talk about the movie without mentioning "the ear scene."

4. To discuss the emerging role of children as ear mutilators in American cinema and speculate whether biting another actor's ear at an early age is a good career move.

First, a bit of history. From the time movies were invented until David Lynch hooked up with Dennis Hopper, ears did not play much of a role in the cinema. Actors used them to hear with, and that was about it. Occasionally, somebody might get yanked around by an ear lobe, or have his or her ears affectionately nibbled on, but for the most part ears, like ulnas and femurs, were left pretty much alone. The single, shining exception to this was Vincente Minnelli's *Lust for Life*, the much-admired, albeit atrocious, 1956 film in which Kirk Douglas, playing the tortured Dutch painter Vincent Van Gogh, chops off his ear after an argument with Anthony Quinn, playing Paul Gauguin. This ponderous load of crap, bloated with every cliché about artists ever concocted, features the predictably dim-witted Douglas as a Dutch doofus who spends the entire film smoking a pipe and dashing around forearms akimbo, looking for all the world like Van Gogh the Sailor Man. The decision to chop off his ear is precipitated by a huge argument with Quinn about the role of emotion in painting, though there is abundant evidence—Douglas's clutching the sides of his head just before he performs the auto-atrocity—that he has in fact been driven to this act of supreme desperation in the foolish hope of escaping from the soaring violin strains of Miklos Rozsa's unbearable score. (Neither Van Gogh nor Douglas is smart enough to figure out that since he still has another ear—a spare, if you will—this tactic will not work.)

Actually, trouble has been brewing between Gauguin and Van Gogh ever since Quinn first showed up at Douglas's rural French house and started complaining about Van Gogh's cooking and housekeeping. In this sense, *Lust for Life* can be viewed as a Post-Impressionist *Odd Couple*, with Paul Gauguin/Anthony Quinn playing the role of the meticulous Felix Unger while Vincent Van Gogh/Kirk Douglas plays the part of the slovenly Oscar Madison. Now that I think of it, both the *Odd Couple* movie and the *Odd Couple* TV series, good as they were, would have been a whole lot more enjoyable had either Walter Matthau or Jack Klugman chopped off his ear and walked around the apartment with a bandage wrapped around his head. Though in the best of all possible worlds, *both* of Jack Lemmon's and Tony Randall's ears would have come off.

Although *Lust for Life* earns innumerable cultural brownie points for being the first major motion picture to feature a severed ear in a prominent thematic position, it is not a very satisfactory mutilation scene, particularly when compared with subsequent ear slashings, such as those in *The Last Temptation of Christ* or *Reservoir Dogs*. For one, we do not actually see the ear get chopped off with the straight razor; Douglas performs the home surgery off camera, and even after the ear has come off, we see only its reflection in the mirror. More disturbing still, one never gets a very clear sense of precisely why Van Gogh was driven to this horrifying act of self-transmogrification, rather than taking things out on someone else. Did he think he was punishing Gauguin by chopping off his own ear? Was he cutting off his ear to spite Gauguin's face? Why didn't he simply chop off Gauguin's ear? Or Gauguin's nose? Another thing: If investors in the late eighties were willing to pay as much as $50 million for a bunch of sunflowers painted by a man most famous for cutting off his own ear, think how much that same painting would be worth if he'd cut off his dick.

Let us leave "Starry, Starry Nightmare" now and examine the subsequent history of cinematic auricular trauma. From 1956 until 1986, the human ear, as a focal point of dramatic action, vanished from the silver screen. Why? Your guess is as good as mine, but good taste certainly cannot be the explanation. For whatever the reason, detached ears did not take center stage in motion pictures again until 1986, when David Lynch released his cult creep classic *Blue Velvet*. The movie opens with placid, reassuring images of Middle American suburban life: attentive crossing guards, friendly firemen, happy schoolchildren, white picket fences, a man having a heart attack. But then a shadow falls across the screen as preppy Kyle MacLachlan, back from college to visit his ailing dad (the guy who had the heart attack), stumbles upon a hairy, moldy, insect-infested ear in the woods. Gingerly inserting it in a plain brown paper bag, Eagle Scout Kyle transports it to the police station where the chief of detectives tells him: "Yes, that's a human ear, all right."

This is where *Blue Velvet* parts company with *Lust for Life*. In *Lust for Life*, the audience knows all along that the ear-chopping scene is coming sooner or later, because we all know that the real-life Vincent Van Gogh did actually chop off his ear. But after the ear has come off, the moviemaker drops the whole unsavory subject; he doesn't try to play it for laughs. Not so in *Blue Velvet*, where the bodyless ear becomes a powerful element in the movie.

"What can you tell about a person from their ear?" MacLachlan asks the town coroner. "Are you the one who found the ear?" Laura Dern subsequently asks the Kylemeister in one of the great pick-up lines of all time. And when the coroner tells MacLachlan, "We'll check the morgue records, but I don't recall anything coming in minus an ear. The person may still very well be alive somewhere," it signals to the audience that something very troubling is taking place here. Surely, the coroner is suggesting, anyone unlucky enough to have had his ear cut off, or anyone unlucky enough to have a loved one whose ear had been cut off, would immediately report it to the police. This isn't the sort of injury—say, a boil, or herpes—that one simply ignores.

In *Blue Velvet*, the severed ear also functions on a metaphorical level when we are introduced to Isabella Rossellini, a mysterious lounge lizardess whose husband has been abducted—and his ear lopped off—by the sex maniac Dennis Hopper. Here, the detached ear is important for two very different reasons. One: After listening to Isabella's brutal rendition of the Bobby Vinton classic "Blue Velvet" during her nightclub act, it becomes apparent to the audience that she will never be able to raise any serious ransom money if she has to depend on her voice. Two: Only a person who was missing at least one ear could possibly derive any pleasure from listening to her singing.

Ears also play an important role in *Blue Velvet*, because without them Kyle MacLachlan would not be able to make any sense out of the dream Laura Dern describes to him after he asks why there is so much evil in the world. Turning archly Hegelian, she replies:

> In the dream, there was our world. And the world was dark because there weren't any robins. And the robins represented love. And so along this time there was just this darkness, and all of a sudden thousands of robins were set free, and they flew down and brought this blinding light of love. And it seemed like that love would be the only thing that would make any difference. And it did. So I guess it means there is trouble till the robins come.

Laura, as usual, is a *big* help.

From *Blue Velvet*, we naturally segue into Martin Scorsese's *The Last Temptation of Christ*. Why? Because *Blue Velvet* is a movie about a small town with big problems where somebody gets his ear cut off, and it also contains a scene where a likable young man (MacLachlan) is kissed on the lips by a creepy guy he would prefer not to be kissed by (Hopper), just as *The Last Temptation of Christ* is a movie about a small town with big problems where somebody gets his ear cut off, and it contains a scene where a likable young man (Willem Dafoe) is kissed on the lips by a creepy guy he would prefer not to be kissed by (Harvey Keitel).

But first, some indispensable biblical background. There are four different versions of Christ's arrest on the Mount of Olives on Holy Thursday (Matthew, Mark, Luke, and John), but only St. Luke's version of the Gospel describes the scene where Christ miraculously reattaches the right ear of the high priest's servant after St. Peter has chopped it off. Perhaps because the ear-cutting scene did not go over so well in *Lust for Life*, or perhaps because they were basing their screenplays on the Gospels written by the other Evangelists, neither Nicholas Ray in his 1961 *King of Kings* nor George Stevens in his 1965 *The Greatest Story Ever Told* include the ear-healing scene. (In Stevens's defense, a director forced to cast John Wayne as the Roman centurion at the foot of the cross, intoning the words, "Surely, this was the son of God," is already trying the audience's patience enough without confusing the issue by introducing audial anguish.)

The Last Temptation of Christ is another story entirely. Clearly the ear-lopping incident was far too wonderful an opportunity for the Roman Catholic Mob-flick Director Marty Scorsese to pass up. Actually, Scorsese's ear-chopping scene is relatively tasteful, considering what immediately precedes it: Harvey Keitel, cast as a red-haired Judas with a Bensonhurst accent, kissing Willem Dafoe (Jesus of Nazareth) full on the lips. After witnessing a scene as unsavory as that—Jesus seems plenty surprised by the kiss—it's hardly surprising that one of Christ's disciples should whip out his knife and hack off the ear of the High Priest's hapless servant. Interestingly, the disciple uses a nifty uppercut to lop the ear off, creating the impression that this may not be the first time he's done this sort of thing. The ear fragment comes off cleanly, bloodlessly, and tumbles to the ground, where Christ, who also seems to be used to this sort of mayhem, picks it up, reattaches it, and then goes on his merry way being taken into custody and crucified. Inexcusably, the man with the restored ear doesn't even thank Jesus. One other thing: Unlike the revolting, hairy ear in *Blue Velvet*, the ear fragment that Dafoe retrieves from the ground in *Last Temptation* looks incredibly cheesy. I mean: Where's the blood? Where's the gore? What were you saving it for: Joe Pesci in *GoodFellas*, Marty?

This might be a good opportunity to say a few words about Scorsese's overall mutilative technique. The first time I saw *The Last Temptation of Christ* I was very impressed by the low-key way in which Scorsese handled this incident, which, in the hands of a lesser director—say Oliver Stone—could have been pretty nauseating, and which, in the hands of a lesser director, Quentin Tarantino, *was* pretty nauseating. Then I had second thoughts. There's something very unsettling about a movie where somebody gets his ear cut off and nobody thinks it's that big a deal. Say what you want about *Reservoir Dogs*, but when Michael Madsen lops off the cop's ear, the victim at least reacts as if something pretty horrible has just happened to him.

Contrast this with the decidedly muted reaction to the auricular butchery in *Last Temptation*. The disciple whips out his knife, lops off the ear, and the victim sort of groans, but he doesn't descend into the kind of full-fledged hysteria we see in *Reservoir Dogs*, and he doesn't even get as upset as Joe Mantegna seems to be in *The Godfather Part III*, when he merely has his ear *bitten*. All in all, I think Scorsese should be censured for pussyfooting around in this scene, and if he ever gets to do one of those restored director's cuts like Francis Ford Coppola or Sam Peckinpah or Kevin Costner, I hope he'll add in some footage he must have lying around somewhere of the victim going completely fucking ballistic. Let's face it: If you got your ear sliced off on the Mount of Olives while you were arresting a man who claimed to be the King of the Jews, I think you'd make a pretty big stink about it. God knows, I would.

I don't want to make too much of this whole ear-lopping business, but I must admit that it's always been the one thing that prevents me from accepting St. Luke's account of the events that transpired on Holy Thursday as Gospel truth. What really rings false is the reaction of the Roman soldiers after Christ has reattached the ear. Put yourself in their situation: If you were sent out in the middle of the night to arrest a man who was supposedly the Son of God, and one of his confederates chopped off one of your confederates' ears, and then the man widely thought to be an itinerant divinity miraculously reattached it, don't you think you'd find yourself saying something like, "Correct me if I'm wrong, but didn't this guy just surgically reattach Maximus Minimus's ear without the benefit of any known medical technology? And if so, don't you think it's a little bit risky to try bringing this guy in, armed only with short daggers, tiny spears, and these fey little tunics?"

Similarly, right after Christ is taken into custody, he is interrogated by a rather poncey Pontius Pilate played by David Bowie, who gets a bit flip with Him. Bowie, sporting what appears to be a first-century A.D. Beatles moptop, treats Christ dismissively, remarking, "It's also said that you do miracles. Is this good magic or bad magic? Could we have some kind of . . . eh . . . demonstration? I mean, could you do a trick for me now?"

By this point, if I'm Jesus Christ, I'm probably going to find myself saying, "Look, asshole, I'm the guy who just reattached a human ear that had been lopped off somebody's head, and you're a two-bit Roman bureaucrat who's been banished to a dead-end job in Judea. Do you really think I'm the sort of person you should be fucking with?"

But, of course, I am not Jesus Christ, so I'll have to let the issue drop and move on to Andy Garcia.

Garcia is our next subject of interest because of the unsettling scene in *The Godfather Part III* where he takes a huge bite out of his arch-rival Joe Mantegna's ear. Mantegna, it will be recalled by the three of us who saw the picture, plays a mobster who has inherited most of Michael Corleone's empire after Al Pacino decides to go legit. Unwisely, he turns up at Pacino's house the day the Don is being awarded a very prestigious medal by the Catholic Church in recognition of the $100 million he has donated to a fund that will succor the poor, aid starving artists, and contribute to the economic revival of Sicily. Mantegna tries to get on Pacino's good side by presenting him with a plaque from a prefab organization called the Meucci Foundation, named after an Italian who purportedly invented the telephone the year before Alexander Graham Bell claimed to have done so. Pacino says he never heard of the guy. The telephone, bear in mind, is a device that involves the use of the human ear. *Symbolism and foreshadowing. Symbolism and foreshadowing.*

The formalities concluded, Mantegna now explains to Pacino that he has been having trouble with a cheap punk who claims to be related to Pacino. The punk in question is one Vincent Mancini (Andy Garcia), the illegitimate son of Sonny Corleone (James Caan), who was killed off in the original *Godfather*. Pacino tells Garcia to join him and Mantegna in his study for a genial chit-chat. Garcia arrives, improperly attired in a leather jacket, glances at Mantegna, and grabs his nuts.

Trouble is a-brewing.

Garcia now tells Pacino that Mantegna has been running around behind his back saying things like "Fuck Michael Corleone." Pacino asks Mantegna if this is true, noting that anyone who would say such a thing is "a dog." Mantegna concurs with the Don's forceful logic, remarking, "Yes, it's true. If anyone who would say such a thing, they would not be a friend. They would be a dog." Pacino ignores Mantegna's deplorable grammar and accepts this explanation, telling his illegitimate nephew to make his peace with his superior. Mantegna and Garcia embrace, but then Mantegna goes one step too far and whispers something in Italian while giving the chastened Garcia an affectionate but condescending chuck on the ear. The next thing you know, Garcia has his teeth firmly planted in Mantegna's external acoustic equipment, in a seemingly ferocious attempt to bite it off.

This scene is important for two reasons. One: It establishes in the minds of the audience that Garcia is a sadistic brute unfit for human company, and thus will almost certainly end up in bed with Bridget Fonda later that same day. Two: More important, the bite on the ear seems to affect Mantegna's ability to act for the rest of the movie. Let us recall that the ear is the center of equilibrium in the human body, and once it has been damaged, however slightly, even a talented actor like Joe Mantegna will find himself muffing his lines. By the time Mantegna, now decked out with an ear patch, makes his farewell speech at the Convention of Tutti Capi in Atlantic City, where he vainly attempts to assassinate Pacino, his acting is so much out of the Rod Steiger on a Bad Day School of Dramatic Art that he can no longer deliver his lines with any trace of credibility, and really must be killed.

At this point, I'd like to clear up a confusing issue about the 1978 film *Midnight Express*. When I first conceived the idea for this story, I told all my friends that I would welcome any tips about movies in which aurally related mishaps occurred. No less than three friends advised me to rent Alan Parker's sordid tale of savagery in a Turkish prison, assuring me that there was a memorable scene where the house rat fink has his ear ripped off by Brad Davis. In fact, I had already seen this all-purpose slimefest at least three times, and seemed to recall that scene myself. Dutifully, I rented the film once again and fast-forwarded to the relevant scene. Alas, the reigning mythology about the film is completely untrue. Just as horror movie buffs always say they can recall the sight of Janet Leigh's red blood vanishing down the bathtub drain in *Psycho* even though the film was shot in black and white, people insist that Brad Davis physically rips off another character's ear in *Midnight Express*. This is not the case. Davis does gouge the rat-fink's eyes, smash his face into a set of stone steps, and rip his tongue out with his own teeth, bringing his performance to a triumphant conclusion by spewing the tongue into the air. But at no point does Davis attempt to rip off the man's ear.

Understandably, many cinephiles have deluded themselves into thinking that a movie scripted by Oliver Stone would almost certainly contain a scene where a human ear is torn off, but in this case their memories deceive them. The fact that three of my friends inaccurately recalled such a scene lends credence to the theory that Oliver Stone is the victim of a vast conspiracy on the part of the media, the ratings board, and even the general public to make him appear to be a far more depraved sadist than he actually is. Or at least it did until Stone made *Natural Born Killers*, where somebody actually does get his ear mutilated.

Although *Godfather III* was not a huge commercial hit, it was probably the largest-grossing film in history to feature a scene where a human ear is mistreated. With this repugnant scene in *Godfather III*, ears finally entered the mainstream of cinema and became an acceptable focal point of dramatic tension. The same year that *Godfather III* came out, Robert Altman released *Vincent & Theo*, yet another look at the life of the doomed, uni-eared Van Gogh, which, like *The Last Temptation of Christ* and *Blue Velvet*, features a scene where one man (Van Gogh) surprises another (Gauguin) by kissing him just before an ear gets hacked off. Two years later, testing the waters a bit further, Quentin Tarantino made his odious *Reservoir Dogs*, which contains the most graphic auricular violence in the history of motion pictures. Ears were here to stay. Though they were probably not going to stay put.

The central theme of *Reservoir Dogs* is the concept of honor among thieves: the belief that even cold-blooded murderers recognize that there are bounds of good taste beyond which even they dare not venture. Harvey Keitel adumbrates this theme when he draws the crucial distinction between ordinary murderers such as himself and psychopaths such as Michael Madsen.

"A psychopath ain't a professional," fumes Keitel after a botched heist turns into a bloodbath because of Madsen's itchy trigger finger. "You can't work with a psychopath. You don't know what those sick assholes are gonna do next."

These lines, it should be emphasized, are uttered *before* Madsen carves off a hostage cop's ear with a straight razor while dancing to "Stuck in the Middle with You," *before* he asks the cop, "Was that as good for you as it was for me?"; *before* he whispers into the severed ear, "Hey, what's going on?"; and *before* he douses the cop with kerosene. For the record, I would just like to say that I cannot remember where I was when Robert Kennedy and Martin Luther King were shot, but I can perfectly recall where I was when I first saw *Reservoir Dogs*. I was at home, sitting in my favorite armchair, poised in front of the television set, wondering what kind of sick fuck makes pictures like *Reservoir Dogs*.

Despite the failure of *Reservoir Dogs* to set the world on fire commercially, other moviemakers have shown no disinclination to integrate auscultatory depravity into their work. In 1993 alone, John Woo had one henchman scissor the earlobe off another in the Jean-Claude Van Damme masterpiece *Hard Target*, while Gary Busey lost stereo in *The Firm*. And only time will tell whether playing the role of a somewhat cuddly kidnap victim who takes a huge bite out of a psychopath's ear in *A Perfect World*, also released in 1993, will lead to a big career for eight-year-old T. J. Lowther; many moviegoers probably wish that the kid's role had been played by Macaulay Culkin, and that it was the murderous jailbird who got to take a bite out of *his* ear. But the fact that two major motion pictures depicting graphic acoustical trauma have already appeared in 1994 strongly suggests that audial savagery is here to stay. *Speed*, in which Dennis Hopper cheerfully jams a knife into a man's ear, and *Natural Born Killers*, where Robert Downey Jr. goes monaural, leave no doubt that auricular mayhem has assumed its rightful place in the *patois* of contemporary filmmaking, suggesting that in the months and years to come we can look forward to many more films in which actors get their ears mutilated. In a sense, there is a poetic justice in all this: Actors have been sticking it in *our* ears for years, so now let's all sit back and enjoy them getting it stuck in theirs.

Or is a remark like that a lobe blow?

Note: Since this prophetic article appeared, ears have continued to go flying left, right, and center, though never with the panache exhibited in Reservoir Dogs *or the metaphorical evocativeness of* Blue Velvet. *Whatever that means.*

TRENCH MOUTH

Hollywood denizens sometimes write memoirs to even old scores, but Lynda Obst's *Hello, He Lied—and Other Truths from the Hollywood Trenches* (Broadway Books, $13, 272 pp.) is the first autobiography I have ever come across whose primary purpose seems to be to kiss old asses. Officially a female producer's heartwarming account of her rise to stardom, the book is actually a clever attempt to stay on the good side of the powers that be by an outrageous public display of servility. Here is Obst, whose wildly uneven producing career ranges from *The Fisher King* and *Sleepless in Seattle* to *Bad Girls*, *Heartbreak Hotel*, and *This Is My Life*, sucking up to—for the lack of a better phrase—David Geffen:

Those players who float many levels above the fray—the Ovitzes, the Geffens, the Murdochs, the Eisners, the Spielbergs—set the field. David Geffen does this brilliantly. For a time—from 1984 to 1986—I watched a master set the field at close range. As head of development for the Geffen Film

Company, I had the extraordinary opportunity to learn at David's feet. Not content to read the field as it is, David is formidable enough to blow certain opponents off the field preemptively with a gruff bluff or shrewd strategy, or even by his mere presence. David is holographic, his advantages multidimensional. He is holding more or better information than his adversary and he is fearless—having owned his own soul all of his career. He is preternaturally instinctive and he is charming: a combination designed to accomplish virtually any objective. He is our Lola in that we have seen over the course of a public, vastly successful career spanning decades that what David wants, David gets.

Homage as electrifyingly fulsome as this is hard to come by these days, so anyone who wants to move to Hollywood and become a full-time bootlicker would do well to read this tidy little volume from cover to cover. (This includes people who would like to come back to Hollywood after crossing Geffen—like, say, a once-powerful superagent.) And would-be memoir writers would also do themselves a big favor by using *Hello, He Lied* as their template. Though still quite young to be casting a backward glance at her career, Obst has proved herself a prodigy of pap, leaving no film industry cliché untapped, no Tinseltown banality unuttered. It is hard to believe that a person so young could already be such a boring old fart. Think of her as a short, distaff Otto Preminger.

Consider the evidence. First, the constant interspersion of Zen wisdom with quotations from people like Barry Diller, a time-honored L.A. literary standby. Next, the hackneyed, utterly idiotic use of military imagery (yes, like 10,000 other Hollywood savants, she actually cites *The Art of War*) to describe the movie industry. (Ever notice that historians never say things like "Napoleon versus Wellington conjures up images of Barry Diller versus Sumner Redstone"?) Most important of all, a ceaseless, pitiless barrage of Polonius-like platitudes and kernels of wisdom, invariably uttered with Copernican glee, as if Obst had just revealed the cure for Hodgkin's disease. Consider some examples:

"Sink or swim."

"Forewarned is forearmed."

"Don't float too high."

"Never go to a meeting without a strategy."

"Hindsight makes fools or geniuses of us all."

"Our job is to keep standing no matter how much force is applied to knock us down."

"Ride the horse in the direction it's going."

"Eat the reality sandwich."

A typhoon of obviousness cunningly meshed with bum-kissing of nigh on Ed McMahon-ian dimensions, all leavened with a gentle sheen of tried-and-true Tao Te Ching bullcrap, *Hello, He Lied* is a masterpiece of late-nineties twaddle. Perhaps the most revealing thing about the book is the subtitle: *and Other Truths from the Hollywood Trenches*. "Trenches" is a word generally used to describe filthy, rat-infested ditches in which men give their lives for something important. There is something endearingly barmy about its appropriation by the woman who brought us *One Fine Day*. It reinforces the conviction that people in Hollywood are not so much nasty as just incredibly *dumb*. As Obst might put it, citing one of her favorite Hindu sayings, "If you sit by the river long enough, the body of your enemy will float by." Yes, but if you sit by the river long enough, the body of the person who produced *Adventures in Babysitting* will also float by.

A COMPLETE LACK
OF DIRECTION

The night before the mega-dud *Last Action Hero* was officially released last summer, one of my best friends called the house around 10:30 P.M. and asked if I would like to attend a midnight preview of the film.

"Do I look like the kind of person who goes to Arnold Schwarzenegger movies?" I replied, somewhat piqued.

"It's a John McTiernan film," my friend corrected me. "His movies are pretty good. He made *Die Hard*."

Oh. Oh, now I understood. A John McTiernan movie. A *film* by John McTiernan. A cinematic project that utilizes the inexhaustible thespianic resources of a semi-literate Austrian weightlifter who's a bosom buddy of retired Nazi Kurt Waldheim to delineate the personal vision of one John McTiernan. Oh, now *that* was different.

My friend, who has a Master of Fine Arts degree from Johns Hopkins University, and who once studied with the famed film critic Mark Miller, is the only person of my acquaintance who has the faintest idea who John McTiernan is, much less knows that he directed *Last Action Hero*. Virtually everyone that I know—and virtually everyone that you know—is the sort of person who couldn't care less who directed the latest Arnold Schwarzenegger, Clint Eastwood, or Tom Cruise movie. Americans are intelligent, sophisticated people, who intuitively understand that the motion picture industry is a glorified form of manufacturing, not unlike the canning industry, where a bunch of interchangeable packagers with interchangeable skills compete to see who can produce the most serviceable, durable merchandise, and who can do it in the most timely, cost-effective fashion. The American people do not know or care who Ridley Scott or Adrian Lyne are, and they haven't the faintest idea which one of them directed *Indecent Proposal*. The American people also do not know or care whether it was Susan Sarandon playing Thelma or Geena Davis playing Louise. They have better things to do with their time than to keep movie trivia straight. They've got kids to raise, lawns to mow, guns to clean, wives to beat.

Or am I just imagining this? Hey, it's all well and good for me to sit here in the refined comfort of my quiet, suburban home and disparage the cinematic efforts of the Messrs. Scott, Lyne, and McTiernan and act like *anyone* could have directed *Last Action Hero* or *Flashdance*. But is my sneering contempt for most directors actually shared by the vast American public? And can that contempt or indifference be calibrated in an empirical, statistically meaningful way? Obviously, the average American does not care who directed the latest *Ernest* movie, nor does he care who directed *Ghoulies III*. But what about serious movies, like oh, I don't know—*Falling Down*? Think about it. If it is true that Americans only go to the picture show to see movie stars they enjoy, or to see the latest installments in series that they have come to love and trust (*Aliens*, *Star Wars*, *Nightmare on Elm Street*), and couldn't care less who directed the most recent episodes, then why do studios insist on taking out big, splashy advertisements that read

DAVE: AN IVAN REITMAN FILM

or

A MARIO VAN PEEBLES FILM

POSSE

Surely, the studios do not pay for such advertisements merely to stroke the egos of directors, merely to make them believe that someone, somewhere, actually cares who directed the latest Kevin Kline movie or gives a hoot who was behind the camera when the latest sociopathic Boyz-in-the-*Zeitgeist* film was being midwifed into existence by some surly film-school putz in a tight-fitting baseball cap. Surely they pay for these extravagant, attention-getting directorial kudos because it helps to sell tickets, because it helps to create product loyalty, because all across America, tired, hard-working people come home every night and say, "Hey, toots, how about loading the kids into the Voyager and checking out that new John Singleton movie?" or "Look, honey, drop everything and let's go see what John McTiernan's been up to lately. You know, John McTiernan? The guy who directed *Die Hard* . . ."

To establish once and for all whether the average filmgoer knows or cares who directed a movie, I spent four days standing outside theaters in New York City asking people pointed questions as they emerged. I attempted, in as scientific a fashion as was humanly possible, to construct my sample in a demographically meaningful fashion, including substantial numbers of teenagers, Hispanics, blacks, and senior citizens, while avoiding foreigners, the apparently homeless, obvious scum-sucking pigs, people who looked like movie critics, and morons. Generally speaking, I asked the first ten plausible-looking people coming out of the theater if they could tell me the name of the man or woman who had directed the film they had just seen. Occasionally, when I elicited particularly unexpected responses, I would expand my sample to as many as twenty-five, just to make sure I had not stumbled upon some sort of demographic Bermuda Triangle that would unfairly skew the results and make people like John Mc-Tiernan (who directed *Die Hard*) seem even less important than they actually are.

For the sake of methodological equilibrium, statistical relevance, and overall journalistic fairness, I narrowed my research to directors with a certain reputation and stature in Hollywood. Thus, I did not ask anyone who had directed *Dennis the Menace* or *Life with Mikey*. I did not want to turn my study into a complete joke.

Instead, I confined my study to major films by major directors (Sidney Lumet, Sydney Pollack, Steven Spielberg), major films by individuals who would like to be thought of as major directors (Nora Ephron, Renny Harlin, Neil Jordan, Adrian Lyne, John McTiernan, Ivan Reitman, Mario Van Peebles), and, of course, films by James Ivory. Then, as a sort of control, I threw into the mix a trio of highly praised foreign films (*Orlando, The Story of Qiu Ju, Un coeur en hiver*) whose aficionados would be familiar with the *auteur* theory, and thus would be more likely to know the identity of the director of this or that film. Finally, I included a movie by a pair of up-and-coming directors (the Hughes brothers) who were taking Hollywood by storm with their new film *Menace II Society*, getting written up almost daily in the *New York Times* and other important publications.

The results of my study are presented herewith.

Last Action Hero by John McTiernan. I spent an hour outside the Loew's Orpheum Theatre VII at Third Avenue and Eighty-sixth Street in Manhattan the Monday after the film opened, and asked the first ten people coming out if they knew who had directed the movie. Not one knew or cared. One man volunteered, "Renny Harlin," then said, "I work in this business and I don't know who directed it. I own six movie theaters. But nobody knows who directs these things."

Actually Renny Harlin, who directed *Die Hard 2*, was a pretty good guess, since John McTiernan, who directed *Last Action Hero*, had directed *Die Hard*. So there was some sort of *Six Degrees of Separation* thing going on here. What's more, *Cliffhanger*, which Renny Harlin *did* direct, was playing in the same theater as *Last Action Hero*. Determined to give McTiernan the benefit of the doubt, I hung around and asked fifteen more people, including a half dozen nerdy Chinese-American high school students, if they could identify the director, but they mostly looked at me as if the question was incredibly stupid. Incidentally, most of the people that I polled did feel that the film sucked, so in the long run, a lack of a high profile is probably going to work in John Mc-Tiernan's favor as a director.

RESULT: 0/25

The Crying Game by Neil Jordan. This artsy affair had gotten lots of attention in New York City, drawing on the huge Irish-American transvestite audience, and had won tremendous praise for its director. It was playing in a snooty, cigar-box theater across from Bloomingdale's in midtown Manhattan, and people coming out after seeing it looked for the most part like your typical art house crowd. But none of the ten people I polled had any idea who had directed it. "Michael Jordan," was the closest I came to getting an accurate identification.

RESULT: 0.5/10

Guilty as Sin. This was the one instance in which even I didn't know who had directed the film I was asking questions about. Because the movie featured an actor who had married Melanie Griffith *twice*, I naively assumed that the director must be somebody with a name like Nick Castle or Shlomo Gildermeister or something. So did my polling group. People emerging from the City Cinemas/Cinema I on Third Avenue at Sixtieth Street in the middle of that sweltering afternoon were amazed that anyone could possibly have the *chutzpah* to ask who had directed a Don Johnson movie, much less a film with Rebecca De Mornay in it. The typical reaction was that of two smarmy Yuppies bulging out of wide-lapelled suits, their visages festooned with gleaming Ray-Bans and incipient pustules. They cracked up when I asked the question.

"Get out of here," said one, good-naturedly.

"What kind of question is that?" guffawed the other.

I didn't find out until I read an article in the *New Republic* the next day that the director was the revered Sidney Lumet. Jesus, was I embarrassed.

RESULT: 0/10

Dave. "An Ivan Reitman Film." You know, like *8 1/2*, "a Film by Federico Fellini"? Or *Ran*, "a Film by Akira Kurosawa"? Obviously, none of the ten people I quizzed outside the Loew's Columbus Circle theater in Manhattan had any idea who had directed this lame political satire. The closest anyone came to a positive I.D. was the thin, middle-aged man who said, "I know he's got a Russian name. Is it Ivan or something?"

"That's right," I replied.

"It's Ivan . . . I don't know the last name."

"Lendl?" I volunteered. "Ivan Lendl? Does that sound about right?"

"Yes," he said. The very next afternoon, the aging Czech tennis player got eliminated in the second round at Wimbledon.

RESULT: 0/10

Sleepless in Seattle by Nora Ephron. (Loew's 84th Street VI at 84th and Broadway in Manhattan). Get real.

RESULT: 0/10

Mario Van Peebles' Posse. You know, like DAVID LEAN'S LAWRENCE OF ARABIA? Or DAVE, AN IVAN REITMAN FILM? Given the fact that I was asking people, "Who directed *Posse*?" while they were standing directly in front of a huge poster reading A MARIO VAN PEEBLES FILM: POSSE, you might have expected the results to come out a bit skewed in Mario's favor. But no, only one of my ten pollees at the Embassy 2, 3, 4 Theater at Forty-seventh and Broadway in New York City could tell me who'd directed this dimwit, affirmative-action cowboy flick. Most just shook their heads. A couple of teenagers shrugged. At least one person didn't seem to understand the question. And a belligerent young man of not inconsiderable girth and swarth got right into my face and said, "Who the fuck wants to know?"

Well, precisely.

RESULT: 1/10

Cliffhanger by Renny Harlin. The first nine people I polled outside the Loew's Orpheum Theater VII at Third Avenue and Eighty-sixth Street seemed to think the question was impertinent. The tenth said: "Renny Harding." Close enough.

RESULT: 0.75/10

Indecent Proposal by Adrian Lyne. Playing at the Loew's 19th Street East at 19th and Broadway, not far from Greenwich Village. Yeah, sure.

RESULT: 0/10

Jurassic Park by Steven Spielberg. This was the one phase of the experiment where the results literally blew me away. I'd turned up at the Cineplex Odeon at Park and Eighty-sixth Street— where the picture was playing in both theaters—convinced that at least 90 percent of the people coming out of the theater would know that *Jurassic Park* was a Steven Spielberg production. No way. The very first person that I asked, a woman in her twenties, confidently said, "Yeah, I know who directed it. Stephen King." Stephen King was also the answer supplied by a fiftyish, dorky guy. Five obvious Manhattanite women shot back "Steven Spielberg" without missing a beat, but three young males, one white, one black, one Hispanic, all said they had no idea who had directed the film. One corpulent woman checked me out carefully after I said, "Excuse me, but I'm doing a study for *Movieline* magazine. Could you tell me who directed the movie that you just saw?"

She simply sauntered off, sneering over her shoulder, "That's the best pickup line I've heard in a long time."

I watched her stroll down the street. Then I reflected on what she had just said. I thought about classic pickup lines, such as "Do you come here often?" and "Do those legs go all the way up?" and "Excuse me, but aren't you Demi Moore's sister?" Then I compared these lines to "Excuse me, but I'm doing a study for *Movieline* magazine. Could you tell me who directed the movie that you just saw?" Then I hollered after her: "If that's the best pickup line you've heard in a long time, you're in big trouble."

She kept walking.

RESULT: 5/10

Menace II Society. Directed by the Hughes Brothers or the Hughes Cousins or Something, and playing at the City Cinema 86th Street East, between Second and Third Avenues in Manhattan. Yeah, right.

RESULT: 0/10

Howards End by James Ivory. My experience standing outside the tiny Cineplex Odeon on East Fifty-ninth Street right up the street from trendy Bloomingdale's was a true epiphany. *Everyone* coming out of the theater knew who had directed the film. *Everyone* coming out of the theater knew who had produced it. *Everyone* coming out of the theater thought the question was stupid. The problem was: *Everyone* consisted of only four people. This made me realize that there is an inverse relationship between the audience's ability to identify the director of a film and the amount of money the movie will probably take in. A movie with 100 percent directorial recognition is almost certainly going to be a movie in which Vanessa Redgrave makes an appearance somewhere. This is no way to run a railroad. What Hollywood wants, what Hollywood needs, is an infinite stream of extremely profitable movies made by directors whose names will never hang on every lip. Or, for that matter, any lip. Hollywood doesn't want four people coming out of a movie house knowing that James Ivory directed the film and Ismail Merchant produced it. It wants two thousand people coming out of a Renny Harlin movie thinking they've just seen a movie by John McTiernan. You know, the guy who directed *Die Hard . . . ?*

RESULT 4/4

Special, Artsy-Craftsy Section. I had launched this undertaking convinced that the only people who really care about directors are pretentious snobs who regularly attend foreign films. Inevitably, this led me to the Lincoln Plaza Cinemas, the one-stop multiplex for all your basic show-offy needs. The afternoon I planted myself at the top of the elevator ferrying audience members out of the bowels of the subterranean cinema (this is what they mean by *underground films*), the proprietors were screening three snooty films: *The Story of Qiu Ju* by Zhang Yimou, *Un coeur en hiver* by Claude Sautet, and *Orlando* by Sally Potter. No one, but no one, could tell me who had directed *The Story of Qiu Ju*. No one, but no one, could tell me who had directed *Un coeur en hiver*, though one woman did say, "Claude something," always a safe bet when discussing French films.

Amazingly, however, five of the ten people I polled knew that Sally Potter had directed *Orlando*. More amazing still: All five people were women accompanied by men who could not identify the director. In retrospect, I realized that because *Orlando* is a film about transsexualism and transvestism, it is very possible that the five women who could identify Sally Potter as the director were actually men in drag, while their five male companions were females dressed up to look like pretentious, male art-film buffs. All things considered, given the enormous numbers of transsexual foreign film buffs based in New York, I do not think we can learn a whole lot from these figures.

RESULT: 5/30

WHAT THE NUMBERS MEAN

All told, over a three-day period, I polled 134 moviegoers coming out of 14 different movies. (I actually asked 25 different people, "Who directed *Last Action Hero*?" without finding anyone who could provide me with the answer, but for purposes of methodological fairness, and out of compassion for John McTiernan, who did, after all, direct *Die Hard*, I used only the first 10 responses in my final tabulations). Similarly, I have included only four responses to the question about the director of *Howards End* because there were only four people in the theater at the time, it was a really hot day, and I didn't feel like hanging around for three hours waiting for the next screening to end, anyway. This is the only methodological blemish on what is otherwise a flawless, seamless work of statistical clarity and, yes, perhaps even beauty.

The results are not pretty. Of the nine conventional, American-made films that I investigated, only 6.75 out of 90 people knew the name of the director. That's 7.5 percent. Throw out the universally famous Steven Spielberg and the percentage drops to 1.75 out of 80, or 2.2 percent. *Pathetic*. And even in Spielberg's case (50 percent), the rate-of-recognition numbers were much smaller than for James Ivory (100 percent). Worse still, Spielberg's 50 percent rating put him in exactly the same class as an obscure, English female director of a drama about cross-dressing that is playing at only about six movie theaters on the entire planet. The inescapable conclusion that must be drawn from this data is clear: Americans could give one (1) fuck who directed *Posse*, and couldn't give even that many fucks who directed *Indecent Proposal*, *Dave*, *Sleepless in Seattle*, *Last Action Hero*, *Cliffhanger*, *Menace II Society*, or *Guilty as Sin*. Proving, once and for all, without the slightest shadow of a doubt, that this is not France.

BUT ARE YOU SURE YOU'RE BEING COMPLETELY FAIR?

As a final test of my hypothesis that even bothering to include a director's name in an American film's credits is a hopeless affectation, if not a huge crock of shit, I decided to wrap up my study by visiting several New York theaters and determining whether any of the theater personnel, as opposed to theater patrons, might be familiar with the *auteurs* in question and capable of rattling off their names.

"What time does the Ivan Reitman film start?" I asked the cashier at the Loew's Columbus Circle theater in New York. The movie house, which only has one screen, had been showing *Dave* for about five weeks.

"Who?" she replied.

"Ivan Reitman. What time is the Ivan Reitman film?"

"We're showing *Dave*," she answered, shaking her head. "We're not showing an Ivan Reitman film."

I moseyed uptown to a neighborhood six-plex, the mammoth Loew's Eighty-fourth Street VI, at Eighty-fourth and Broadway.

"Two tickets for the John McTiernan film," I told the cashier.

"Who?" she asked, puzzled.

"John McTiernan. Two tickets for the John McTiernan film."

She consulted her computer screen, visibly confused.

"I don't know the name of that actor. What movie is it?"

"The John McTiernan movie. My girlfriend said to meet her at this movie-house and get tickets for the John McTiernan film."

"Well, I don't know the name of that actor."

I got out of line for a few minutes, asked ten people if they could tell me who had directed *The Firm*, which had just opened that day, did not get a single "Sydney Pollack" in response, then went back to the cashier's booth.

"Can I have two tickets for the John McTiernan film?" I asked.

The cashier looked at me, sleepy-eyed, a grim glimmer of recognition in her stare.

"I don't know the name of that actor."

"Okay, then let me have two tickets for the Nora Ephron film."

"I don't know the name of that actor, either."

I think that says it all.

FOR MEMBERS ONLY

One night last spring, I rented *White Men Can't Jump*, the elegant, understated plea for racial harmony starring Wesley Snipes, from my local video store. Toward the end of the film, in which Woody Harrelson quite convincingly portrays a Caucasian basketball player who isn't very smart, the flaxen-haired *Cheers* alumnus is apprehended by a pair of vicious-looking gamblers he has been eluding for most of the movie. Dragged to a deserted area and stripped to his Marky Mark undershorts, Harrelson kneels helplessly at the feet of the sinister Stucci brothers as they prepare to do him irreparable bodily harm. Begging for one last chance to come up with the thousands of dollars he owes them because of his failure to tank a basketball game, Harrelson looks on in dismay as one of the Stucci brothers jams a sawed-off shotgun into his underpants and warns what will happen if he fails to come up with the money.

Shortly thereafter, the gamblers get their money.

The very next night, I rented *Honeymoon in Vegas*, the quirky comedy in which Nicholas Cage quite convincingly plays a Caucasian who isn't very smart. Warned what will happen if he does not come up with the many thousands of dollars that he owes sinister gambler James Caan after an ill-advised poker game, Cage persuades his fiancée (Sarah Jessica Parker) to spend a weekend with the odious dirtball in exchange for the complete cancellation of his debts. In a winking aside to the audience, apprising them of what might happen to Cage should he fail to live up to his part of the bargain, Caan very early in the movie grabs the testicles of a hotel manager who has been foolish enough to tell him that his usual suite is not available, and proceeds to squeeze them with great dexterity, force, and, apparently, delight.

Shortly thereafter, Caan gets his room.

The very next day, I went out and saw *El Mariachi*, Robert Rodriguez' quirky, elegantly understated $7,000 movie in which the unknown Carlos Gallardo quite convincingly plays a Mexican who isn't very smart. About halfway through the film, the nightclub proprietress in whose bathtub Gallardo finds himself plunges a sharp letter opener into the water between his spread legs and tells him to take out his guitar and perform a traditional mariachi number. If he plays the song with the gusto and panache one has long associated with practitioners of this colorful idiom, it will prove that he is a harmless mariachi musician and deserves to live. If he does not play the song with traditional *elan*, or if he messes up a lot of notes, it will prove that he is a hit man who always conceals his weapons in a guitar case. In that case, she will cut off his balls.

Shortly thereafter, the woman gets her serenade.

Robert Rodriguez has garnered a lot of kudos recently, first by winning the coveted Audience Award at Robert Redford's Sundance Film Festival, then by getting signed to a two-year "first-look" deal with Columbia. Much of the media attention has focused on the director's maverick vision. But the bald truth about *El Mariachi* is that it is a low-budget but nonetheless formulaic comedy about a dimwitted male who keeps getting himself into trouble and that at some point in the film, true to formula, somebody gets threatened with having his nuts blown off, squeezed into putty, or meticulously diced with a letter opener.

I think Hollywood will suit Mr. Rodriguez just fine.

The fact that it was possible for an ordinary moviegoer like me, a person with no ax to grind, no hidden agenda to promote, no soapbox to fulminate from, to view, on three consecutive days, three films that all dealt in graphic fashion with a direct threat to the male reproductive organs, suggested that there was something disturbing transpiring in the national *zeitgeist* that we should all be closely monitoring. Or at least that all men should be closely monitoring.

My suspicion that testicular paranoia was loose in the American subconscious was further strengthened in the next few weeks, when I noticed a direct threat to the organ that I hold most dear in every single movie that I attended, with the single exception of *Howards End*. In *The Dark Half*, a man's balls are cut off and stuffed into his mouth—the last place anyone would think of looking for them. In *Three of Hearts*, Tony Amendola threatens to cut off Billy Baldwin's nuts and "use them for a necklace." (Actually, given that the rodent-faced Baldwin is sharing an apartment with Kelly Lynch, who plays an unsuccessful lesbian, this is not such a bad idea, since Lynch obviously has no use for the Baldwinic balls.) The final vindication of my theory about balls on the brain occurred when I saw the trailer for *Lost in Yonkers* and realized that even in a hopeless morass of ethnic hokum like this there is nevertheless a groin-threatening scene: when Richard Dreyfuss stuffs a revolver down his trousers and then jokes that if it should accidentally go off, he'd be turned into a ballerina.

Tickets are still available for the 9:20 showing.

The concept of penises and testicles getting chopped off, blown into smithereens, pummeled by direct kicks, or transmogrified into offbeat jewelry is not a new concept in the movies, or, for that matter, in life. What *is* new is the *dimension* of the crisis—the fact that cinema goers are now being exposed to a veritable tidal wave of misfortune involving the male reproductive organ. The simple fact of the matter is this: The menacing of the malleable male member has now become as much a cinematic cliché as the cloying Motown soundtrack and the close-up shot of shoes descending from a parked car. (The generic shot of the 1990s is somebody named Baldwin or Quaid dropping his feet out of a car and getting kicked in the balls while Aretha sings "Chain of Fools" in the background.)

How did we arrive at a point in our history when virtually every film made in this country contains at least one scene in which the male member is bent, folded, spindled, mutilated, or at the very least threatened with such indignities? And what does it say about the American psyche that our most popular art form now routinely depicts severe mistreatment of the human cock? And that men have to pay the same price as women to see it? To answer these questions, we must first go back and survey the history of ball-busting films.

Until the 1950s, Hollywood tried to pretend that the penis did not exist. This was, it must be remembered, the post-war era of wholesome entertainment, and the penis, whatever its other charms, can hardly be described as wholesome. Also, it was easier for Americans to forget that penises existed in the era of Pat Boone and Danny Kaye.

Penises did not begin to assert themselves in the American psyche until Tennessee Williams, who was obsessed by cocks and mutilation, hit it big with such depressing plays as *Cat on a Hot Tin Roof*, which is about impotence, and *Sweet Bird of Youth*, which is about the sweet bird of a youth. Although there are no explicit castration scenes in the screen versions of these plays, an ominous mood of genital foreboding looms over each of them, like a tumescent Lord Roger poised to explode. Whatever that means.

It was not until *Goldfinger* (1964) that riveting images of the jeopardized male member could actually be used in film stills to advertise a movie. The famous scene in which a spread-eagled

Sean Connery is threatened with penile bifurcation by an overhead laser beam constitutes a pivotal moment in the history of popular entertainment because it was the first time that a motion picture had addressed, in a meaningful cinematic fashion, the most deep-seated male fear. For it was only then that men came to the terrifying realization that if someone as resourceful, virile, and cool as James Bond could have his nuts cut off, then *anyone* could have his nuts cut off—meaning, no more pussy galore.

Connery is perhaps the only movie star in history to have his genitals directly threatened in two different films (though Woody Harrelson is still young enough to eclipse this dubious record). Halfway through *Never Say Never Again*, the somewhat portly Connery is menaced by the hyperactive Barbara Carrera, who forces him to sit on the ground and spread his legs, then points a gun at his crotch and sneers, "Guess where you get the first one."

Real tough question, Babs.

In discussing the subject of penis-threatening motion pictures, films that the Germans refer to as *das porkenfilm*, and that French film buffs call *le cinema aux couilles*, it is important to distinguish between films in which one or more penises play a major role in thematic development and films in which people get kicked in the balls or castrated purely for the sake of amusing the audience. Into the first category fall films as varied as *Sudden Impact*, *In the Realm of the Senses*, *Stealing Heaven*, *The World According to Garp*, *Born on the Fourth of July*, and *History of the World—Part I*, the last being a movie in which the penis plays such a large part (eight distinct scenes involving castration, circumcision, kicks in the balls, or urination) that it ought to get mentioned in the credits right below the words "Madeline Kahn."

The second category consists of films such as *Last Rites*, *A Prayer for the Dying*, *The Evil That Men Do*, and *The Dark Half*, in which genital misfortune is merely one more revolting element thrown into an already revolting motion picture to make sure that the audience doesn't come away with the wrong idea. Thus, one can readily imagine the producer of *Last Rites* peeking at the rough cut of the film and telling the director, "Look, asshole, you've already got mob priests, incest, drug dealers, and women who murder their spouses, so the least you can do is have the bitch ice him with a .38 slug right in the cock. What kind of picture do you think we're making here?"

For similar reasons, one has no difficulty visualizing the director of *A Prayer for the Dying* reading the riot act to the scriptwriter after looking at his shoddy first draft.

"We've got blind virgins, bad Irish accents, affable child murderers, terrorists masquerading as priests, crucified funeral directors, a whore with a heart of gold, and Liam Neeson all in one film," the director would point out, "so I think that if you forget to include a scene where somebody gets his nuts menaced by a sawed-off shotgun, the audience is going to get a little antsy. As convicted Watergate conspirator Charles Colson once said: 'Once you've got them by the balls, their hearts and minds will follow.'"

To which the scriptwriter would almost assuredly reply: "What's Watergate?"

On the other hand, it would be a mistake to argue that every movie containing gratuitous attacks on the crown jewels is automatically a worthless, mindless film. One of the most memorable kicks in the balls in the history of cinema occurs in *Butch Cassidy and the Sundance Kid*, an entertaining movie that is otherwise devoid of gonadal mayhem. Similarly, James Caan's protracted nut crunching during that early scene in *Honeymoon in Vegas* is really the only somber, tasteless moment in an otherwise peppy, understatedly elegant film. And the mere fact that a jazz musician ends up with his balls stuffed into his mouth halfway through *Angel Heart* does not automatically ruin the movie; Lisa Bonet's acting takes care of that. In fact, after forcing the audience to sit through a couple of scenes involving Robert De Niro with a pony tail and Charlotte Rampling trying to act, Alan Parker may have included the scene about the man with his balls stuffed into his mouth as some kind of black comic relief. Personally, the thing I most enjoyed about *Angel Heart* was the possibility that the fate of the jazz musician might eventually befall Mickey Rourke.

In films dominated by a brooding element of penile peril, it is possible to distinguish between three basic types of nutcracking films: those where the male organs are tormented at the very beginning; those where they are subjected to immense physical pain at the end; and those where the damage to the penis or testicles continues pretty much straight through the film. Into the first subcategory fall such films as *The Evil That Men Do*, a very bad Charles Bronson movie that opens with a journalist in a South American torture chamber having electrodes applied directly to his nuts. The clear intention of the director in kicking off his film with this nauseating scene is to first traumatize his audience, shock them, paralyze them with revulsion, and then reassure them by letting them know that nothing they will witness throughout the remainder of the film will be anywhere near as disgusting as the opening scene. Including Bronson's acting.

In the second sub-category can be found films such as *Lipstick*, *War of the Roses*, and *The World According to Garp*. In each of these movies, the big, climactic scene involving the mutilation or potential mutilation of the male organ is a payoff that the audience has been looking forward to from the get-go. In *Lipstick* Margaux Hemingway plugs Chris Sarandon right in the dick in retribution for his having raped her earlier in the film. In *War of the Roses*, Kathleen Turner first lulls her schmuck hubby, convincingly played by Michael Douglas, into a false sense of security by agreeing to suck his cock (nicknamed "The Bold Adventure"), then takes a big bite out of it. Only then, two hours into the film, does he realize that Turner is no longer his friend. Finally, in *The World According to Garp*, Mary Beth Hurt accidentally bites off the penis of her overly aggressive teenaged lover while giving him what proves to be the final blow job in their up-and-down relationship. The calamity wrought by the appropriately named actress is a sort of metaphor for Garp's entire existence, though I have no idea what that metaphor means. But it does inspire John Lithgow, convincingly cast as a transsexual who used to play tight end for the Philadelphia Eagles, to remark: "I had *mine* removed under general anesthetic. But to have it bitten off in a Buick is a nightmare."

Salvador falls into a somewhat different category than these other motion pictures, in that it is the only film in recent memory in which a major American actor almost gets his balls cut off in a foreign language. This near-disaster occurs towards the end of Oliver Stone's powerful 1986 film, when an uncharismatic El Salvador death-squad leader wearing—what else?—an Oakland Raiders T-shirt and brandishing a sharp machete tells the unbelievably annoying James Woods, *"Me gustan los huevos rancheros,"* which is Deathsquadese for "I'm going to cut off your balls." The man's failure to do so remains, for my money, the single most disappointing finale in any movie made in this country in the past 50 years. With the climax of *Angel Heart* a close second.

In sharp contrast to *Lipstick*, *Salvador*, and *The World According to Garp*, where the brutalization of the male member takes place at the very end of the movie, we have Clint Eastwood's 1982 film *Sudden Impact*, where cock fragments start flying all over the screen almost from the moment the opening credits have finished rolling. This fast-paced psychological thriller, which had a tremendous linguistic and philosophical influence on President Ronald Reagan, deals with a disoriented young rape victim, played by Sondra Locke, who methodically avenges herself by luring her assailants to out-of-the-way places and then emptying a concealed revolver into their privates, inflicting what she daintily describes as "a .38-caliber vasectomy."

Sudden Impact is also noteworthy because of the disturbing scene toward the end of the film when Eastwood, reprising his Dirty Harry psycho-cop role from the early 1970's, offers Locke a can of Budweiser. Although it has become commonplace for manufacturers of fine consumer products to pay movie studios tens of thousands of dollars to have their goods displayed prominently in large-budget movies, it is impossible for me to believe that

Anheuser-Busch actually paid to have Locke quaff a Bud on camera. Not unless the quirky St. Louis brewery was trying to zero in on that fast-growing, twenty-something, beer-guzzling, female rape-victim market.

At this point, the casual reader may find himself wondering aloud: "Gee, you seem to know an awful lot about movies where guys get their cocks shot off, but why are you telling me all this?" The answer is simple: This essay is written in response to voluminous inquiries from *Movieline* subscribers about the subject of penile-dominated films. Recently, veritable scores of readers have written in and said: "We're very interested in movies about castration and what-not, and you guys seem to be pretty up on this stuff, so are there any recommendations you would make to a guy or gal who's trying to build a home library made up of the finest nutcracker films?"

The answer is a resounding yes. Every cinephile interested in this particular genre positively *must* own a copy of *Midnight Express*, in which Randy Quaid loses not one but two testicles during a series of severe beatings in a Turkish prison. *The Big Chill*, where the appropriately named William Hurt can't harpoon Meg Tilly because of something that happened to him back in Vietnam, is optional, as is *Born on the Fourth of July*, but no serious student of cock-related cinema will want to be without *Sudden Impact*, *Last Rites*, or *El Mariachi*—all of which contain impressive phallophobic footage—much less *Caligula*, the big-budget 1980 porno film in which a man's penis is chopped off and fed to a pack of dogs. (This is a metaphor for what happens to people in Hollywood when their movies don't earn out.)

Other must-haves include *Lipstick* (buckshot in the balls), *The Dark Half* (balls stuffed in the mouth), *Butch Cassidy and the Sundance Kid* (good, solid kick in the nuts), and *The World According to Garp* (penis bitten off during ill-timed blow job; penis caught in trouser zipper; various other penile mishaps). More recent works you'll want in your collection include *What's Love Got to Do With It?*, in which the long-suffering Tina Turner, played by Angela

Bassett, nails Ike, played by Laurence Fishburne, right in the nuts, and *Total Recall*, in which Arnold Schwarzenegger barely notices getting kicked and punched in the groin by Sharon Stone. Meaning one of two things: Either Arnold has steel balls, or he's a eunuch.

Several readers have also asked, "Are there any good self-circumcision movies you could recommend for people who might want to practice at home?" The answer is again a resounding yes. Peter Greenaway's quirky, elegantly understated film *Drowning by Numbers* contains an excellent scene where a young girl persuades a boy named Smut to circumcise himself. For viewers who want to go one step further and explore the mysterious world of self-castration, there is *Square Dance*, the quirky, elegantly understated Winona Ryder vehicle in which Rob Lowe tries to jump-start his dying career by playing a retarded fiddle player with a pronounced Southern accent who cuts off his own dick after Ryder, cast as an impressionable adolescent, discovers him in bed, boning an over-sexed female hairdresser.

In addition to its electrifying story line and fine acting, *Square Dance* is also distinguished by its crackling dialogue. Particularly memorable is the scene where Lowe beseeches Winona, "Read me a story, one about them bears, and they're eatin' their cereal." Even less forgettable is the scene where Jane Alexander, playing Ryder's long-suffering hairdresser mother, tells her daughter that she must clear out quickly, lest the police implicate her in the tragic demise of Lowe's penis.

"I got to get you outa here," rasps Alexander. "I gotta take you somewhere. . . . Aggie [Alexander's fellow tonsorial specialist] took me in there and I just about got sick. Her hanging there like shoddy plumbing, and him laying here bleeding, and my haircutting scissors on the floor next to your Bible. Baby, you're in big trouble."

One final question remains. Are there any motion pictures readily available in the VHS format that would be of any use to a person interested in castrating or gelding a man? Again, the answer is yes. *Stealing Heaven*, the elegantly understated 1988 Anglo-

Yugoslavian film that deals with the most famous eunuch of them all, Peter Abelard, contains an excellent scene illustrating how to quickly, efficiently castrate a man (though you will probably need four or five strong men to hold the castratee down while you are doing it).

Of course, nothing in *Stealing Heaven* could possibly compare to the final scene from *In the Realm of the Senses*, the quirky, elegantly understated 1976 Japanese film in which the leading lady, a geisha girl appropriately named Sada, strangles her lover, then hacks off his cock, and then spends four days wandering around the streets of Tokyo with a big smile on her face. This film probably has as much to say about female attitudes toward penises as any film ever made, and once seen will probably permanently cure any American tourist of the desire to take up with a hooker while visiting Japan.

What can the reader learn from this brief history of ball-busting, nut-cracking movies? And what does Hollywood's current obsession with the vulnerability of the penis say about our society? Basically, this: As long as there are men who have penises there will be women who will want to cut them off. What's more, many of these men will deserve to have them cut off. But is the fear of castration primarily a fear that is limited to the serially emasculated men who live and work in Hollywood, or does this veritable geyser of films involving crushed testicles, mandatory gelding, and groinocentric gunshot wounds reflect a wider, deeper fear on the part of all American men, a primal dread that our balls are right there on the chopping board with the blood-drenched meat cleaver poised directly above them? Probably the latter. Films are direct reflections of society's deepest neuroses, and nothing worries the average American male more than the nagging fear that, when all is said and done, his balls are only out on loan and his dick can be repossessed at any time. Deep down inside, every American man secretly fears that someday, somewhere, someone is going to stick a sawed-off shotgun down his jockey shorts and threaten to nuke the crown jewels. He just has to keep hoping that the person with the shotgun will be one of the sinister Stucci brothers, and not his wife. At least *they* can be bribed.

Note: Since this article appeared in 1993, genital mayhem has become such a Hollywood cliché that it's not even worth mentioning anymore.

THE REMAINS OF
THE DAZED

In the many years I have been dealing with *Movieline*, the magazine's editors have repeatedly saddled me with life-threatening assignments just to see what kind of mettle I was made of. One time they asked me to impersonate the blind character Al Pacino plays in *Scent of a Woman* and literally walk directly into New York City traffic, where I risked being killed by an oncoming fleet of taxis. No problem, I told them. Another time they asked me to re-enact the opening scene from *Vertigo*, where Jimmy Stewart risks life and limb by leaping across the rooftops of San Francisco to apprehend a minor criminal. Again, I told them, no problem. On yet another occasion, they asked me to act out one of the cannibal scenes from *Alive*, just to see what human flesh tasted like. And once again, I came through with flying colors. It was no picnic, but I survived.

One day, the editors of *Movieline* called me with yet another death-defying assignment. Right off the bat, they warned me that it would be the most physically demanding work I had ever undertaken, requiring weeks, perhaps months, of physiological *and* psychological wear and tear.

"You want to me to re-enact Stallone's stunt work from *Cliff-hanger?*" I asked. No, they did not. The assignment they had in mind would be far more physically demanding than that, far more draining on the human psyche. The assignment they had in mind would try my patience, jangle my nerves, rupture my relationship with my family, and possibly cause me to be permanently insti-tutionalized. The assignment they had in mind would plunge me into the dark night of the soul, forcing me to spend countless sleepless nights wandering the corridors of my house, desperately seeking an escape from the engulfing darkness. The assignment they had in mind was so terrifying that it would turn ordinary mortals' knees to jelly, their intestines to mush, their lily livers to, well, lily liver.

Suddenly, in a blinding flash, I realized what they were sug-gesting. They were not proposing something of a pedestrianally horrifying nature, like spending a day with Steve Guttenberg. They were not proposing a run-of-the-mill stomach-turning as-signment like reading the collected interviews of Nicole Kidman. They were asking me to do something that could very easily cost me my livelihood, my sanity, my marriage, my life.

They were asking me to watch the complete works of Ismail Merchant and James Ivory.

From the moment *Movieline*'s editors made this obscene overture, I knew my relationship with them had changed forever. Asking me to get run over by automobiles or splattered when I fell from tall office buildings had been good, clean fun—prankish stuff sug-gested in a spirit of puckish goodwill. But in asking me to watch the complete works of Merchant and Ivory—every single video-tape from beginning to end, without fast-forwarding even once— my erstwhile friends were no longer being playful. Now, for what-ever the reason, they were out to destroy me.

When the assignment was first suggested, my immediate reaction was a resounding no. The speed with which I refused was prompted in part by the antipathy of my wife, who had actually seen quite a few Merchant-Ivory films and recognized the grave dangers that lay ahead. Months earlier, I'd told her I was thinking of doing a story for GQ about swimming in shark-infested waters just to get that rush from being on intimate terms with the tigers of the deep. She'd begged me not to do it. Then I told her I was thinking of doing a story about ice scuba-diving—wriggling into a rubber suit and checking out all those neat fish under a frozen lake in northern Michigan in the middle of January. Again, she'd implored me to reconsider. But now that I was talking about watching the complete works of Merchant and Ivory, she changed her tune completely.

"Joe, you're only doing this because I talked you out of swimming in shark-infested waters or being frozen to death as the icy mantle of death closes around you scant inches below the surface of Lake Superior," she said. "But I was wrong. By all means go to the South Pacific and swim in shark-infested waters. Feel free to travel to the Yukon and cut a hole in the ice and jump in for a dip when the temperature, with wind-chill factor, in northern Manitoba is fast approaching fifty degrees below zero. But for God's sake, don't watch all of Merchant and Ivory's movies. If you won't think of me and the children, at least think of yourself."

I listened politely to what she said, but at some primal level I knew that I had already made my decision. For years, I'd been garnering grudging praise from other journalists after returning from my zany adventures. But in the back of my mind, I knew that I was still viewed as a lightweight. Sure I was an iconoclastic, courageous, fabulously talented journalist. But I hadn't raped and pillaged with Pancho Villa the way Ambrose Bierce had. I hadn't climbed into the ring with a professional boxer the way Papa Hemingway had. I hadn't tried out for the Detroit Lions the way George Plimpton had. I hadn't ridden with the Hell's Angels the way Hunter Thompson had. Nothing I had attempted to date— impersonating Mickey Rourke for a day, having lunch with Keanu

Reeves—was anywhere near as daring as what I was contemplating now. By watching all twenty-two Merchant-Ivory movies from beginning to end, I could finally stake my claim to immortality. Years from now, people would still be telling upstart journalists, "So what if you scaled Mount Everest blindfolded with both hands tied behind your back and a family of rabid ferrets lodged inside your trousers while you were suffering from cholera and missing both legs? Joe Queenan watched all of Merchant and Ivory's films."

And so, the die was cast.

As soon as I told the editors of *Movieline* that I would accept the assignment, we finalized the arrangements. The basic stipulation was that I watch each and every movie that had been produced by Ismail Merchant and directed by James Ivory from the first frame to the last. The movies did not have to be watched in any particular order, nor did I have to watch them straight through—I could pause the movies while I went to the bathroom or took a three-month trip to Peru—but once I had begun watching a film, I could not start watching another until the previous one had reached its conclusion. To ensure that I would not cheat by fast-forwarding through the films and polishing them off in two days, my editors said there would be a quiz at the end of the assignment in which I would be asked difficult questions such as "Which character in which film uttered the words, 'Helen, you're a ripping girl' or 'Simcox, the boathouse is all at sixes and sevens'?" These guys were playing for keeps.

My editors, of course, didn't think there was a chance in hell that I would complete this assignment. Forget about watching *all* of Merchant and Ivory's movies, they taunted me; there is no historical evidence that any one person has ever sat all the way through *Slaves of New York*. You'll never get through *Jane Austen in Manhattan*, they sneered at me. No human being could possibly watch *Savages*. And even if you do make it all the way through *Heat and Dust*, *The Courtesans of Bombay*, and *Shakespeare Wallah*, you'll still have Emma Thompson waiting for you in both

The Remains of the Day and *Howards End*. You'll never make it, chump. This time, you've finally bitten off more than you can chew.

How confident were my editors that I would not be able to complete this assignment? Consider this. Just before I wandered off to the video store to rent a dozen movies about doomed maharajas and women in crinoline with unbelievably stiff upper lips, I asked what kind of time frame we were talking about. A week? Two weeks? A month? One day per film? I can still hear their guffaws ringing in my ears.

"Take the rest of your life," they jeered. "Take from here till eternity. That *still* won't be enough time."

I planned to prove them wrong. My battle plan? Identify the least watchable Merchant and Ivory movies and save them until last, when my nerves would have been steeled by weeks of watching other, less cerebrally draining films. Obviously, at this early stage in the project I could not possibly watch anything starring the unbearable Bernadette Peters, the foppish Hugh Grant, the Medusa-like Emma Thompson, the dissolute Denholm Elliot, or the saucer-eyed Helena Bonham Carter. But I also couldn't watch anything starring the Twin Corpses: Maggie Smith and Vanessa Redgrave. So I decided to quickly get some points on the scoreboard by polishing off that ultra-hideous Raj material.

First stop: *Autobiography of a Princess*. One of Merchant and Ivory's earliest collaborations, this raftload of Hindu hooey stars James Mason as a decrepit old colonial reminiscing about the good old days in India when his world-weary maharini friend was still young and perky. Mercifully short, *Autobiography of a Princess* introduces most of the principal themes that would resurface again and again in the score of movies to follow: decrepit old colonials, world-weary maharinis, old men hitting on young girls.

The same day that I watched *Autobiography of a Princess*, I also took in *The Householder*. Another one of Merchant and Ivory's earliest collaborations, this raftload of Hindu hooey spends nearly two hours depicting the plight of an Indian wanker who can't get his wife to clean the house and who is too nervous to ask his boss for a piddling raise. Finally, he gets his mother-in-law to read his wife the riot act. Hideously long, *The Householder* introduces all the other themes in the score of movies to follow: the inability of heterosexual men to satisfy their wives, an old woman's unhealthy interference in the life of a woman many years her junior, the difficulty in finding good domestic help.

Autobiography of a Princess and *The Householder* bored me to tears. But there was a plus side to things. By the end of my first full day of watching Merchant and Ivory films, I already had two down with twenty to go. At this rate, I would easily finish the assignment within two weeks. No, it wasn't going to be a pleasant two weeks—or what people back in the days of the Raj might have called a fortnight—but I could tough it out. At this point, I saw no earthly reason why I should not be able to get through the rest of their movies.

I still felt confident of my ultimate success by the end of the second day of my ordeal. I started the day by watching *Roseland*, a trilogy set in New York's famous Roseland dance theater whose most interesting vignette stars Christopher Walken as a gigolo trying to keep three different women happy. This is not possible, since Geraldine Chaplin is one of them. With its corny old music, fat men in madras jackets, conga lines, senior citizens reminiscing about the good old days, and an older woman hitting on a younger man, *Roseland* is a direct descendant of the two Indian monstrosities I'd watched the day before.

But *Roseland* also featured two other elements that I would come to know and dread in the days to come. Dramatically, it is framed as a kind of pseudo-documentary, an appalling technique that has worked well in exactly one film—*This Is Spinal Tap*. More ominously, the film is set in New York. And the one thing I would learn from my experiences as I ventured deeper and deeper into the heart of Ruth Prawer Jhabvalaian darkness was this: Nothing in the world is more deadly than a Merchant-Ivory production set in New York City.

Nothing.

It took me three days to finish watching *Roseland*. By this time, I realized that this assignment was not going to be a can of corn. Actually, it *was* going to be a can of corn—22 cans of corn. What it would *not* be was a piece of cake. Still reeling from the emotional torpor of watching a battalion of geriatric pinheads doing what appeared to be the Hustle in *Roseland*, I had only enough energy to trudge through two more Merchant-Ivory films that week. The first was *The Wild Party*, a pseudo-documentary set in the Flapper Era, which stars the loathsome James Coco as an aging silent film star who is hitting on a couple of younger women—first Raquel Welch, then a teenybopper—neither of whom he can possibly satisfy because he's James Coco. This film introduces the final element that can be found in almost every subsequent Merchant and Ivory film: When all else fails, have somebody go over to the piano and bang out a tune. The film is awful.

The week thus ended on a disturbing note. Yes, I had knocked off four deadly Merchant-Ivory films. But I had eighteen more to go. And Emma Thompson and Maggie Smith loomed on the horizon. At this rate, I figured to be living and breathing Merchant and Ivory for another full month. This wasn't going to be pleasant.

I started the next week by watching *Shakespeare Wallah*—more Rubbish from the Raj—and *The Courtesans of Bombay*, a pseudo-documentary about exotic dancers trying to provide pleasure to repressed Indian men under the stern eyes of their domineering mothers. It too was appalling.

By the middle of the week, my dreams of systematically hacking my way through this celluloid swamp lay in ruins. Four days after I loaded *The Bostonians* into the VCR, it was still sitting there. The movie, which opens with an organ recital, stars Vanessa Redgrave as a sexually repressed, aging suffragette spinster who has an unhealthy fascination with a young girl who is deeply in love with Christopher Reeve. I will say no more. With characters named Basil and actresses named Linda Hunt and Jessica Tandy reading aloud to each other from musty 19th-century books at endless tea parties while Wagner's *Lohengrin* plays languorously in the background, *The Bostonians* quickly proved to be the cinematic equivalent of the rack. It was Bustle Hell.

Nevertheless, deeply encouraged by the fact that the movie actually ended, I started the next week by watching *Heat and Dust*, a movie about a young Englishwoman who comes to India seeking wisdom; *Bombay Talkie*, a movie about a young Englishwoman who comes to India seeking wisdom; and *Hullaballoo Over George and Bonnie's Pictures*, a movie about a young Englishwoman who comes to India seeking wisdom. In each case, I kept scrupulous notes to make sure that I was not actually watching the same movie over and over again.

Bombay Talkie is the one filled with a lot of corny music where the Englishwoman ends up in bed with a lecherous adulterer played by Shashi Kapoor, but there's no good sex. *Hullaballoo Over George and Bonnie's Pictures* is the one filled with a lot of corny music where an old Englishwoman totally dominates her young companion who ends up in bed with a lecherous adulterer played by Saeed Jaffrey, but there's no good sex. And *Heat and Dust* is the one filled with a lot of corny music where Greta Scacchi ends up in bed with a lecherous adulterer played by Shashi Kapoor, but there's no good sex. Are we clear?

By the fourth week of the assignment, I was starting to gather speed. I went to the local art house and guffawed through *Jefferson in Paris*, Merchant and Ivory's numbskulled, revisionist portrait of the intellectual, if not the actual, father of our country. This laughable film, freighted down with more wigs and harpsichords and bustles than a *Wuthering Heights* pajama party, is the one where a slave played by Thandie Newton ends up in bed with an adulterous lecher played by Nick Nolte, but there's no good sex. When *Jefferson in Paris* was released, critics jumped all over Merchant and Ivory because they had capriciously, idiotically cast Nick Nolte as Thomas Jefferson, possibly the smartest, most cosmopolitan American ever. So what? Six years earlier, these upmarket bozos had cast Bernadette Peters—Carol Channing-in-waiting—as a super-hip young downtown chick in *Slaves of New York*. Let's face it: These guys were capable of anything.

Buoyed by my ability to sit through *Jefferson in Paris*, I decided to go at this project hammer and tong, and, as the cricketers say, hit them for six. Alas, Week Number Four quickly turned into sheer torture. First I watched *Quartet*, a flapper-era concoction in which Alan Bates plays a lecherous adulterer who, to the immense dismay of his wife (the decrepit, sexually repressed Maggie Smith, who seems to have her own unhealthy fascination with the far younger woman), keeps hitting on Isabelle Adjani, but there's no good sex. And, worse still, someone is always tinkling the ivories. Next, I steeled my nerves for *The Europeans*, where Lee Remick plays a conniving continental cousin who comes to the United States seeking romance, tinkles the ivories a few times, then goes back to Europe because the young man she's hitting on is too sexually repressed, and there's no good sex. Finally, I staggered through *The Guru*, a film about a sexually repressed young Englishman who goes to India looking for romance or the meaning of life or whatever. Yes, he is a musician. And yes, the music is appalling.

"Do you want me to wake you up when you fall asleep?" my eight-year-old son Gordon asked me innocently as I attempted to blowtorch my way through *Savages* at the beginning of Week Number Five. Yes, I told him, gloomily rewinding to the part where I'd drifted off. Up until this point, I had found this assignment purely horrifying, the critic's equivalent of Christ's Crucifixion, with eight more Stations of the Cross. But unlike Christ, I wasn't sure I could make it all the way through to the Crucifixion. I mean, at least He had the Romans to put Him out of His misery. Only by asking my two children to tie me to the BarcaLounger, like Odysseus before the Sirens, was I able to survive the film, which features croquet matches, butterfly nets, monocles, harps, *and* the vocal stylings of Bobby Short. And the kids literally had to sit at my side force-feeding me tureens of coffee and smelling salts to get me through *Jane Austen in Manhattan*, a film loaded with corny piano music in which Anne Baxter plays a septuagenarian drama teacher who seems to have an unhealthy fascination with the far, far, far younger Sean Young.

I used the same technique to machete through *Mr. and Mrs. Bridge*, a film loaded with corny piano music and Blythe Danner, in which Paul Newman seems to have an unhealthy fascination with his daughter Kyra Sedgwick, and people keep reading aloud to one another from books at languorous garden parties, and there's no good sex. And only by using extra-tight ropes and pleading with my children to help me stay awake during my private cinematic Gethsemane by sticking toothpicks under my fingernails could I possibly sit through *Maurice*, a dreary tale of sexual repression in the Edwardian era with lots of pianos and cricket, but no good sex, not even Hugh Grant paying somebody for a fast blow job.

But by the beginning of Week Six, when I started watching *A Room with a View*, I was beginning to fear that this was all a lost cause. This fear was confirmed at the end of Week Six, when I still hadn't finished watching *A Room with a View*, a story about a repressed young Englishwoman who comes to exotic Italy seeking romance but instead is trapped under the thumb of the ancient Maggie Smith, who seems to have an unhealthy fascination with a woman two generations younger, while Daniel Day-Lewis plays a twit who reads aloud from musty old 19th-century books during a bunch of interminable garden parties where there's no good sex.

According to every screenplay book I've ever read, the filmmaker must use the first ten minutes of the film to introduce the major characters of the drama and explain what the film is all about, or the audience will lose interest. But ten minutes into *A Room with a View*, Maggie Smith, Denholm Elliott, and Helena Bonham Carter were still arguing about who was going to get the room with a view. At this point, I finally understood why the American Revolution had been fought in the first place. No quantity of blood was too much for us to spill in order to emancipate ourselves from the cultural hegemony of these repressed tight-wads.

My hopes momentarily surged at the beginning of Week Number Seven when I actually managed to get through *The Remains of the Day*, where Anthony Hopkins plays a repressed old lecher who has an unhealthy fascination with the lethal Emma Thompson, and there's no good sex. Yes, it took three whole days, but I finally did it. Now the Grail was in sight. I had fought my way through the dreary Raj films. I had polished off two of the three films set in New York. I had met and subdued, in rapid succession, Maggie Smith, Denholm Elliot, Julian Sands, Michael York, Linda Hunt, Jessica Tandy, the entire Newman Salad Dressing Family, and Dame Peggy Ashcroft. I had singlehandedly watched five films starring the reptilian Shashi Kapoor. I had survived countless boating parties, cricket matches, Edwardian balls, piano recitals, poetry readings, and museum tours. Most important of all, I had escaped unscathed from one of the two Merchant-Ivory movies starring Emma Thompson.

Alas, it was that final Emma Thompson film that would take the measure of this man. What I had never taken into account when I'd undertaken this assignment was the cumulative, deleterious effect of seeing the same horrible people surfacing again and again in a group of films. There are only so many times in a person's life that he should be forced to watch a prissy fop like Simon Callow—what a name!—or James Wilby, and when I saw these refugees from a bevy of previous Merchant-Ivory movies lurch onto my screen once more, I sensed that I was a goner. Yes, I managed to fight my way through to the last scenes in the movie. But by the end of the seventeen days it took me to finish *Howards End*, I knew that my energy was spent. There was nothing left in the tank. There was no way on earth that I—or anyone—could sit through *Slaves of New York*.

I knew that *Slaves of New York* was poison from the moment I spotted the film's video box. To my mind, the video box for *Slaves of New York* is one of the scariest objects in motion picture history, a taunt, a dare, a warning, a threat. And not just because it has

Bernadette Peters on it. Think about it. A movie *by* Merchant and Ivory, written *by* Tama Janowitz, and starring Bernadette Peters. That's like a rhinoplasty by Michael Jackson and Jimmy Durante as adapted by Barbra Streisand with help from Karl Malden. Yes, the notes on the back of the video box tell all:

> *Slaves of New York* is a caustic, comic portrait of Manhattan's bohemian scene, complete with an eclectic ensemble of artists struggling to succeed at their work and love lives. Bernadette Peters stars as Eleanor, a struggling hat designer desperately seeking a "normal" life in the casually cruel, concrete world of New York City. Stuck in an unfulfilling relationship with a narcissistic pop artist, Eleanor sets out on a tentative journey of self-discovery. From one ramshackle SoHo loft to the next, Eleanor gamely endures an assortment of hilariously disastrous encounters with pretentious performance artists, manipulative MBAs, and social-climbing fashion seers, only to be caught *off avant-garde* [*sic*] by her own growing sense of confidence and self-esteem.

Still not scary enough? Read on.

> *Slaves of New York* features impeccable design and production, along with a striking contemporary soundtrack peppered by performances from Iggy Pop, Billie Holiday, Boy George, and Diana Ross and the Supremes.

Cutting fucking edge.

I tried to stay awake. Oh God, I tried to stay awake. But ultimately, life *is* too short. As I sat there in the reclining chair with my kids lighting matches to my feet, I realized that God had created Merchant and Ivory for only one reason: because otherwise the concept of death was too terrifying. Yes, as was the case with Nick Nolte in *Jefferson in Paris*, Merchant and Ivory had performed a miracle of bad casting by positioning Broadway munchkin Bernadette Peters at the center of the action. Peters, the quintessential, heart-on-her-sleeve chantoozy, is about as downtown as Lucie Arnaz. Casting her as a trendy downtown chick makes about as much sense as casting Dana Delany as a dominatrix.

I honestly tried to watch *Slaves of New York* all the way through. I had it cued up on my VCR for three weeks, and every four days or so I would go in and watch a minute or two. But in *Slaves of New York*, I knew that I had finally met my Waterloo. When the Supremes impersonators dressed in skin-tight, orange dresses turned up, I realized that I wasn't going to make it. And then when the entire cast assembled for a softball game, I finally gave up the ghost. A softball game in a Merchant-Ivory movie? Time to turn off the VCR.

What did I learn from my two-month descent into Merchant-Ivory Hell? Basically, to go a whole lot easier on people like Sylvester Stallone. Movies like *Judge Dredd* may be fascistic and sadistic and evil and stupid, but at least nobody ever says, "You have your vicar's benediction?" or "You're a ripping girl" in them.

But that's not the most important thing I took away from my experience. For in a very real sense I have been humbled by my Promethean undertaking. True, I managed to sit through twenty-one Merchant-Ivory movies, and, true, I came within nineteen minutes of actually polishing off their entire *oeuvre*. But at the critical moment, when I had to stand in the fire and look directly into the eye of the tiger, I blinked. At the critical juncture when journalistic immortality was right there within my grasp, I panicked. I choked. Perhaps there was a part of me that realized that I was not worthy of the triumph I was seeking. Perhaps a reservoir of Christian humility told me that I was not yet ready to be assumed into the Pantheon of the Immortals. Perhaps I really couldn't bear the thought of watching Bernadette Peters for nineteen more minutes. Most likely, I recoiled at the last minute because I feared that watching *Slaves of New York* straight through to the very end could destroy me as a human being. The person who had set out to watch all twenty-two of Merchant and Ivory's movies was, at the end of the day, still only a frail mortal. The person who could sit through *Slaves of New York* would have to be a god.

Or Satan Himself.

Note: Since this article appeared in 1995, Ismail Merchant and James Ivory have continued to make Merchant-Ivory movies, as there is no law against it.

THAT'S ENTERTAINMENT?

In a year that the Academy of Motion Picture Arts and Sciences has seen fit to honor a movie about a charming Australian pig, a movie about a semiliterate, incompetent communist postman, and Sharon Stone, one can easily make the case that our pudding has no theme. This would be a foolish oversight. More than any year in recent history, the films nominated for the 1995 Academy Awards are characterized by a number of clear, unifying elements. They are:

1. Virulent hatred of the English aristocracy.

2. Preposterous accents.

3. Civil servants forced to take early retirement.

4. Rampant crucifixion imagery.

5. Kilts.

6. Leading men who no one is all that sorry to see go at the end of the film.

7. Even more hookers than usual.

But first, an overview. The 1995 Academy Awards will be remembered as the year that everything came in duplicate. Mel Gibson was nominated for Best Director for *Braveheart*, a movie about English mistreatment of the Scots, and Tim Roth was nominated for Best Supporting Actor in *Rob Roy*, a movie about English mistreatment of the Scots. Sharon Stone was nominated for Best Actress in *Casino*, a movie about the difficulty of finding love in Las Vegas, and Elizabeth Shue was nominated for Best Actress in *Leaving Las Vegas*, a movie about the difficulty of finding love in Las Vegas. Meryl Streep was nominated for Best Actress for her role as a lovelorn Italian whose drab, rural existence is changed forever by a chance encounter with a globe-trotting "artiste" in *The Bridges of Madison County*, and Massimo Troisi was nominated for Best Actor for his role as a lovelorn Italian whose drab, rural life is changed forever by a chance encounter with a globe-trotting "artiste" in *Il Postino*.

The pattern does not end there. Both Joan Allen (*Nixon*) and Kathleen Quinlan (*Apollo 13*) are up for Best Supporting Awards for playing tight-lipped women whose husbands' careers run aground during the Nixon Administration. Both Mira Sorvino and Elizabeth Shue have been nominated for Oscars after playing prostitutes with hearts of gold who fall in love with complete losers in *Mighty Aphrodite* and *Leaving Las Vegas*. Finally, both Anthony Hopkins in *Nixon* and Richard Dreyfuss in *Mr. Holland's Opus* have been nominated for Best Actor Awards for playing sixty-year-old men who are forced into premature retirement due to outside political pressure.

Hatred of the English upper class is one of the most noticeable themes to surface in the film industry this year. One of the biggest box office winners was *Braveheart*, the Mel Gibson film which depicts the valorous struggle of the courageous Scots against the duplicitous, libidinous, sadistic English back in the early 14th century. Gibson, who directed the film, made English males in particular look so bad that he was nominated as Best Director.

One is tempted to dismiss the rampant anglophobia of *Braveheart* as a complete fluke, reasoning that the Scots' oppressors might just as well have been Vikings or Normans or Jutes, until one considers the strange case of *Rob Roy*. *Rob Roy* is a film which depicts the valorous struggle of the courageous Scots against the duplicitous, libidinous, sadistic English back in the early 18th century. Tim Roth, playing a particularly villainous English fop, was so convincing as a horrible Brit that he was nominated by his peers for Best Supporting Actor.

Again, one is sorely tempted to dismiss the rampant anglophobia of *Rob Roy* as a complete fluke, reasoning that Tim Roth might just as well have been a Belgian or a Saracen or a Sri Lankan or a Jute until one considers the strange case of *Sense and Sensibility*. The film, based on the Jane Austen novel of the same name, deals with two charming young sisters who are unlucky enough to fall in love with a pair of English gentlemen, one an ineffectual fop, the other a complete scoundrel. Again, we are dealing with a film that depicts the English male aristocracy as a pack of scheming, avaricious, backstabbing scoundrels.

One is sorely tempted to dismiss the rampant anglophobia of *Sense and Sensibilty* as a complete fluke until one considers the strange case of *Nixon*, the Oliver Stone movie about the disgraced ex-president. Could it possibly be a coincidence that when Stone went out to find an actor capable of portraying the duplicitous, wheedling, oily, smarmy, backstabbing, generally horrible Richard Nixon that he chose an Englishman? Think about it.

A second common characteristic of Oscar nominees this year is absurd foreign accents. In *Braveheart*, the Australian Mel Gibson speaks with a Scottish accent. In *Nixon*, the Oxbridgian Anthony Hopkins speaks like somebody who went to Whittier College. In *Dead Man Walking*, Sean Penn and Susan Sarandon's torpid southern accents strongly suggest that they prepped for their roles by taking classes at Berlitz's Johnny Reb annex. Meanwhile, in *The Bridges of Madison County*, Meryl Streep sports the most rambunctious Italian accent since Cher whooped things up in *Moonstruck*, and in *Il Postino*, Philippe Noiret, a Frenchman, plays Pablo Neruda, a Spanish-speaking Chilean who conducts all his conversations in Italian. Although the movie has been shown in America with those annoying little yellow subtitles at the bottom of the screen, whenever Noiret opens his mouth in the film, he appears to be speaking not Italian—and certainly not Spanish—but his native French. Meaning that he has been dubbed. Meaning that the movie, which lionizes a lazy, semiliterate commie poet, is both dubbed and subtitled. For this, I need to pay $8.50?

Hapless hookers were out in force this season, with Elizabeth Shue snaring a Best Actress nomination for her portrayal of a call girl who gets involved with a complete jerk in *Leaving Las Vegas*, while Mira Sorvino was nominated for Best Supporting Actress for her portrayal of a call girl who gets involved with a complete jerk in *Mighty Aphrodite*. Also worthy of note is Sharon Stone's nomination for Best Actress for her portrayal of a call girl who gets involved with a whole regiment of complete jerks in Las Vegas in *Casino*. Of all the Academy's nominations this year—lovable Australian pigs, lovestruck commie postmen, Brad Pitt—this is the only one that makes no sense whatsoever.

Premature retirement was a theme that dominated *Nixon*, *Leaving Las Vegas*, and *Mr. Holland's Opus*. In *Leaving Las Vegas*, Best Actor nominee Nicholas Cage plays a Hollywood agent who drinks himself to death after being forced out of his job. In *Nixon*, Anthony Hopkins plays a politician who goes on to write a lot of boring books and do David Frost interviews after being forced out of his job. And in *Mr. Holland's Opus*, Richard Dreyfuss plays a high-school music teacher who is forced to step down from his position after he publicly sings the horrendous John Lennon song "Beautiful Boy" to his deaf son Coltrane.

Kilts were all over the place in 1995—in *Braveheart*, in *Rob Roy*, and in the unjustly neglected *Clueless*—as was crucifixion imagery. In the last scene of *Dead Man Walking*, rapist/murderer Sean Penn, strapped to a gurney, has his arms spread wide, the director obviously intending some arcane link with the death of Jesus Christ. Jesus Christ, when last I checked, was not crucified for any crimes resembling those of the character played by Mr. Penn. But never mind.

Crucifixion imagery also surfaces in *Braveheart*, where Mel Gibson, playing the Scottish patriot William Wallace, is strapped to a crosslike structure and has his entrails yanked out. And, naturally, Oliver Stone flashes an image of Christ crucified shortly before the finale of his interminable *Nixon*, though in Nixon's case, the crucifixion imagery probably refers to the plight of the Good Thief.

The demise of Sean Penn and Anthony Hopkins at the end of the films for which they have garnered Best Actor nominations focuses our attention on another dominant theme in this year's awards: the rapture the audience experiences once these depraved human beings finally leave the stage. Ranging from Nicholas Cage, a louse who drinks himself to death in *Leaving Las Vegas*, to rapist-murderer Penn, who ends up succumbing to a lethal injection, to Tim Roth, who ends up with his body sliced in half by Liam Neeson at the end of *Rob Roy*, to Hugh Grant, who ends up having to marry Emma Thompson at the end of *Sense and Sensibility*, I can't remember a single year in recent history when so many movies ended with a complete bum getting his just deserts.

Purists may argue that this is not the case in *Mr. Holland's Opus*, where Dreyfuss torments the audience for at least two minutes by singing the horrible "Beautiful Boy" to his deaf son and then gets to leave the stage—and the movie—without having his entrails torn out. I disagree with this assessment. Let me explain why.

Mr. Holland's Opus deals with an aging high-school music teacher forced into early retirement because of local budgetary constraints that are almost certainly the fault of people like Dick Armey. As the film draws to its sappy conclusion, a dejected Mr. Holland is seen dragging himself out of his office for the very last time when suddenly he hears a hubbub in the assembly hall. To his amazement, the legions of well-meaning but inept students he has taught for the past three decades have come back to give his long forgotten First Symphony its very first and, one hopes, very last performance. The symphony—a mishmash of the best of Gustav Holst and the worst of Ludwig van Beethoven—is so awful it makes you wish that the hoods who beat Joe Pesci to death with baseball bats at the end of *Casino* would pop by to knock some sense into Holland.

Nevertheless, it is clear from the panache with which Mr. Dreyfuss wields his baton in front of this sea of tin ears that the scene is intended to send the audience home from the theater with an uplifting sense that Mr. Holland's career has not been a complete washout.

But then the movie springs a big surprise. Just before Mr. Holland takes the podium, the state's governor, also one of his old students, bursts into the auditorium to deliver an electrifying send-off speech. She then demurely, self-effacingly takes her place as oboist with the orchestra—the way New York lieutenant governor Betsy McCaughey would—and puckers up. At this point, *Mr. Holland's Opus* seems to cleverly shift gears and become a searing indictment of school boards everywhere. Let's face it: Big send-off or no big send-off, at the end of the film Mr. Holland still ends up getting booted right out onto the street.

The film thus lends itself to two entirely different interpretations. From the point of view of bleeding-heart liberals, it seems to say, If one of your woodwind students grows up to be governor but still doesn't pack enough punch to save your job, who cares how well she plays the oboe? With friends like this, who needs gubernatorial oboists?

Budget-slashing conservatives, on the other hand, can derive an entirely different moral from the picture: If you fritter away all the time you could have spent grading term papers or rehearsing the glee club for the past thirty years writing symphonies as rotten as Mr. Holland's *Opus*, the school board probably should have fired you a long time ago.

What can we learn from all this? It has long been my belief that motion pictures are the subconscious expression of the beliefs, aspirations, fears, and neuroses of the American people. Based on the evidence supplied by this year's slate of Academy Award nominees, this society, from a psychological point of view, is in very good shape indeed. In movies nominated for Academy Awards in 1995, drunks died, mobsters got beaten to death with baseball bats, rapists/murderers were subjected to lethal injections, and English fops were either slain by heroic Scotsmen or forced to marry Emma Thompson. All in all, it was a very good year: The Forces of Righteousness prevailed on the silver screen. My only quibble? I really do wish that Richard Dreyfuss had been drawn and quartered at the end of *Mr. Holland's Opus*.

But that's show business.

MATINEE IDLE

Down through the ages, wise men have vainly striven to understand seemingly inexplicable, apparently irrational human actions. Why did Hitler allow the British army to escape at Dunkirk? Why did Custer attack the largest gathering of American Indians in history with just 225 men under his command? Why did the Aztecs allow Cortez to imprison their emperor? Why did Attila the Hun, with all Europe in flames and nothing standing in his way, turn back at the gates of Rome? And why did otherwise sane Americans agree to pay $9 to see that Joe Pecsi film *Gone Fishin'* last summer?

It is this last question that will concern us here. Let me confess that I am one of those people who has never lost his childlike belief that the next motion picture he sees could be the worst film ever made. That's why I go to all of them. So you can imagine my euphoria on May 6, 1997, when I spied an ad for the film *Gone Fishin'*. Starring those reliable old hams Joe Pesci and Danny Glover, *Gone Fishin'* dealt with a pair of Jersey-bred poltroons who go on a fishing trip in Florida and wind up in a whole passel of trubble. The dead giveaway that the movie was going to suck— aside from the fact that both Joe Pesci and Danny Glover were in it—was the series of blurbs used in the newspaper ads:

"Holy Mackerel—You'll Laugh Your Bass Off!"
                                        —*The Sandshark Sentinel*
"Thank cod for this movie!"
                                        —*Saturday Evening Pike*
"Bring Your Whole Grouper to This Movie!"
                                        —*Barnacle and Seaweed Monthly*

In other words, the studio couldn't even get Medved and that other idiot to say something nice about it. Clearly, *Gone Fishin'* had the potential to be the worst film of this or any year, so I made a mental note to see it as soon as humanly possible.

But then I got a brainstorm. According to my newspaper listings, the Sony Lincoln Square complex at Sixty-eighth and Broadway had scheduled an 11:40 A.M. screening of the motion picture. As soon as I saw that early-morning listing, I became obsessed with finding out what kind of person would turn up for an 11:40 A.M. screening of a film that was transparently unwatchable, and that had already been panned by every critic in America.

So instead of going to see the movie the day it opened, I decided to wait until the following Thursday, the last day of its run. This way, I could be certain that the film had been out long enough that anyone who went to see it would already know that it sucked. My intention at the time was to wait until the end of the film and then ask departing patrons how they had reached such an abject juncture in their lives where they had nothing better to do with their time than to attend the 11:40 A.M. screening of a Joe Pesci movie. Costarring Danny Glover. By eliciting an answer to this question, I felt that I could penetrate to the core of one of the deepest mysteries of human behavior: Why do human beings so often subject themselves to wounds that are entirely self-inflicted? This would stand me in good stead if I was ever asked to do a story about why people live in rural Arkansas, buy season tickets to see the San Diego Padres, or marry women who went to law school.

Things did not work out exactly the way I had planned. When I arrived at the theater that morning, there were five of us in attendance, all men. The film started rolling, and, as I had expected, it sucked to the ninth power of suckitude. About a third of the way through the movie, one guy got up and left. I figured he was probably a salesman and had just been killing time, so his purchase of a ticket signified nothing. Ten minutes later, another guy left. He too I ignored. Then, about twenty minutes before the end of the film, a young man way up front who had been the only person to laugh at anything said during the film also departed. Since he had not technically sat all the way through the movie, I had to assume that he also had simply been killing time. That left me and a somewhat taciturn African-American senior citizen in the last row who did not seem to think the film was a laugh riot. This was the guy I needed to talk to.

But at the end of the film, as the man dragged himself out of his seat and trudged out into the lobby, I had a sudden change of heart. It was obvious from the man's body language that he had come to the movie house expecting a barrel-load of chuckles and had been cruelly disappointed. Here was a guy who had lived through the Great Depression and had probably served in World War II and had maybe even been wounded at Guadalcanal or Anzio and who had lived through the whole civil rights crusade and all that other neat stuff, yet who now, in the autumn of his years, found himself with nothing better to do than to attend a Joe Pesci movie at 11 o'clock in the morning. Watching him straggle off, I felt that it would be ignoble to subject him to one of my cruel, wise-assed journalistic pranks. Instead, for reasons I still do not fully understand, I decided to bring some much-needed sunshine into his life.

"Excuse me, sir, may I talk to you for a second?" I asked.

"Yes?" he said, mildly suspicious.

"Sir, I represent the Joe Pesci Cultural Indemnification Institution and I have been personally authorized to refund your nine dollars for sitting through this horrible movie."

The man looked at me in disbelief as I handed him a five and four ones.

"Are you serious?"

"I am."

I will never, ever forget the radiant smile that cascaded across his face as he took the money.

"Man," he said, beaming up at me, "this is just so *nice*."

It was, it really was. Although I had been contributing to philanthropic organizations like CARE, MADD, and the New York State Democratic Party for years, I had never gotten any visceral gratification from my generosity, because I had never gotten to see the whale, manatee, or small, tubercular Guatemalan child that my infinite largesse had rescued from perdition. But after I saw that wonderful smile surge onto the old man's face, I decided that this newly discovered grassroots selflessness was the way to go. At long last, after all those years of jaded detachment, I had turned myself into one of the thousand points of light.

I am not a compassionate person, and people who have been invited over to my house for dinner are well aware that I am not a generous person, either. But from the moment that elderly man flashed me that headlight smile, I realized for the first time in my life that generosity is a two-way street. Sure, I was taking nine dollars out of my own pocket just to make another human being feel good about himself. But in doing so I was also pouring water on the hot fires of cynicism that raged in my savage breast. Or something. Never before in my jaundiced adulthood had I felt such an emotional jolt. And let me tell you, I liked the feeling I was getting.

For the rest of the day, I positioned myself outside motion picture theaters whenever a screening of *Gone Fishin'* had just finished, and gave refunds to patrons who looked like they were in distress. Sometimes I said I was from the Joe Pesci Cultural Indemnification Institute. Other times, I identified myself as a representative of the American Celluloid Retribution Society who was authorized to give patrons complete refunds for sitting through very bad movies in the hope that word would spread throughout the community that not everyone in Hollywood was completely demonic. By the end of the day, I had given away ninety crisp one-dollar bills.

Most of the beneficiaries of my altruism seemed overjoyed to get the money. But oddly enough, not all of them acted completely surprised. Typical was the exchange I had with a sixty-something woman, a rugged, chain-smoking type whom I immediately sized up as a native New Yorker.

"Ma'am, I represent an organization called the League of Cinematic Retribution, and I have been personally authorized to refund you the price of this appalling film," I explained.

"Thanks," she said, tucking the money away in her bag. "You do this a lot?"

"I do."

Her eyes lit up.

"Like, where?"

"Like, all over the place."

"Well, could you tell me, what other films are you doing?"

I took my cue.

"Ma'am, wherever there's a movie starring Dan Aykroyd, look around and I'll be there. Wherever there's a movie starring Adam Sandler, Chris Farley, David Spade, or Pauly Shore, look around and I'll be there. Wherever people are being forced to watch movies starring Jennifer Anniston, David Schwimmer, Courteney Cox, or any of the members of the cast of *Friends*, with the possible exception of *Scream*, where Cox has only a bit part and which was directed by cult favorite Wes Craven, look around and I'll be there."

The woman remained nonplussed.

"Well, I'll be looking out for you."

I cannot adequately put into words the joyous feeling I came home with that day after restoring so many unsuspecting persons' faith in the American movie industry. I felt like Black Jack Pershing at Belleau Wood, like MacArthur returning to the Philippines, like Jesus at the marriage feast of Cana. Joe Pesci will do that to you. But as I lay down on my pillow that evening, I began to more closely examine my motives for this sudden munificence. And the more I thought about it, the more I realized that for as long as I could remember, I had always dreamed of the moment when a complete stranger would walk up to *me* and give *me* a complete refund for the odious movie I had just seen. Subconsciously, by compensating all these anonymous individuals for their suffering, I was trying to repay myself for the hours, days, and even years I had spent looking at stupendously horrible motion pictures. At some deeply buried level of my consciousness, I was seeking vindication, compensation, and yes, perhaps even closure.

The next day, I mentioned my experiences to a friend.

"Oh, you're like the Guardian Angels!" she giggled. "Only you're the Bad Movie Angel."

That's right. That's exactly what I was. I was the Bad Movie Angel. And to be a truly effective Bad Movie Angel, it was vital that I have the appropriate uniform. So later that day, I bought myself a beret and a red shirt and had the words BAD MOVIE ANGEL painted onto it. Then I armed myself with a fistful of fives and singles, arranged them in wads of nine dollars each, and headed back out into the streets.

For the next three months, I was the Bad Movie Angel: a mild-mannered reporter by day, an Angel of Mercy by later in the day. Whenever I found some free time, I would duck into a men's room, don my garish costume, and slip into dark, depressing movie houses, distributing refunds to long-suffering film lovers. It was surely one of the happiest times in my life, one of the few periods during my sojourn on this planet when I actually felt that I was doing something useful. The only time, in fact.

But being the Bad Movie Angel was not as easy as I thought.

One problem was that the public and I could not always agree on what constituted a bad movie. One afternoon, I purchased a ticket for *Out to Sea*, a Jack Lemmon/Walter Matthau vehicle that seemed to have all the earmarks of high suck. In fact, the movie was not nearly as bad as I expected it to be. Although Lemmon was his usual unbearable self, Matthau was reasonably funny, and the film was ultimately redeemed by Brent Spiner's star turn as a supercilious cruise ship entertainment director. What's more, when the film ended, I could tell by the happy expressions on the dozen or so audience members' faces that they had thoroughly enjoyed the motion picture.

This being the case, it was impossible for the Bad Movie Angel to give anyone a refund. For the Bad Movie Angel to become the stuff of modern urban legend, he had to be known as a creature who only gave refunds to people who had sat through truly appalling movies. If the Bad Movie Angel started giving refunds to people who had sat through merely mediocre films, he would quickly go broke. What's more, his generosity would encourage the public to believe that they would be rewarded not only for watching totally unwatchable films, but for watching partially unwatchable films. This was not the way the Bad Movie Angel operated. The Bad Movie Angel wanted to restore a smile to the lips and a song to the heart of those who had been totally ripped off by Hollywood, innocent victims who felt like stooges, clowns, patsies. The Bad Movie Angel had no interest in perking up moviegoers who were merely slightly miffed.

This was not the only problem faced by the Bad Movie Angel. A far bigger problem was the logistical element: finding the time to sit through lots of *seemingly* bad movies just to make sure that they were *genuinely* bad. Luckily, years and years of experience in writing about bad movies had given the Bad Movie Angel pretty good intuition in this area. For example, The Bad Movie Angel instinctively knew that *A Smile Like Yours*, starring Greg Kinnear, had to suck, because if the studio was interested in making a good movie, why would they have hired Greg Kinnear to be in it? But

A Smile Like Yours was not the cakewalk the Bad Movie Angel had expected. At the end of the film, the Bad Movie Angel gave a man who had sat all the way through the film without laughing his full $9 refund. Immediately, the Bad Movie Angel was approached by one of the other patrons in the theater and asked if she too could have a refund.

"No," replied the Bad Movie Angel. "You came in two thirds of the way through the film and you laughed at the part where the nurse put on the surgical gloves for the rectal exam, which wasn't funny."

"Oh," she said, glumly. Reluctantly, the Bad Movie Angel gave her a $3 refund for the one-third of the film she had sat through, but told her not to expect such rules-bending in the future. She didn't seem too pleased.

"The Bad Movie Angel does not grade on a curve," the woman was curtly warned. "Be advised."

The worst part about being the Bad Movie Angel was having to sit through horrible movies and then finding that there was nobody to give any money to because everyone had enjoyed the film so much. This is what happened when the Bad Movie Angel went to see the latest Shaquille O'Neal offering. *Steel* was an idiotic shoot-'em-up that had absolutely no redeeming features, yet the eighty or ninety kids in the room, not to mention the eight adults, enjoyed it immensely. There was no way the Bad Movie Angel was going to reward that kind of cultural depravity. Sure, the Bad Movie Angel had been sent to earth to spread a message of good cheer. But asking the Bad Movie Angel to give complete refunds to people after they had laughed merrily through an idiotic film was like asking Saint Teresa of Avila to visit Planet Earth and reward people for masturbating or fibbing. No way you were going to catch *this* Bad Movie Angel pulling crap like that.

As the weeks passed, the Bad Movie Angel's heart began to grow heavy. One thing that bothered him was that fewer and fewer people expressed surprise when he approached them, wads of fresh dollar bills in his hand. It was as if they knew that the

Bad Movie Angel was out there and figured it was only a matter of time before they ran into him. Typical was an exchange outside a Times Square movie theater in early September, when the Bad Movie Angel approached a young man of about nineteen. "Did you just sit through *The Texas Chainsaw Massacre IV*?" the Bad Movie Angel asked.

"Yes," came the reply.

"How was it?"

"It sucked."

"Well, I'm the Bad Movie Angel and I'd like to give you a complete refund for sitting through this revolting motion picture."

"*Kewl,*" the young man replied. And then he simply walked away.

Little by little, the Bad Movie Angel came to realize that his time on Earth was drawing to a close. When he approached two seventy-year-old women after a screening of the joyously moronic *G.I. Jane*, they honestly reported that the movie was a disappointment, then stuck the money into their handbags, never once breaking stride on their way to the ladies' room.

"You didn't have to do that," said one of them, which was a nice enough reply, but whatever happened to: "[GASP!] Thank you, Mr. Bad Movie Angel! Thank you a thousand times! And may the road rise to meet your feet in the morning!"

When the Bad Movie Angel recounted this experience to a friend, she got him even more ticked off by pointing out that senior citizens didn't have to pay the full $9 to see a movie, especially not one shown early in the day. Yet not one of the lucky seniors had pointed this out to the Bad Movie Angel, cagily pocketing enough cash to cover not one, but two cinematic outings. The Bad Movie Angel was getting ripped off by his very own flock.

One day the Bad Movie Angel decided to return to the original premise of this entire undertaking and to find out what possessed seemingly intelligent people to throw away their money on irredeemably horrible movies. Buttonholing a middle-aged couple who were coming out of *A Smile Like Yours*, he asked if they had just seen the movie with Greg Kinnear and if so, why.

"No special reason," she replied.

"I slept through it," he replied. "So I really can't say."

Determined not to reward such indifferent moviegoers, the Bad Movie Angel now spotted another man coming out of the theater.

"Why did you go to see *A Smile Like Yours*?" the angel inquired.

"It looked like it would be good. And I liked other things he was in."

The Bad Movie Angel then asked what these other things were, and the man said he couldn't remember. In fact, the "other things" was *Sabrina*.

Now the Bad Movie Angel got a tad personal.

"Do you always go to movies without knowing what they're like?"

"Not usually."

"But sometimes?"

"Yeah, sometimes."

"Let me ask you a question. Do you ever ride the subway?"

"Sure."

"Before you get on the subway, do you ever check to see where the train is going? Or do you have a specific location you're headed towards?"

"I see the analogy you're trying to make, and it's valid," said the man.

"So . . . ?"

The man kind of shrugged his shoulders. "It's not that big a deal. You know?"

"Does that mean you don't want the nine dollars?"

"No, I want the nine dollars."

Based on this and a few other experiences like it, the Bad Movie Angel came to realize that nine goddamn stinking bucks wasn't enough to impress most people. Sure, the disappointed movie-goers were happy to have a visit from the Bad Movie Angel. But it wasn't like they'd been visited by Bob Barker or Madonna or something, or had been handed a free microwave. Nine bucks one way or the other wasn't going to make much difference in the lives of people who had nothing better to do with their time than to go see universally panned Greg Kinnear films in the middle of the afternoon.

For some time, the Bad Movie Angel had suspected that when people took his $9 refunds, they did not learn anything from the experience, but simply used the cash windfall to finance an expedition to a movie starring Steven Seagal or costarring Charlie Sheen. This premonition was confirmed in a dramatic, heartrending manner when the Bad Movie Angel gave a $9 refund to a man who had just confirmed that *G.I. Jane* sucked, then watched in horror as the man bounded up the street and disappeared into a porno palace.

One day the Bad Movie Angel approached a young Chinese-American man and his Hispanic girlfriend, and asked if they had just seen the dreadful Alicia Silverstone vehicle, *Excess Baggage*. They had. He asked if it was any good. They replied that it was not. As usual, the Bad Movie Angel whipped into action, pulling out eighteen crisp one dollar bills. The woman was clearly thrilled at the sight of the money. But the man gave the Bad Movie Angel a cold, blank, dead-eyed stare.

"You just do this?" the girl asked.

"Yes, I'm the Bad Movie Angel and I give away refunds to people who have just sat through bad movies in the hope that the experience will not wreck their faith in cinema."

"We don't want the money," the young man said.

The Bad Movie Angel was totally floored. Did they think this was a Letterman-type prank? Some kinky kind of sexual turn-on? Or perhaps the old, Bad-Movie-Angel-gives-you-eighteen-dollars-but-as-a-show-of-good-faith-you-have-to-withdraw-$5,000-from-your-bank-account scam?

"You don't want the money?" said the Bad Movie Angel, aghast.

"No," said the man. "Thank you."

And then they vanished from the Bad Movie Angel's life for good.

That night, the Bad Movie Angel dragged himself back to his home and stripped off his Bad Movie Angel T-shirt and beret forever. That seraphic, never-to-be-forgotten expression of joy on the old man's face the morning he had seen *Gone Fishin'* was now but a distant memory. The Bad Movie Angel had alighted on this planet in the hopes of bringing hope and sustenance to a downtrodden public, but had now become a figure of scorn, a creepy old turd skulking around Times Square trying to give unwanted money—probably still moist—to young guys' foxy girlfriends. The Bad Movie Angel could live with being taken for granted. But he could not live with being despised.

Along the highways and byways of mighty Gotham, there are people touched by the Bad Movie Angel who still keep his legend alive. Some say that the Bad Movie Angel has just taken a breather. Others say that he is dead; still others that he is merely asleep. Some people claim to have sighted him in Tarrytown, New York. The truth of the matter is, the Bad Movie Angel lives no more. Yet his work lives on in the hearts of the people who briefly crossed his celestial path. One day, perhaps, when cineplexes show nothing but Demi Moore and Greg Kinnear movies, when the entire nation cries out for deliverance from films starring Emilio Estevez and Pauly Shore, when an entire race of once proud people need the balm of Gilead applied to their wounds, the Bad Movie Angel will return. But I wouldn't count on it. The Bad Movie Angel is already out about three hundred bucks on this deal, and even he knows a losing proposition when he sees one.

AND THEN THERE
WERE NUNS

In every human being's life, there comes a moment when he finds himself trapped in the epicenter of the vortex of the eye of the storm of the most viscerally and emotionally disequilibrating experience he will ever encounter. For many of us, this will occur when we take our marriage vows; for others, when we make the belated discovery that the person sharing our bed in the Econo-Lodge this evening is not of the gender we initially thought he/she/it was. For still others, it is the moment when we agree to spend a night at Michael Jackson's house. And then, of course, there is the moment of death itself: often a surprise, usually a bummer.

In my own life, the most emotionally discombobulating experience I have ever undergone is watching Mamie Van Doren erupt into tears in the back of a chapel at a Catholic girl's reform school while Paul Anka sings "Ave Maria" to her. *You would cry too, if it happened to you.* This scene occurs toward the end of the acrobatically awful film *Girls Town*, in which the top-heavy Van Doren, easily pushing thirty, perhaps from the other side, plays a wayward teen sent to a Roman Catholic halfway house for alleged psychopaths while the local police investigate charges that she murdered her boyfriend Chip. Eventually, we learn that Chip was actually pushed off a cliff by Mamie's kid sister during one of those botched rape attempts for which people named Chip, Kip, Skip, Flip, and Rip are justifiably famous. Mamie's kid sister is played with consummate verve by Cathy Crosby. There have, of course, been other, worse Cathy Crosbys since then, though most of them spell their name with a *K*.

Sis ultimately seeks refuge in the same halfway house as Mamie, no doubt hoping that Frankie Avalon will show up and sing "Tantum Ergo" or "Adeste, Fidelis." But before anything this sublimely ludicrous can happen, she is kidnapped by Mel Torme—the aging crooner, the paleolithic lounge lizard, the *capo di tutti schmucki*, and one of the strangest-looking people to ever inhabit this planet—who plays a lecherous, hot-rodding teen who finally gets popped in the kisser by Anka, an even uglier actor, an even more annoying singer, an even more pre–Jurassic-era lounge lizard, and an even shorter human being. At which point, Torme swoons into a velvet fog.

All of this lunacy is finally brought under control when Mamie gets down on her knees and prays to Saint Jude, the patron saint of hopeless causes. (Apparently, her prayers have something to do with Paul Anka's voice.) Run to earth by a contingent of vigilantes headed by a nun armed with a large wooden mallet, Torme's reign of terror finally ends. Shortly thereafter, Mamie is sprung from the spiritual slammer, Sis is cleared of all pending charges for homicide, Anka agrees to call off his doomed liturgical singing career, and everyone else lives happily ever after.

If the preceding plot line sounds completely insane, that's because it is. How then, one wonders, did the people involved in the manufacture and distribution of this cultural anomaly ever stray so far from their psychic and cinematic moorings that they could end up filming a scene in a dimly lit chapel in which Paul Anka sings "Ave Maria" to Mamie Van Doren, she of the nuclear bosom, who doesn't give the impression that she actually understands what Anka is singing, and probably thinks he's warbling something like "My God, you've got amazing tits" in Latin?

The easy answer to this question is: It was 1959, the Russians had just sent up their first manned rocket ship, everyone was zonked out by fear of nuclear war, Castro had just taken over Cuba, Nixon looked like a pretty safe bet to become the next president of the United States, everybody in America was completely bananas. But this is not an acceptable answer. Elvis Presley appearing in a movie about a youngster whose dad wants him to become a pharmacist? *Stupid.* Creatures from another planet invading serene, middle-American communities and destroying the delicate fabric of society as we know it? *Wacky.* Charlton Heston cavorting in a loincloth and pretending to be a likable Jewish chariot driver? *Definitely peculiar.* But Paul Anka singing "Ave Maria" to a lachrymose Mamie Van Doren in a chapel shortly before she gets down on her knees and prays that Saint Jude will give Paul Anka a voice like Neil Sedaka's?

Now, that's insanity.

How did all of this mental illness come about? The answer to this question is surprisingly simple: The filmmakers were making a nun movie and all nun movies ultimately descend into a dark abyss of lunacy. Whether the setting is 17th-century France (*The Devils*), late–20th-century Detroit (*Sister Act*), the highest reaches of the Himalayas in the 1940s (*Black Narcissus*), contemporary Madrid (*Dark Habits*), Belgium in the mid-1960s (*The Singing Nun*), or 12,000 feet above Salt Lake City circa 1974 (*Airport 1975*), all movies that feature nuns in prominent roles ultimately end in a teeming cesspool of incurable dementia.

Of course, most of them *begin* in a teeming cesspool of incurable dementia. Shirley MacLaine as a roving, polylingual missionary cantering around on a little burro during a civil war in

19th-century Mexico in *Two Mules for Sister Sarah*? (My, that's a new twist.) Kathleen Byron as a neurotic nun sequestered in an abandoned harem in the Himalayas who gets her jollies by dolling herself up behind closed doors in a little black cocktail dress she purchased mail-order from Calcutta, then tries to push Mother Superior Deborah Kerr off a bell tower in *Black Narcissus*? (Gee, that sounds plausible.) Vanessa Redgrave as a hunchbacked, sex-crazed, demon-possessed lunatic in *The Devils*? (What a refreshing change of pace.) A bunch of East German and Hungarian nuns marooned in the Arizona desert waiting for Sidney Poitier to show up and build them a chapel in *Lilies of the Field*? (Well, we certainly haven't tried filming that one in a while.) Whoopi Goldberg as a person who a large group of white people—or anyone—would cheerfully welcome into their midst in *Sister Act*? (Terrific idea.) And while we're at it, how about Helen Reddy as a nun who sings to Linda Blair in Australian shortly before an epic aviation disaster in *Airport 1975*?

Credible.

Believable.

Bankable.

Sane.

The most interesting kernel of truth about nun movies is that in the entire history of the genre, there has never been a movie that accurately portrays nuns the way they really are. As a Roman Catholic who has *only* attended Roman Catholic schools and universities in his lifetime, as a person who has *never* set foot inside a nonsectarian institution of higher learning, and as a person who has watched twenty-nine nun movies in the last two weeks, I can say with complete confidence that there are no nuns on this planet who look anything like Ingrid Bergman in *The Bells of St. Mary's*, Audrey Hepburn in *The Nun's Story*, or Deborah Kerr in *Black Narcissus*.

There are also no convents on this planet that house nuns with names like Sister Manure and Sister Rat, as depicted in Pedro

Almodovar's *Dark Habits*. Nor are there any religious orders I know of that would willingly accept into their community a fruit loop like Meg Tilly in *Agnes of God*, a ding-dong like Mary Tyler Moore in *Change of Habit*, or a sex-addled maniac like Vanessa Redgrave in *The Devils*. The portrayals of nuns in these movies are complete and utter misrepresentations, and everyone associated with these products will burn in Hell for all eternity. Of course, everyone who works in the movie business is going to burn in hell for all eternity anyway, so this is no big threat.

Interestingly, what makes nun movies so outrageously inaccurate is not the obsession of the directors and screenwriters with the nuns' imagined sexual problems, but the persistent failure of Hollywood to depict nuns as the remorseless terrorists that they truly are. In preparing this article, I watched twenty-nine movies in which nuns play a prominent role. In vain did I wait for the truly explosive violence that is an intregal feature of all nuns' lives. True, Kathleen Byron did try to push Deborah Kerr off that bell tower at the end of *Black Narcissus*, Meg Tilly did strangle her newborn baby in *Agnes of God*, and the surprising crepuscular arrival of a shadowy group of nuns at the end of *Vertigo* did scare Kim Novak so much that she plunged to her senseless death hundreds of feet below. Yet in not one of these movies was there a single scene in which anyone gets hit with the ruler.

This is preposterous. As anyone who has ever attended parochial school can tell you, a movie that attempts to portray a day in the life of the average nun without including at least one scene in which a recalcitrant student gets worked over with the ruler or yardstick is like a movie about the Mafia in which not a single person gets whacked. The closest any of these twenty-nine movies comes to portraying nuns as the remorselessly vindictive papal enforcers that they are is *The Devils*, in which Vanessa Redgrave's false testimony against Oliver Reed leads to his having his tongue impaled with a red-hot torture implement, his legs smashed to smithereens by a deranged inquisitor, and his body set ablaze in the public square while his own illegitimate, two-month-old son looks on. Which is still a lot less painful than being hit by a nun with a ruler.

Why are nun movies so hopelessly estranged from the reality of religious life? And why do all nun movies eventually plunge into a dark whirlpool of lunacy? The easy answer is: Oliver Reed and Meg Tilly are on the set. But that only applies to a couple of movies. The reason that all the other nun movies go completely off the rails is much simpler. *It's the music.* Go to see virtually any nun movie and at some critical juncture a group of sisters will be spotlighted in a grotesque, stomach-turning musical number, often featuring a lethal stringed instrument intimately associated with Joan Baez. Shortly thereafter, a senseless, horrible tragedy will occur, and the film will spin hopelessly out of control.

For example, in *The Sound of Music*, not very long after spunky novice Julie Andrews strums a god-awful number on the guitar, the Nazis rise to power in Germany, annex Austria, and wreck the 20th century for everyone except Melanie Griffith, who still gets to infiltrate the Nazi high command in *Shining Through*. In *The Devils*, Oliver Reed's misfortunes occur shortly after Vanessa and her fellow nuns are seen chanting vespers in the chapel. " 'Cause I'm goin' to the chapel, and I'm gonna get in-cin-e-ra-ted." And in *Airport 1975*, it is only after Helen Reddy picks up Linda Blair's guitar and begins to sing a song with the lyric "I am my best friend to myself"—a statement I have no trouble whatsoever believing—that a private plane crashes into the cockpit of the jet, kills flight engineer Erik Estrada and copilot Roy Thinnes, and blinds Efrem Zimbalist Jr., thus leaving the aircraft in the hands of the cross-eyed stewardess Karen Black. Only then do the passengers realize that they should have flown United or Delta, rather than Air Bimbo.

The intimate connection between singing nuns and senseless human tragedy is a staple of virtually every nun film ever made. Take *The Singing Nun*. Moments after Debbie Reynolds wreaks carnage with her avenging guitar, a little Belgian boy is hit by a truck, apparently while trying to get out of earshot. In *Sister Act*, not very long after Whoopi Goldberg induces a group of dowdy, prune-faced nuns to abandon their tired old Gregorian chants and sing a bunch of tired old Motown songs, Harvey Keitel, quite justifiably, attempts to murder her. *Stop! In the name of love,* indeed.

And that's not even mentioning *Change of Habit*, the curious project in which Elvis Presley plays a crusading Johnny Reb physician who has fled the backwoods of Tennessee for the inner city of Detroit. Not long after the King of Kings has taught Mary Tyler Moore how to play the guitar, a local loser shows up and tries to rape her. *Hey, what goes around, comes around.* And while it is true that Kathleen Byron has been gradually slipping over the edge since the very beginning of *Black Narciccus* (in part because of her obsession with David Farrar, a failed Stewart Granger impersonator who wears a Jolly Green Giant hat throughout the movie, making him look like an Annapurnan Robin Hood), her final catapult into the abyss of mental illness occurs shortly after Deborah Kerr and her fellow nuns sing a preposterous Irish yuletide carol called "Lullay My Liking."

What is most troubling about the demented music in nun movies is the staggering variety and styles of horrendous numbers conjured up. In *Agnes of God*, it's Meg Tilly chanting in Latin. (Apparently, just as Spanish is the loving tongue, Latin is the appropriate idiom for nuns who have strangled their illegitimate children.) Nuns with guitars—truly the single most frightening sight in the entire solar system—surface in *Lilies of the Field*, *Change of Habit*, *Airport '75*, *The Sound of Music*, and *The Singing Nun*, whereas nuns armed with pianos rear their ugly headdresses in *Nuns on the Run*, *Sister Act*, *Sister Act 2*, and *Black Narcissus*.

In an especially unnerving sequence in Almodovar's *Dark Habits*, a nun armed with a pair of bongos begins banging on them in the backyard of the convent. Luckily, she is interrupted in mid-bongo by her pet tiger, who reaches out with his paw and forces her to stop. Almodovar's symbolism is clear: The nun with the bongos symbolizes the boundless power of Almighty God, who can fuck around with us as much as He likes, and there's nothing any of us can do about it. The tiger, on the other hand, symbolizes tortured humanity, who would like Almighty God to give us all a break. I admit this pattern of symbolism might be a bit hard to follow.

Dark Habits is worthy of mention in another context, because it is the seminal nun movie of the post-Mamie Van Doren era, the nun movie of which at least two other nun movies are a direct rip-off. Released in 1984, *Dark Habits* is a film in which a destitute lounge lizardess takes refuge in a convent after her lover O.D.s on heroin, and then ends up transforming the grim old convent into a veritable Isle of Capri with her pep, her personality, and her capacious stash of cocaine. Also bear in mind that the climactic scene in the film features the lounge lizardine performing her cabaret act in the convent itself, in front of a bunch of rapturous communicants, with musical accompaniment provided by three nuns, one even armed with an electric bass guitar. Does this sound a little bit like *Sister Act*, or what?

Or consider *Change of Habit*, the 1969 film in which Mary Tyler Moore plays a feisty upstart nun who comes to an urban ghetto where she does not exactly blend in and is initially greeted with frosty disdain by her aging, conservative superior, but who ultimately manages to win over her aging, conservative, disdainful religious superior with her gusto and oomph and all-around musical expertise. Does this sound a little bit like *Sister Act*, or what?

Or consider *Nuns on the Run*, the 1990 British comedy in which Eric Idle and Robbie Coltrane play two bozos who hide out from the mob by disguising themselves as nuns in a convent headed by the crusty old Janet Suzman, who doesn't actually like them. Does this sound just a teensy-weensy bit like *Sister Act*, or what?

Besides insufferable music and crusty old Mother Superiors played by frosty British actresses, the one other staple of all nun movies is a scene where a miracle occurs. In *Lilies of the Field*, there are actually two miracles: the first, when the bricks needed to build the chapel miraculously appear out of nowhere; the second, when the German-speaking nuns learn to speak English by singing Negro spirituals with Sidney Poitier. In *The Bells of St. Mary's*, a miracle occurs when the church is saved from demolition by the change of heart of a hardened businessman who takes a shine to Bing Crosby. In *The Song of Bernadette*, a miracle occurs when the Blessed Virgin Mary appears to a dim-witted peasant girl in a grotto in France in the middle of the 19th century and the town is miraculously turned into a booming tourist attraction, a sort of Niagara Falls for Catholics. And in *Airport '75*, a miracle occurs when Helen Reddy picks up Linda Blair's guitar and begins strumming a song called "I'm My Own Best Friend," yet none of the other passengers try lynching her. What's more, a second miracle then occurs, when cross-eyed actress Karen Black keeps the aircraft aloft long enough for Charlton Heston to attempt a daring, midair helicopter-to-airplane pilot exchange. This, of course, is just the sort of thing that eventually drove Laker Airways out of business.

Why does Hollywood always go so far awry when it makes movies about nuns? In part because there are too many people in Los Angeles named Sid and not enough people named Clotilde. But a more pressing reason that the film industry has so much trouble realistically portraying the life of the average nun is because people in Hollywood cannot understand how a woman could voluntarily make the decision to spend her entire life without the benefit of male sexual companionship.

Ironically, the explanation for this puzzling lifelong chastity can be found in two recent movies. The first is *Sister Act*, in which a group of nuns headed by Maggie Smith seems to manage perfectly well without the services of Harvey Keitel, the male lead. The second film is *Bad Lieutenant*, in which a young, beautiful nun is raped and sodomized with a crucifix by two young Hispanic men to whom Harvey Keitel, the male lead, eventually gives $30,000 and a pair of bus tickets out of town. When you get right down to it, most men really are a lot like Harvey Keitel—or one of the two rapists—so it isn't hard to understand why women would decide to become nuns and remain nuns rather than go out into the real world, where they're only going to end up getting involved with somebody like Harvey Keitel or worse. Incidentally, for all you Abel Ferrara buffs, nuns also get raped in *Dark of the Sun*, *Salvador*, and *The Devils*.

As the above makes frighteningly clear, nun movies are basically all the same, following a fixed formula in which the same plots, characters, costumes, wimples, and venial sins occur over again and again. Here's a skeletal outline of the all-purpose nun movie:

A bunch of white nuns are stranded in *Detroit/Las Vegas/the Himalayas/Southern France* in a neighborhood where they clearly do not belong. Their mother superior is played by a tight-lipped English actress *(Maggie Smith, Vanessa Redgrave, Janet Suzman, Greer Garson, Deborah Kerr)*, who is always having trouble with a feisty youngster played by *Audrey Hepburn/Hayley Mills/Whoopi Goldberg/Mamie Van Doren/Debbie Reynolds/somebody named Gemma*. Into their midst comes a dashing ne'er-do-well played by *Peter Finch/Sidney Poitier/Elvis Presley/Satan/Oliver Reed* who immediately turns the convent topsy-turvy with his raffish *headwear/impressive harmonica-playing/enormous sideburns/huge dick*. After an innocuous musical interlude featuring *guitars/recorders/bongos/harmoniums*, a complete lunatic played by *Meg Tilly/Kathleen Byron/Helen Reddy/Mary Tyler Moore* commits some unforgivable act such as:

- getting dolled up like Alice Cooper and then trying to toss Mother Superior off Mount Everest.

- not keeping an eye on Elvis when he goes back into the drug dispensary to prepare a prescription.

- strangling a newborn infant.

- befriending Linda Blair.

- singing any Motown song.

Obviously, very few people reading this essay are going to go out and rent twenty-nine movies that feature nuns in them any time in the near future, just as very few people reading this essay are likely to go out and read the Holy Bible. Still, most of us like to have at least a passing acquaintance with the great stories from the Good Book—Salome's dance for Herod, the last nights of Sodom and Gomorrah, Balaam's ass—and in all likelihood most readers would like to have a passing familiarity with the great scenes and memorable moments from the World's Greatest Nun Movies. To fulfill that wish, we have prepared the following list:

Best scene with nuns putting on stockings. Mary Tyler Moore and two colleagues can be seen dressing and undressing as the opening credits roll in *Change of Habit*. Sorry, it's the best we can do.

Best scene of nuns stripped to ravishing black underwear. Towards the end of *Nuns on the Run*, which features Eric Idle and Robbie Coltrane as gangsters masquerading as nuns, a policeman rips open a very pretty nun's habit to reveal a lacy black garter belt and bra-and-panty set. This is the only good scene in the movie.

Best name for a nun in a movie that is a complete rip-off of every Luis Buñuel movie you've ever seen. (Tie): Sister Rat of the Sewers and Sister Manure in *Dark Habits*.

Dumbest actress to appear in starring role in a dumb nun movie. Jennifer Jones in *The Song of Bernadette*.

Actress appearing in a nun movie on whom God Almighty is least likely to show mercy at the Last Judgment. Debbie Reynolds in *The Singing Nun*.

Most convincing infanticidal nun. Meg Tilly in *Agnes of God*.

Most persuasive performance as a chain-smoking bitch of a nun. Anne Bancroft in *Agnes of God*.

Most terrifying supporting cast in a nun movie. Ricardo Montalban, Agnes Moorehead, Chad Everett, and Katherine Ross in *The Singing Nun*.

Best performance by an actress playing a nun riding a very small burro. Deborah Kerr in *Black Narcissus*.

Best performance by an actress playing a whore masquerading as a nun riding a very small burro. Shirley MacLaine in *Two Mules for Sister Sarah*.

Worst lyric in a nun movie. "I'm sticking to my God like a stamp on a letter." Whoopi Goldberg in *Sister Act*

Second worst lyric in a nun movie. "Come praise the Lord, for He is good." Elvis in *Change of Habit*

Second best line in a nun movie. "Buy some coke, too. It would do the convent good." Mother Superior to the itinerant lounge lizardess in *Dark Habits*.

And, of course, the single greatest line ever uttered in a nun movie occurs in *Girls Town* when Mamie Van Doren asks one of her fellow reform school detainees, "What's holy water?" and is told, "It's plain, ordinary water with the hell boiled out of it."

That's what they mean by Gospel truth.

IT'S ALL GREEK TO ME

When Woody Allen was a young man, he repeatedly amused his audiences by playing a nerdy, putzy, ditzy *schlemiel* who somehow managed to wind up in bed with characters played by Diane Keaton, Louise Lasser, or Susan Anspach, none of whom looked like they had trouble getting dates. There was something endearingly democratic about Allen's unlikely amatory conquests in films such as *Take the Money and Run*, *Bananas*, *Sleeper*, *Annie Hall*, and *Play It Again, Sam*, perhaps because it held out hope for lonely geeks everywhere that if someone as twerpy as Woody Allen could get these babes into the sack, anything was possible.

But one day, a dark shadow fell across the landscape. In his 1979 film *Manhattan*, Allen played a character who was no longer willing to hit on women ten years his junior. This time out of the chute, the Man of Wood wanted to start knocking off Lolitas. At the time, no one could have known how profoundly autobiographical this film would turn out to be, just as no one could have known that Allen's subsequent obsession with the subject of marital infidelity in *Hannah and Her Sisters* and *Crimes and Misdemeanors* masked a level of personal duplicity that would only come to light during his legal battles with longtime companion Mia Farrow. Looking back, one recognizes *Manhattan* as a watershed film in Allen's career because his earlier fascination with women too beautiful for him now gave way to an obsession with women too young for him. Women far too young for him. Like, girls.

By and large, Woody Allen's movies do not do huge box office business in the United States, his appeal being confined to New York, Los Angeles, and certain trendy neighborhoods in Boston and Philadelphia. Aficionados attribute Allen's lack of commercial success to the alleged "sophistication" of his work, putting him in the same class as the deified foreign filmmakers Bergman, Fellini, and Antonioni, because the characters in Allen's films regularly attend the ballet, know who Schubert is, spend a lot of time queuing up for Akira Kurosawa movies, and eat sushi.

I prefer another explanation. I think the reason Woody Allen has failed to catch on commercially in recent years is because he keeps casting himself in movies opposite young, alluring females who would not be caught dead in an embrace with him were he not who he is, and that the American people do not want to see this decrepit ass bandit ogling, pawing, and bedding women young enough to be his granddaughters. I think that the American people have correctly identified Allen as the planet's most famous dirty old man and simply don't want to see this long-in-the-tooth Lothario onscreen anymore. Neither do I.

Yet he plods on. In *Mighty Aphrodite (The Goddess of Love)*, Allen plays an aging sportswriter browbeaten into adopting a child by his radiant young wife Helena Bonham Carter, who is, of course, a chic Soho art gallery owner. As is usually the case in Woody Allen movies, being married to a Helena Bonham Carter or a Diane Keaton or a Judy Davis isn't enough to quell the old testosterone sacs; this world-class nighthawk needs to get something going on the side with a Mariel Hemingway or a Juliette Lewis or somebody else who's barely out of rompers.

This time out, the target cupcake is his adopted son's mother, a hooker played by Mira Sorvino, daughter of the talented character actor Paul Sorvino. Initially, Allen fixates on Sorvino because he wants to find out more about his son's gene pool, but as time goes by he actually becomes romantically involved with her because she is a completely passive, helpless idiot, and thus is right up his alley.

Throughout Allen's descent into the *demi-monde* occupied by hookers, gangsters, and bookies, his *hubris* is denounced by a Greek chorus led by F. Murray Abraham, the prodigious ham most famous for his portrayal of Mozart's rival, Antonio Salieri, in the film *Amadeus*. At several points in the film, the members of this irksome chorus even engage in a few Broadway-style dance numbers, hoofing along to that tiresome, overplayed big-band-era music that has become a staple of Woody Allen films. Like everything else in this impossibly slight film, this joke starts out being funny, but quickly wears thin.

In last year's amusing *Bullets Over Broadway*, Allen seemed to have solved the problem of being an over-the-hill screen satyr by casting John Cusack in the role he himself would have played twenty years earlier. Though Cusack was completely overshadowed by Chazz Palminteri, Jim Broadbent, Jack Warden, and Dianne Wiest, he was at least credible in the role of the whiny, pretentious playwright tormented by the eternal questions of life and love that people who drop out of college after two years—as Woody Allen did—never seem to be able to get out of their systems. Most important of all, he solved the one really big problem in a romantic comedy by Woody Allen: finding a leading man who could kiss young women without making the audience gag.

But in *Mighty Aphrodite*, Allen has reversed field and gone back to his old tricks. The results are creepy: Watching Woody Allen kiss Mira Sorvino is like watching Benny Hill kiss anybody. The nervous system can't take it. There comes a point where no audience, no matter how accommodating, can completely suspend its sense of disbelief. Not for this joker.

Twenty years ago, when Allen made *Take the Money and Run*, *Bananas*, *Sleeper*, and *Love and Death*, he was far and away the funniest, most likable person working in the U.S. film industry. In 1996, with *Mighty Aphrodite*, he comes across as just another self-indulgent old lecher running on empty. Stripped to its core, *Mighty Aphrodite* is another Damon Runyon rip-off—not unlike *Bullets Over Broadway*—a corny whore-with-a-heart-of-gold fable about a 55-year-old man whose fling with a 24-year-old hooker teaches him the enduring value of his marriage to a 28-year-old wife. *Mighty Aphrodite*, like its author and screenwriter, is pathetic.

Note: *Since this article appeared in 1996, Woody Allen has made* Everyone Says I Love You, *where he nails Julia Roberts, and* Deconstructing Harry, *where he nails everybody. Plus ça change, plus c'est la même chose.*

THE 4000 BLOWS

When the fiercely handsome Ralph Fiennes first appears on the screen in *The English Patient*, his face is a hideous collage of burns and lesions, the result of a plane crash in the Sahara. Though the pre-transmogrified visage of this fine British actor is on display throughout most of the film (since the story is told in a series of flashbacks), there are nevertheless long stretches of the movie when Fiennes, approaching death, is seen sporting his hideous scars, rendered yet more stomach-turning by odious tufts of sheeny marsupial fur that seem to have sprung up across his face.

While studying Fiennes's appalling countenance, it occurred to me that the actor had made a very wise move in accepting this role at a relatively early point in his film career. Though no one likes to speak about it, there is literally nothing that the moviegoing public enjoys more than seeing a terrific-looking guy get completely jacked up. For reasons that are not entirely clear, but which probably have an awful lot to do with the fact that most male moviegoers don't look anywhere near as good as Ralph

Fiennes, it can be stated unequivocally that the public will not confer its full blessing on an actor until they have seen him get bludgeoned, lacerated, pistol-whipped, filleted with razors, burned, flogged, splattered with acid, crucified, or beheaded. And generally speaking, they like to see plenty of abuse in the facial area.

This is the main reason that male movie stars command higher salaries than their female counterparts: Female stars get sexually molested all the time, but when was the last time you saw Goldie Hawn get her teeth kicked in?

I am certainly not arguing that the public *only* wants to see good-looking guys get their faces smashed in, or even that the public *primarily* wants to see gorgeous guys gouged and garroted. What I am saying is that major-league face-bashing and/or obscene torture is a sine qua non of the cinematic arts, a rite of passage that all male movie stars must endure if they ever hope to attain true greatness. The public does not demand that its idols get their faces worked over in every one of their films, or even in most of their films. But if a star is not willing to get that perky puss pounded in at least one film, he can pretty much resign himself to loitering forever in the penumbra of superstardom. Ask John ("Sir") Gielgud why he never became as big a star as John ("Duke") Wayne and he will almost certainly tell you, "Because I was never willing to get my face bashed in."

Anyone who doubts the logic of my argument should spend a bit more time at the video store. There he will discover a single harsh truth: It is almost impossible to name a major movie star of this or any other era who did not sooner or later get his face smashed in. Jimmy Cagney got his face busted up good by the Gestapo in *13 Rue Madeleine*. Kirk Douglas, already worked over in *The Champ*, got himself whipped and crucified in *Spartacus*. Paul Newman got jacked up in both *The Hustler* and *Cool Hand Luke*. Charlton Heston got his face smashed in with a ring of keys early in *Ben-Hur*, then was flogged and had a whip cracked across his face during the film's climactic chariot race. Why did these stars meekly agree to endure this kind of abuse? Because they understood that before the public would embrace them as screen idols, they first had to pay their dues.

The record speaks for itself. Dustin Hoffman was subjected to gut-wrenching orthodontic torture in *Marathon Man*, Al Pacino got his face smashed in by Sterling Hayden in *The Godfather*, and Jack Nicholson had his nose sliced open in *Chinatown*. Harrison Ford got the shit beaten out of him in *Indiana Jones and the Temple of Doom*, Tom Cruise got that fantastic face brutalized during the improbable barroom brawl in *Far and Away*, and in *Lethal Weapon*, Mel Gibson had his chest torn by electric shocks while his sidekick Danny Glover was getting his face rearranged by a bunch of heroin-smuggling goons.

The list of prominent pummeled-pusses does not stop there. Kevin Costner got his face kicked in during *Revenge*. Ditto Nicholas Cage in *Raising Arizona*. Kurt Russell was beaten senseless, bound, suspended, and electrocuted in *Tango & Cash*. Bruce Willis got thumped good in *Pulp Fiction* and *Die Hard 3*. And in *Black Rain*, one of cinema's most memorable two-fers, Michael Douglas had his face wrapped in a plastic bag by a Japanese thug who would later chop off Andy Garcia's head. Finally, in one of the most stomach-turning examples of facial brutality ever filmed, Jeff Bridges repeatedly had to kiss Barbra Streisand in *The Mirror Has Two Faces*.

Indeed, one of the most interesting developments in recent years is the rise of the *recidivist face-bashee*. In the good old days, you took a few ass whippings early in your career purely to satisfy the public's dark, primordial, sadomasochistic urges and then moved on to roles that allowed you to be a bit more debonair. This was the course charted by Humphrey Bogart, who adeptly leaped from playing psychopathic gangsters in *The Petrified Forest* and *The Roaring Twenties* to guys who smoke pipes and wear homburgs in films like *The Two Mrs. Carrolls* and *Sabrina*.

On a much smaller scale, this is exactly what happened to Charles Bronson, who started out by getting his face battered into hamburger patties in a number of mostly undistinguished American films until the French decided that he could really act and turned him into a brooding, existentialist antihero in a series of undistinguished films where he did not need to get his face battered into hamburger patties. As usual, the French got things wrong.

This clearly defined career path underwent a seismic shift with the arrival of Sylvester Stallone in *Rocky*. No, Stallone was not the first actor in history to become famous by having his face bashed in; Marlon Brando had already done this in *On the Waterfront*, as had Clint Eastwood in *A Fistful of Dollars*, and Jack Nicholson, who first came to the public's attention by getting a baseball bat smashed across his face in *Easy Rider*. Nevertheless, Stallone is, to my knowledge, the first actor in history who is *only* remembered for films in which he gets his face bashed in.

Rocketing to stardom by getting his head handed to him in *Rocky*, Stallone was then battered senseless in *Rocky II*, mercilessly thrashed in *Rocky III*, pummeled into a stupor in *Rocky IV*, and beaten to a pulp in *Rocky V*. And that's not even mentioning all the pulps he got beaten to in films as varied as the three *Rambos*, *Tango & Cash*, and *Cliffhanger*. Since Stallone conspicuously failed to get his face bashed in during the filming of *Rhinestone*, *Oliver*, and *Stop! Or My Mom Will Shoot*, all of them flops, it is probably safe to say that in Sylvester Stallone Hollywood has finally found a movie star that the public *only* wants to see getting his eyes gouged out and his teeth knocked loose. And, to his credit, writer/director/producer/star Stallone seems to understand this.

Despite Stallone's complicity in his own face-bashings, I am a bit concerned about possible anti-Italian bias on the part of the public, which only requires fair-haired boys like Tom Cruise and Ethan Hawke to get beaten up once or twice in their careers, but keeps forcing persons of a more swarthy complexion—or Australians—to make repeated visits to the Ass-Whipping Store. I feel the same way about the peculiar arc of Denzel Washington's career.

Though Washington is without question one of the finest actors of his generation, he has already been beaten senseless in *Ricochet*, horsewhipped in *Glory*, and had his face bashed in with his own trumpet in *Mo' Better Blues*. In this film, the public was not satisfied with a good old-fashioned thumping where the jangled threads of flesh dangle hideously from the hero's cheeks. No, this time out they wanted to go the whole nine yards. They wanted to see the guy get his face totaled. They wanted to see the guy get his face violated. They wanted to see the guy's lips literally explode across the surface of the screen. This time, the public was out for blood.

Frankly, I can think of no more damning indictment of the virulent racism that permeates Hollywood and eats away at the very soul of this nation than the fact that golden boys like Brad Pitt get off with a couple slaps upside the head in their films, while the suave, charismatic African American Denzel Washington repeatedly has to get the shit kicked out of him. This suggests that at some subliminal level, the American moviegoing public doesn't really like good-looking black men. This being the case, it's no wonder that so many African Americans have ditched Christmas for Kwanzaa.

Savvy movie stars, cognizant of the public's secret desire to see them pulverized, usually opt to take their beatings early in their career, just to get them out of the way. In certain instances, one can even make the argument that it is the beating that enables the movie star to vault to major stardom. This was certainly the case with Marlon Brando, victim of a horrendous butt-stomping in *The Wild One* and an even worse thrashing in *On the Waterfront*. In the climactic scene of this memorable film, Lee J. Cobb and his nefarious henchmen beat Brando so badly that his face literally looks like minute steak, with huge gobs of viscous material dangling from his eyes, brows, nose, and cheeks, creating the unnerving impression that the actor is sporting a Fu Manchu made entirely out of blood.

A less calculating movie star might have said that this was enough carnage for one career. Not Brando. Just to make sure that the public wouldn't write off these debut ass-whippings as a fluke, Brando arranged to get himself bullwhipped in the disturbing film *One-Eyed Jacks*, and then, just to be on the safe side, also encouraged Karl Malden to break his shooting hand. In this manner, the actor sealed a lifelong covenant with the public: I took my whuppings when I was young, so you have no right to complain about how fat, cranky, and self-indulgent I get when I am old.

Clint Eastwood chose a similar career path to Brando's. Having started out as a TV cowpoke of no great distinction, Eastwood rocketed to stardom by getting his face kicked in by a bunch of ornery varmints late in *A Fistful of Dollars*. The public liked this, particularly the eye half closed by a sea of caked blood, a much-admired grace note. They immediately made Eastwood a star. But Eastwood, like Brando before him, wanted to make sure that he had completely satisfied the public's blood lust. So he quickly came back for more in *Hang 'Em High*.

In the opening scene of this film, Clint is cornered by a bunch of obnoxious, self-involved vigilantes who rope him like a steer, drag him across a river, beat his face in, and hang him from a tree. Miraculously rescued by the ubiquitous Ben Johnson, Eastwood spends the rest of the movie tracking down this passel of substandard lynchers, periodically exposing the garish rope marks around his neck just to get innocent bystanders cranked up. Indeed, in this smorgasbord of physiognomic abuse, Eastwood later has his face repeatedly smashed into the ground by the crafty Bruce Dern. But he survives—prevails even. Why did Eastwood agree to take so much crap in these films? Because he knew that by sating the public's sadistic urges early in his career, he could maneuver himself into a position where he would be able to wreak vengeance on his tormentors many years later. And in such dark, lugubrious, rain-soaked films as *Bird* and *The Bridges of Madison County*, he has done just that. By cleverly manipulating French critics and their American vassals into proclaiming him an *auteur*, the perpetrator of *Coogan's Bluff* and *Dirty Harry* has given it right back to the public in spades. You stick it in my ear, says Clint, and I sure as hell am going to stick it in yours. Incidentally, Eastwood is the only certified *auteur* to ever costar in a movie with Charlie Sheen.

Most movie stars realize that getting the shit beat out of them onscreen is not a once-in-a-lifetime thing. For the mid-level star to ensure a long, healthy career, it is imperative that he occasionally return for a second session where he gets his head stove in. Thus, Burt Lancaster, worked over early in his career in several films, was later beaten and crucified in *Valdez Is Coming*. Charlton Heston, flogged in *Ben-Hur*, was later beheaded in *Khartoum*. Jack Nicholson, beaten to death in *Easy Rider*, later had his nose slit in *Chinatown*. And Mel Gibson, brutalized in the *Mad Max* films and the *Lethal Weapon* series, and jacked up from Jump Street in the self-directed *The Man Without a Face*, later got the mother of all whompings in *Braveheart*, where even before he gets his innards ripped out he is subjected to a brutal clubbing by a horde of treacherous Brits. Though I have never seen any of these stars discuss this subject in print, all of them seem to intuitively understand that the public periodically demands the ritual desecration of its most treasured icons. The American public, in this context, is best looked upon as 250 million sick fucks.

Is a major face-bashing an inevitable event in a successful actor's career? Yes. Again and again, it has been demonstrated that if you don't get your face busted up early in your career, you're simply going to have to do it later. This has led to some of the most disheartening moments in motion picture history, the most famous being Jimmy Stewart's heartrending bullwhipping at the hands of Lee Marvin in *The Man Who Shot Liberty Valence*.

By the time he made this film, Stewart was well into his fifties, far too old to be taking this kind of abuse. But because he had conspicuously failed to get his teeth knocked out or his nose smashed to cauliflower in early films like *The Philadelphia Story*, *Destry Rides Again*, and *It's a Wonderful Life*, he had to backtrack and get his ass kicked much later in his career. *Jawohl*, we get too soon old and too late smart.

In fact, one of the most disturbing developments in recent years is the rise of the senior citizen as beating victim. Richard Harris, early in his career, got thumped pretty good in the rugby classic *This Sporting Life*. But that was fine, because he was young. Then he got his body ripped to pieces during that weird Indian ritual in *A Man Called Horse*. That was also okay, because he was still young. But in 1992, with his career clearly in eclipse, Harris returned for some additional fine-tuning in *Unforgiven*, where Gene Hackman kicks him in the head so hard and so often that his face starts to resemble a pink grapefruit. Harris, by the time the film was made, was fast approaching retirement age, way too old for this kind of nonsense. It just goes to show to what lengths an old trouper will go to please the public. Just the same, it was a tad pathetic.

At this juncture, I would like to say a few words about non-facial ass-whipping. Generally speaking, the public would really prefer to see a guy get his face kicked in and his teeth knocked out. But if this is not a possibility, the public will sometimes accept a flogging, a crucifixion, or a ritual beheading as a substitute, provided the victim seems to be suffering immensely. Yet, here it is important to draw the distinction between sadistic behavior that the public views as psychologically and even morally acceptable, and pain that is sullied by a disturbing, perhaps even gross, homoerotic undercurrent.

Consider, for example, the hideous torture sequence at the end of *Braveheart*. Just before he is ripped to pieces, Mel Gibson is asked by the royal executioner if he would like to take this opportunity to confess to his treason and thus be granted a more merciful death. Gibson immediately makes eye contact with a tiny boy in the crowd. Even in his woozy condition, he can see that the wide-eyed boy, the symbolic stand-in for the moviegoing public, really doesn't want to get cheated out of a good show. So Gibson agrees to be hung, have all his bones broken by being stretched on the rack, have his stomach torn open and his entrails ripped out, and then get beheaded. It's all very disgusting, but at least it's disgusting in a traditional, costume drama, boys-will-be-boys, macho way. Because Gibson's dismemberment is handled in a fashion the public can view as somehow *wholesome*, no one has to feel guilty about enjoying it.

An entirely different situation prevails in movies where the torture scenes contain a homoerotic subtext. Think of Tyrone Power getting whipped by George Sanders in *Son of Fury*. Think of Peter O'Toole getting caned in *Lawrence of Arabia* while flirty José Ferrer gets his rocks off behind a partially closed door a few feet away. Most important of all, think of Brando's bizarre flogging at the hands of surrogate father Karl Malden in *One-Eyed Jacks*. In each of these movies, there is a psychosexual subtext to the punishment because one or both of the participants seems to be enjoying things too much. This kind of stuff makes the public feel a bit creepy. Put it this way: The public knows that it is sick, but it would prefer to think that it is straight.

Anyone who doubts the validity of my theory about the public's passion for seeing leading men getting fucked over should take a look at Martin Scorsese's rambunctious remake of *Cape Fear*. The unsophisticated viewer could easily be forgiven for thinking that *Cape Fear* is a movie about revenge, sexual repression, class warfare, or glaring inequities in the judicial system. But in reality *Cape Fear* is a movie about two good-looking guys who get a rush from fucking up other guys' faces. That's it: game, set, match.

Cape Fear is a bonanza for closet sadists because it features not one, but two, leading men getting physiognomically nuked. First, Robert De Niro, previously fucked up royally in *Raging Bull*, gets the shit beaten out of him by a bunch of goons in Nick Nolte's employ. But then De Niro turns the tables on his adversary by pistol-whipping him, kicking him in the head while he lies bound helplessly on the ground, and, just to add a little flourish, spitting some revolting cigar fragments into his face while getting in the mood to rape Nolte's entire family. Take it from me: Guys find this stuff very humiliating.

Luckily, Juliette Lewis, never to be trusted in situations like this, surprises De Niro by setting his face on fire. *Ouch*. By the time the surprisingly resilient De Niro reemerges from the watery depths into which he has plunged to cool himself off, he really looks bad—worse than he looked in *Mary Shelley's Frankenstein*. But he soldiers on. The movie ends with the men battering each other's faces with heavy rocks, and actually seems ready to achieve a highly satisfying apotheosis when Nolte raises a boulder high above his antagonist's head and prepares to smash it wide open.

But just then, the boat fragment that De Niro is chained to drifts off into the storm, and we never get to see the blood and guts and fragments of the sinus cavity and caved-in orbital lobes that we've all been waiting for. This is a classic case of what is known in the trade as *coitus interruptus cinematicus*: The audience feels cheated because it doesn't get to see De Niro's brains trickling out of his eye sockets. Next time out, Marty should bear in mind the words of Henry Miller: If you're going to start with the cannons, you've got to finish with dynamite.

At this point, I would like to say a few words about unsatisfactory cinematic face-bashings. One thing I have come to admire about superstars like Mel Gibson, Kevin Costner, and Clint Eastwood is their stoic acceptance of the principle that if you're going to get your head stomped in, you might as well get your head stomped in good. Stars such as these men understand that the public doesn't want to see a few nicks and scratches; they don't want to see a couple of black eyes; they want to see a major facial. They want to see a cranial meltdown. They don't want to see the shit hit the fan; they want to see the face hit the fan.

This is why I find Christian Slater's beating at the hands of John Travolta in *Broken Arrow* so unsatisfying. It is not as if Slater is a stranger to physical abuse; he gets blown up at the end of *Heathers*, and gets his ass kicked good and proper in *True Romance*, a film where he literally ends up with one eye. But for some inexplicable reason, Slater wimps out in the extended fist fight that opens John Woo's action flick about a deranged Air Force officer who steals two thermonuclear devices just for chuckles.

Sure, Slater gets stomped and whomped all over the ring by his taller, bulkier nemesis, but when the fight is over, there are no bruises, no blood, no teeth flying across the ring. This defeats the whole purpose of Slater's getting his ass kicked: If you're going to do it, do it right. Slater's beating at the outset of *Broken Arrow* is the worst case of onscreen pussying-out I have ever seen. Such fulsome wimpery makes me doubt that he will ever become a bona fide superstar now.

Let me emphasize one point here: I am not arguing that all on-screen beatings are a sign of psychosis on the part of the movie-going public. Nor am I suggesting that movie stars getting beaten or mutilated is always a bad thing. I was happy to see Eric Roberts get his thumb chopped off in *The Pope of Greenwich Village*. I have never been upset by the amount of abuse Steven Seagal takes in his films. I, like many other viewers, was more than happy to see Spike Lee get his face smashed in near the end of *Mo' Better Blues*. And personally speaking, Jean-Claude Van Damme couldn't get crucified often enough to suit me.

Nor am I arguing that a good beating or mutilation is always a passport to international stardom. Kyle MacLachlan got beat up pretty bad in *Blue Velvet*, and he's still scuffling around in the vestibule of stardom. Jeff Daniels got the shit kicked out of him by Ray Liotta in *Something Wild*, then took a weird detour into comedy where he literally ended up on the shitter. Chuck Norris has been whipped on good for more than two decades, yet he still remains little more than a poor man's Charles Bronson. As for Mickey Rourke, well, I'm sorry I brought it up.

In this context, it is fitting that we take a brief look at the 1978 film *Midnight Express*. A cornucopia of depravity, this film contains a number of graphic scenes in which Brad Davis is stripped naked, suspended upside down, and beaten on or about the soles of his feet until he cannot walk. Oddly enough, succumbing to all this degradation did virtually nothing for his career. This brings us back to my central point: The public does not automatically canonize an actor just because he gets his ass kicked. But without getting his ass kicked at least once, it is nigh on impossible for an actor to achieve lasting fame.

Midnight Express is valuable for one other reason: because of the strange case of Randy Quaid. Halfway through this horribly depressing film, Randy Quaid gets beaten so badly that he loses a testicle. At this moment, there occurs one of the great lost opportunities in the history of motion pictures. Had Randy Quaid been beaten so badly that he lost a testicle onscreen, and had the audience been treated to close-ups of the testicle he lost, I believe that Randy Quaid would today be a bigger star than Tom Cruise or Mel Gibson. And had he lost both testicles on the screen, we might very well be talking about him in the same terms as we speak of Cary Grant. Alas, Randy Quaid did not lose a testicle onscreen. And that's why he's still making movies with Chevy Chase. There's a lesson in this for young actors everywhere: For the want of a ball, a career did stall.

Since physical abuse does not guarantee a successful career, I would discourage young actors who might be reading this article from deliberately subjecting themselves to onscreen beatings in their upcoming projects. Although it would be nice to see Luke Perry get his teeth knocked out, it cannot be stated with absolute certainty that such activity would make the public any more receptive to his films. The public is cruel, but it is also fickle. As for David Schwimmer: Hey, don't even bother trying to salvage this career with an ass-whipping. The public is cruel, but it is not stupid.

Throughout this essay, I have repeatedly drawn attention to the public's creepy yen to see great-looking guys get totally jacked up. In doing so, I have perhaps created the impression that I myself am impervious to such dementia. Nothing could be further from the truth. I love to see movie stars get worked over by a two-by-four. I love to see a handsome guy's head get opened up with a power saw. I love to see a glamour boy go headfirst into the wood chipper.

Where I part company with the public is in the choice of people

I'd like to see worked over. Most Americans, being xenophobic little toads, only want to see homegrown movie stars get their faces smashed in. Perhaps because I studied at the Sorbonne, have read the complete works of Pierre Corneille, and have spent years learning how to pronounce the words *Notre Dame*, I prefer to see French movie stars get jacked up. For as long as I can remember, I have always harbored a secret desire to see Gérard Depardieu, that stupid, fat frog, get his teeth kicked in. I would also love to see Jean-Louis Trintignant get utterly totaled before he retires. Indeed, one of my greatest regrets in life is that I never got to see classy, elegant bon vivant Yves Montand facedown in the gutter getting his head stomped in by malevolent street urchins.

On the other hand, I did get to see Streisand kiss him.

HAIR FORCE

One hour into Philip Kaufman's tough, honest, uncompromising, putrid *Henry & June*, actor Fred Ward, playing the globetrotting smutmeister Henry Miller, pounces on Maria de Medeiros, playing the sparrowlike Anaïs Nin, author of some of the least erotic erotica ever published. The lovemaking scene, shot from overhead, allows the audience a full view of the top of Ward's head, transformed by makeup artists into a bald dome resembling that of the famous writer he's playing.

Unfortunately, the rectangular patch on the crown of Ward's skull has been made up so studiously that the actor comes away looking not like an expatriate lecher known to have screwed anything that moved, but like one of those Powder Pete magnetic toys that children use to heighten their manual skills at age three. What's more, viewed from overhead, Ward looks not so much like a middle-aged Henry Miller, one of the greatest writers America has ever produced, but like an aging Joe Garagiola, the obsequious, emphatically bald baseball player turned announcer. Thus, while Kaufman intended this scene to be supremely passionate and romantic, what actually seems to be taking place on the screen is the ravishing of an anorexic European tart by a middle-aged chrome dome who bears an uncanny resemblance to a scrub catcher who couldn't even start for one of the worst teams in baseball history.

What we have seen in *Henry & June* is a phenomenon that has occurred again and again throughout the history of cinema: the inadvertent but irremediable sabotaging of a major motion picture by a disruptive hairstyle. Though purists may argue that *Henry & June* was fatally flawed from the beginning by a horrible script, Uma Thurman's cryptic Brooklyn accent, the weight of its own pretensions, Uma Thurman's cryptic Brooklyn accent, Richard E. Grant's habit of referring to his porn queen wife as Pussywillow, and Uma Thurman's cryptic Brooklyn accent, a case can be made that *Henry & June* could have survived all of these drawbacks and emerged from the editing room as a palatable *bagatelle*, a charming *bonbon*, a harmless wisp of Franco-American *froufrou*. But once the cinematographer made the fateful decision to use an overhead shot of Ward's gleaming pate, the film passed far beyond the realm of salvation. Forever.

We raise this troubling issue here because seditious, disruptive, subversive hairstyles have been appearing with alarming regularity in films in recent years, and now seem to be exerting a cata-strophic effect on the box office. Though many critics would argue that *Jimmy Hollywood* bombed because no one was interested in seeing a movie where Christian Slater has to keep visiting the hospital for a brain scan (surely they weren't hoping to find one), the real reason for the failure of Barry Levinson's earnest film about a ninth-rate actor who lands the role of a lifetime as a vigilante patrolling the streets of Hollywood is the havoc un-leashed by Joe Pesci's heavy-metal blond wig, which typecasts him as a short Bon Jovi roadie or the world's plumpest, shortest, oldest Renny Harlin impersonator.

Pandemonium-inducing hairstyles have also exerted a ruinous

effect on *Barton Fink*, where John Turturro appears to have a removable vacuum cleaner suction nozzle glued onto his head; *Kalifornia*, which showcases not one but two young actresses coifed in a garish Louise Brooks getup; *This Boy's Life*, in which Robert De Niro's semi-skinhead makes the gifted actor look even more hideous than he does in real life; and *The Vanishing*, where what appears to be a dead otter has been glued onto the right side of Jeff Bridges's head, making it impossible for all but the most focused moviegoers to concentrate on the film's other fine qualities: the lush Pacific Northwest settings, the nuanced convolutions of the plot, Kiefer Sutherland's superb acting.

I am not suggesting that movies featuring insurgent hairstyles are always disasters. Despite Kevin Costner's I-didn't-know-the-lawn-mower-was-running-when-I-stuck-my-head-inside-it hairdo in *The Bodyguard*, the film was a huge success, primarily because Whitney Houston's fine acting and the haunting refrains of Dolly Parton's anthem "I Will Always Love You" were powerful enough to neutralize the effects of his absurd coiffure. Similarly, *Cape Fear* and *Scarface* were box office smashes, despite the presence of enough mutinous hairstyling to sink a dozen less worthy films.

Nevertheless, it is fair to say that obtrusive hairstyles—Diane Keaton's anachronistic perm in *Mrs. Soffel*, Gary Oldman's Veronica-Lake-goes-to-Hell's-Kitchen look in *State of Grace*, Mickey Rourke's Tangerine Dream greaseball cut in *A Prayer for the Dying*—have torpedoed a sufficiently large number of quality motion pictures in recent years that Hollywood should at least be sensitive to the burgeoning problem of hilarious hair and perhaps consider hiring mane monitors whose job it would be to scrutinize the daily rushes from films to ensure that no big-budget enterprise will be doomed to failure from the very moment of its conception by a militant hairstyle that operates at cross-purposes to the intentions of the director, the producer, the screenwriter, and even the players themselves.

In the following pages, we will have much to say about a growing cadre of movie stars, loosely known as the Hair Force, for whom dissonant hairstyles have become a mark of distinction. These include De Niro, Pesci, Juliette Lewis, John Malkovich, Whoopi Goldberg, Gary Oldman, Mary Elizabeth Mastrantonio, and the vastly underrated Jeff Bridges, all of whom have consistently used disruptive hairstyles to upstage their fellow actors. We will also make passing reference to such Lifetime Achievement Award winners as Cher, whose pioneering hair work is legendary, and Keanu Reeves, the only living movie star who can actually act with his hair.

But first, a bit of history. Hair has always played a major role in films, in part because so many people have had so much of it. From the trailblazing days of Theda Bara straight through to the Veronica Lake era, where enormous amounts of visually arresting hair literally held entire films captive, what an actor has on his head has always been at least as important as what he has in it. But, for the purpose of this article, we will limit our discussion to incongruous, seditious, or infuriating hairstyles that unwittingly, without malice aforethought, undermine the audience's ability to concentrate on the rest of the film.

Emphasis here should be placed on the word "unwittingly," in the sense that the directors of the films did not realize at the time they were shooting that the hairstyles in question would exert a devastating effect on the finished product. On the other hand, deliberate barberific buffoonery, such as Brad Pitt's pompadour in *Johnny Suede*, Nick Nolte's Tarzan-the-surfer look in *Farewell to the King* or Dana Carvey's spaghetti mop in *Wayne's World*, will not be discussed, nor will we have anything to say about ludicrous wigs in period pieces such as *Dangerous Liaisons*, where everyone has a stupid 'do, and it isn't simply a case of Malkovich hamming it up.

Similarly, for reasons too obvious to mention, we will completely avoid any discussion of films featuring mohawks (*Taxi Driver*, *The Last of the Mohicans*), razor cuts (*An Officer and a Gentleman*), Friar Tuck coiffures (*Robin Hood: Prince of Thieves*, *The Name of the Rose*), scalpings (*Little Big Man*), or deliberate cross-cultural weirdness such as Wesley Snipes as a blond, pompadoured assassin in *Demolition Man*, looking like a short, blond, male Grace Jones, if such a horrifying concept can be countenanced.

Also omitted from the discussion will be films such as *Eraserhead*, which are in and of themselves movies about cranial chaos, and any movie starring Lyle Lovett, who looks no more ridiculous in the movies than he does in real life. (Bear in mind that Lovett, unlike say, Lou Diamond Phillips, is not really an actor, so he cannot be held to the same lofty standards.) Finally, all mention of Yul Brynner and his spiritual descendants Telly Savalas (*Kelly's Heroes*) and Sigourney Weaver (*Alien 3*) will be avoided, since the skinhead look, as opposed to partial baldness, is a cheap publicity stunt, and perhaps even a marketing scam to sell more tickets to bald eagles seeking role models on the silver screen.

Instead, we will center our attention on a handful of recent films in which one or more puzzling hairstyles have usurped the traditional role of the screenplay and taken center stage as the basic talking point of the film. A good place to begin is the Coen Brothers' 1991 dud *Barton Fink*. *Barton Fink* stars John Turturro as a left-leaning young playwright who goes to Hollywood in 1941 in search of fame and fortune, but discovers, to his complete amazement, that people in Hollywood are incredibly vulgar and only care about money. The Coen Brothers' tiresome film is severely hampered by a screenplay that recycles a bevy of tired old clichés about F. Scott Fitzgerald, William Faulkner, and the once famous, but now largely forgotten, Clifford Odets.

But what really stops *Barton Fink* dead in its tracks is Turturro's failed Afro, which makes him look like a Sicilian Clarence Williams III. With his head crowned by a bristly tuft of kinky black hair, Turturro could easily pass for a human autobody buffer, and despite John Goodman's game efforts to compete with that hideous 'do by delivering a bravura performance as a traveling salesman who turns out to be Satan, the audience can never really get its mind off that economy-sized fright wig poised on Turturro's skull.

A similar situation prevails in Joel Schumacher's tough, honest, uncompromising, putrid 1993 film *Falling Down*. In this clumsy, racist attempt to do for white commuters what *Rocky* once did for white boxing fans (create a fantasy world in which goofy white people get to beat the shit out of muscular ethnics), Michael Douglas plays a weary divorcé who abandons his car on a crowded freeway in Los Angeles and begins a deadly walk across the city, maiming everything in sight. Which in itself is not a bad idea.

What sets off Douglas's murderous spree is an ugly confrontation with two Hispanic men who allegedly object to his entering private property, i.e., the ghetto. But what really pisses them off is not Douglas's mere presence—after all, white people have rights too—but the naked effrontery of his daunting, porcupine-quill hairdo, which clearly poses a direct threat, cultural iconography-wise, to the bushy, Annette Funicello ponytail sported by one of the Hispanic thugs. To the unsophisticated film critic—say, the guy who wrote that *Newsweek* cover story about the film—the Boyz in the Barrio resent the interloper's affluence, his respected position in society, and his cool demeanor. But what really motivates their attack on him is much more complex, consisting of three separate elements:

1. Secret resentment that Hispanics are in some ways bouffantally challenged, in the sense that they are follically incapable of growing hairdos that will make them look like Ozzie Nelson.

2. A nagging fear that an epidemic of copycat Latino porcupine haircuts could undercut the power of major East Los Angeles gangs by making an entire subculture look silly.

3. Deep, nay, implacable rage that Michael Douglas has contemptuously ignored clearly marked graffiti which, translated from gang patois into conventional English, states: "No Revenge-of-the-Nerds haircuts beyond this point."

Up until now, we have largely spoken of films in which one performer sports a hairstyle that cuts a movie adrift from the port of plausibility and reduces the audience to tears of laughter. But a far more insidious development in recent cinema is the outbreak of dueling hairstyles, where not one, but two, actors compete for tonsorial hegemony on the screen. A case in point is *Cape Fear*. The first two people seen in this film are Juliette Lewis, armed with the heaviest set of bangs since Audrey Hepburn was a teenager, and De Niro, coifed in a greasy, prison-issue ponytail, which creates the impression that a rat marinated in Vaseline has been surgically grafted onto his neck. The viewer instinctively senses that a deadly *mano a mano* between these two hairstyles will inevitably take place, and that Nick Nolte and Jessica Lange's primary function in the film is merely to delay as long as possible the frightening moment when the ultimate barberial brouhaha erupts.

In the hands of a lesser director, *Cape Fear* would have become a monotonous free-for-all between Lewis and De Niro, with the fur flying from Tallahassee to Pompano Beach. But it is a mark of Martin Scorsese's extraordinary craftsmanship that he keeps the pair away from each other until about halfway through the film, when they collide in the infamous thumb-sucking scene. Up until that point, I personally felt that De Niro was the hands-down favorite to blow Lewis right off the screen, especially after he calls her on the phone while hanging upside down from an exercise beam, looking like a fiftysomething werewolf gymnast. But such is the awesome power of Lewis's stringy bangs that the actress very nearly demolishes her only coiffureal competition in the film.

Lewis's quiet emergence as one of the superstars of the Hair Force is confirmed by her fine work in *Kalifornia*, where she duels with serial killer Brad Pitt, also a charter member of that august group. At the start of the movie, Pitt and Lewis are coifed in traditional redneck chic, he with stringy biker hair, she with your basic white-trash 'do. But, forty minutes into the film, Lewis asks Michelle Forbes, decked out like Louise Brooks on a very bad day, to "fix her hair."

Obligingly, Forbes gets out her scissors and turns Lewis into Louise Brooks on an even worse day. This is what they mean by the expression, "Do unto others what you would have them do unto you." Not long after this scene, an enraged Pitt, realizing he cannot possibly compete with two Louise Brooks aficionados occupying the same screen, kills Lewis, restoring a measure of tonsorial sanity to the film. The subtle undertones of hairdressing angst that dominate this troubling cinematic enterprise are confirmed in the final scene, where Forbes, with both Lewis and Pitt long dead, abandons her twenties flapper look for something more sensible: a triptych hairdo that looks like a cross between Cleopatra, young Cher, and Kathleen Sullivan. The movie thus seems to suggest that when bad people die, their bad hair dies with them, but good people's bad hair lives forever.

That Lewis's hair should dominate *Cape Fear* and *Kalifornia* inevitably leads us to a discussion of the harmonic convergence of bad hair. By this I mean that actors and actresses who have already sabotaged one film with their hair will inevitably sabotage others, often by encouraging their costars to ravage their future projects with mutinous hairstyles. One can even go so far as to theorize that the Hair Force is a sort of invisible repertory theater whose members actively seek out one another in the hope of taking over otherwise worthwhile movies and turning them into *Night of the Living Mr. Christophe's.*

Look at it this way: Juliette Lewis stars in *Kalifornia* with Hair Force commando Brad Pitt, who has an extremely problematic hairstyle in *True Romance*. Included in the cast of *True Romance* is Gary Oldman, whose woeful hairstyles have already seized control of *Criminal Law*, *Bram Stoker's Dracula*, and *State of Grace*. *True Romance* also features Hair Force hero Christian Slater, who costars with Hair Force generalissimo Joe Pesci in *Jimmy Hollywood*. Pesci made an unforgettable Hair Force appearance bedecked with an orange Brillo pad passing for a wig in *JFK*, which costars Oldman of *True Romance* and *Bram Stoker's Dracula*. *Dracula* not only stars Hair Force field marshal Keanu Reeves, but Winona Ryder, whose blond cheerleader locks in *Edward Scissorhands* virtually brought that film to its knees.

Ryder subsequently appeared in *The Age of Innocence* (directed by *Cape Fear*'s Martin Scorsese), a film which is utterly dominated by Michelle Pfeiffer's plangent perm, which itself can claim a direct lineage from *Mrs. Soffel*, in which Diane Keaton plays the long-suffering wife of a prison warden trapped in a remote region of western Pennsylvania, where seemingly there are no competent hairdressers. Keaton was once romantically linked with Woody Allen, who gives Lewis a bad-hair assignment in *Husbands and Wives*. The lingering suspicion that Hair Force members all want to work together makes it almost inevitable that Ryder, Reeves, Oldman, Pitt, and Lewis will one day work with Forelock King Andy Garcia, Big Hair High Priestess Cher, and Pesci's only serious toupee rival, John Malkovich, who has, of course, already appeared with Garcia in *Jennifer Eight*, which stars Uma Thurman, who worked with Fred Ward in *Henry & June*. Bear in mind that towards the end of *Cape Fear*, De Niro expresses disappointment that Lewis has not brought along a book entitled *Sexus* that he had intended to read aloud with her—one of the scariest thoughts ever. It just so happens that *Sexus* was written by Henry Miller, the bald smut king played by Fred Ward in *Henry & June*. Coincidence, you say?

One subject we have not discussed is the Rites of Passage Hairstyle Syndrome, in which an actor decides that he has arrived at the point in his career where he is famous enough and powerful enough to adopt the moronic my-bangs-got-caught-in-the-electric-fan look immortalized by Laurence Olivier in *Hamlet*. Like a ceremonial torch passed from one generation to the next, Lord Larry bequeathed that bizarre hairstyle to Richard Burton in *Becket*, who then passed it along to Steve McQueen in *Bullitt*. Even before McQueen had passed from the scene, Donald Sutherland felt confident enough to adapt that close-cropped look in *Klute*, and before long Al Pacino was giving it a Cuban spin in *Scarface*, Harrison Ford had the *cojones* to use it in *Presumed Innocent*, and most recently, Kevin Costner took to it for his role in *The Bodyguard*, a film originally written for Steve McQueen. It should be noted that all of these movies in question were hits, largely explaining why the stars would be willing to subject themselves to such hair-raising humiliation. The moral is clear: If it's already broke, don't fix it.

It is ironic that Brad Pitt is cast as a serial killer in *Kalifornia*, because in their own quiet way Hair Force vets really are the beauty parlor equivalent of serial killers: If you don't kill them the first time out, they're bound to kill again. Emboldened by the hairy havoc he wrought in *Cape Fear*, De Niro soon turned up in *This Boy's Life* sporting a hairstyle that fused the very worst elements of the mohawk, the ducktail, the Marine Corps brush cut, and concentration camp chic in an awesome display of tonsorial schizophrenia. Pesci's wigwagging in *My Cousin Vinny*, *JFK*, and the *Lethal Weapon* series is legendary, but it is the failure of Hollywood to rein in his barbershop bodaciousness that has goaded him into even more lavish displays of subversive hairstyling in *Jimmy Hollywood* and *With Honors*.

Yet, in many ways, the most amazing Hair Force capers of all time do not involve performers who have resorted to disruptive hairstyles in consecutive films, but performers who use *more than one disruptive hairstyle in the same film*. Here we are talking about such peerless troupers as Whoopi Goldberg, who is first seen in *Fatal Beauty* wearing a mane so long and thick it could force the King of the Jungle himself to hire a new barber; who then switches to dreadlocks and then to the early Supremes look; and who ultimately escapes being crushed to death by a collapsing ceiling because her hair is so thick and awesome that it reduces the tumbling beams and plaster to harmless rubble.

Here we must also pay tribute to Barbra Streisand in *The Way We Were*, an unbelievably awful film in which Ms. Glamourpuss is first seen as a slightly cross-eyed Andrews Sisters impersonator whose hair has more bounce in its flounce than Rita Hayworth's; then as a pinko Shirley Temple, rallying support for Joseph Stalin while sporting a headful of cherubic curls; and finally going with a short fifties cut that makes her look like everyone's drab Aunt Ethel. Or drab Aunt Mabel. Or drab Auntie Mame. Or, for that matter, Streisand.

Yet neither of these performances can hold a candle to Mary Elizabeth Mastrantonio's astonishing work in *Scarface*, probably the greatest dueling hairstyle movie of all time. Remember, if you will, that the most memorable scene in *Scarface* occurs when Al Pacino's drug-dealing compadre is cut to ribbons with a chain saw wielded by Central American scumbags. What few people realize is that the same electrical appliance almost certainly had been used to give Pacino his disastrous haircut before the movie went into production, and that witnessing this haircut so terrified Mastrantonio, playing his sister, that her hair exploded into a humongous bride of Frankenstein fright wig.

Early in the movie, Pacino and Mastrantonio are on relatively equal tonsorial footing: He has an incredibly bad haircut, she has an incredibly bad haircut. But as the movie goes on, Mary Elizabeth's hair continues to expand, getting bigger and fuzzier and wilder, growing at an uncontrollable pace, annexing vast sections of her face and neck. This infuriates Pacino to no end, because:

1. He can't grow hair like that.

2. He really wants to fuck his sister.

The situation comes to a head when Mastrantonio disappears into a men's room to snort some coke and perhaps give a blow job to a lowlife named Fernando who also has seriously bad hair. Pacino doesn't mind his sister screwing a guy in the bathroom, and he certainly doesn't object to her using coke, his main source of income. But there is no way on earth that he is going to let his own flesh and blood go down on a guy who has even worse hair than he does. So he pummels the shit out of both of them.

Shortly after loverboy is dispatched, Mastrantonio tearfully returns home in the company of Pacino's best friend and partner. Delicately, he tries to explain Pacino's brusque behavior towards her back in that men's room.

"Come on, Gina," he says, "put yourself in his place, okay? Right now you happen to be the best thing in his life, the only thing that's any good, that's pure."

He then refers to her boyfriend as an "asshole."

"Hey, I like Fernando," Mastrantonio objects. "He's a fun guy, and he's nice. And he knows how to treat a woman, all right?"

By this point, it is clear that the hair follicles have grown directly into Mastrantonio's brain and are now affecting her sanity. But the movie doesn't end there. Nor does her hair. Some time later, driven insane by jealousy, Pacino guns down her new husband, his former best friend. Mastrantonio, after a nuclear meltdown following her beloved's death, appears in her brother's office wearing nothing but a bathrobe, skimpy panties, and more hair than Iron Maiden, Motley Crue, and Metallica rolled into one. She begins firing at him with a pistol. He ducks, and a gunman appears directly behind him. Fearing that Mary Elizabeth is hiding several hand grenades—and perhaps even a mortar launcher—in her hair, the assassin blows her away. This sends Pacino into a final paroxysm of rage, during which he kills everything in sight, including a killer with very long, very bad hair. Hair today, gone tomorrow.

I would like to conclude this essay by paying homage to one of the very brightest stars of the Hollywood Hair Force: Jeff Bridges. Bridges started out his coiffureal career in a fairly conventional style, but in recent years he has done some of the most interesting hair work of anyone on the current scene. His massive ponytail in *The Fisher King* kicked major ass, and his bizarre haircut in *The Vanishing* surely sent many moviegoers home from the theater asking themselves, "What kind of woman would be stupid enough to get into a car with a guy who seems to have a dead marsupial attached to the side of his head?" (Answer: Anybody stupid enough to live with a character played by Kiefer Sutherland.)

But for my money, Bridges's best Hair Force work is in *American Heart*, the tough, honest, uncompromising, putrid film that opens with Bridges in a bus station men's room, stripped to boxer shorts, with a mass of blond hair wafting about his shoulders, which, with his big, bushy, walrusy mustache, makes him look like the seventh reincarnation of Duane Allman. Confronted in the washroom by his adolescent son, Bridges says, "Well you look good—other than your hair." Then he thinks about it and adds: "Of course, I should talk . . ."

Precisely, Jeff. Precisely.

Note: Since this article appeared in 1994, seriously seditious hair has contaminated films as varied as Boogie Nights, The Fifth Element, Pulp Fiction, In the Line of Fire, Casino, Hook, Restoration, The Man in the Iron Mask, The Saint, *and* Basquiat, *but no hairstyle has never commanded more of the spotlight than Bruce Willis's gay caballero's blond wig in* The Jackal. *My hat is off to him.*

SPIKE LEE DOES NOT BITE

I don't know any white people who like Spike Lee. I know white people who used to like Spike Lee, but that was before his prefab antiwhite tirades, his outbursts at New York Knicks' basketball games, his going to bat for the likes of Mike Tyson and Albert Belle, and a general sense that he had become excessively ubiquitous caused him to wear out his welcome with practicing Caucasians. In saying this, I am aware that I cannot speak for all white Americans, just as Lee cannot speak for all black Americans. But I can speak for a lot of them.

From the moment his career took off, Spike Lee has been dogged by two irksome paradoxes. On the one hand, he has become the champion, perhaps even the spokesman, of an underclass to which he does not actually belong. This got the media on his case, because once they discovered that Lee was not an oppressed inner-city youth, but the product of a thoroughly middle-class background, many journalists decided that the irascible filmmaker was a bit of a fake, a conclusion their white readers wholeheartedly endorsed.

Nor did Lee's public masquerade as a pop revolutionary win many plaudits from the mainstream press, if only because real revolutionaries do not do Nike commercials, do not direct award-winning videos on MTV, do not hang out with Michael Jordan, and do not have courtside seats at Madison Square Garden. In the eyes of many, perhaps most, whites, nobody with courtside seats at Madison Square Garden has the right to criticize American society. People sitting up in the cheap seats can criticize American society all they want. But you Woody Allens and John McEnroes and Alec Baldwins better keep your damn mouths shut. You too, Spike.

Playing the devil's advocate, or, in this case, the white devil's advocate, I would like to say a couple of things in Spike Lee's defense. In portraying the misfortunes of a class (the poor) to which he does not actually belong, Lee has done nothing that has not been done a million times over by novelists, painters, playwrights, rock stars. What, you think Springsteen actually worked in a factory?

More pertinently, Lee deserves credit for not going Hollywood like Eddie Murphy, Whoopi Goldberg, and Michael Jackson. Unlike many African-American artists and entertainers who are black when it is useful to be black, but then retreat into the amorphous race of Show Biz, Spike Lee is black twenty-four hours a day. Had he chosen the obvious career path after his hilarious *School Daze* was released, Lee would now be churning out formulaic $45-million comedies about the misadventures of lovable African-American suburbanites (*Home, Black and Alone II*), instead of a $2.8-million film about fifteen black men riding on a bus to the Million Man March in Washington last fall. Instead of becoming a dark-skinned Chris Columbus or the African-American Joe Dante, Lee has continued to make interesting, complex, thought-provoking films. Money-losing films, to be sure, but interesting films. When white people shun Hollywood and persist in making interesting, complex, thought-provoking, money-losing films, they get good seats at Elaine's and totally undeserved Academy Award nominations. When Spike Lee does it, he gets dissed.

That pretty much constitutes my entire defense of Spike Lee the Man. The Spike Lee who pillories white America and then shills for sweatshop operators ("I wish interviewers would refer those questions to the folks over at Nike"), the Spike Lee who volunteers to make an HBO feature about the Cleveland Indians' slugging dickhead Albert Belle, the Spike Lee who pauses in the middle of an interview conducted at his 40 Acres and a Mule Productions in Brooklyn's Fort Greene to tell me how glad he is that the lowlife sex offender/college hoop star Richie Parker "got a second chance" is either a complete enigma or a complete . . . well, let's not get personal.

Look at it this way: Either Spike Lee has devised some personal philosophy whereby all these contradictions cohere in some heretofore unintelligible fashion, or he just does this stuff because he knows that it really annoys people. Personally, I think that he does it because he knows that it really annoys people. At no time during our forty-five-minute *tête-à-tête* in the stately, gorgeous converted firehouse that is the base of his operations do I get the sense that Spike Lee cares about annoying people. But he's not mean or coarse or vulgar or belligerent or even unfriendly. He's just annoying.

The tradition of annoyingness from which Spike Lee descends is a European rather than a Brooklynian one. Generations ago, the French developed the concept of *épater la bourgeoisie*, which, loosely translated, means: "Do everything humanly possible to get on middle-class people's nerves." The Dadaists did it, the Surrealists did it, the Absurdists like Eugène Ionesco and Jean Genet did it all the time. Tellingly, one of the things that the bourgeoisie always found so annoying about this practice was that the offending artists depended for their livelihood on the very people they were annoying. The artists didn't care. They weren't being annoying because of the hours or the benefits. They were just being annoying for the hell of it.

I think that Spike Lee falls squarely into this group of highly annoying artists. I do not think that Lee is simply a "world-class hustler," to use one critic's dismissive term, a cunning huckster who does and says annoying things because he thinks it will sell more tickets to his films. *Obviously, that hasn't worked.* I think that Lee honestly believes that artists have a sacred obligation to get under the public's skin, to constantly rock the boat, to say and do unbelievably stupid things, to boldly don the mantle of annoyingness. It is a mantle he wears quite well.

Unfortunately, Spike Lee the Man has drawn so much attention to himself that he has diverted attention away from Spike Lee the Filmmaker. So much has been made of Lee's hot-blooded rhetoric that almost no one has noticed how thoroughly intelligent, thoughtful, and even-handed his films are. Looking at *Do the Right Thing, Jungle Fever, Malcolm X,* and the more recent *Clockers,* you really have to wonder what all the fuss about Spike Lee's take on race relations is about. As opposed to Spike Lee the Public Figure, Spike Lee the Director makes films that are nuanced, sensitive, and remarkably free of political cant. Indeed, in a society where white people get all bent out of shape about the way whites are depicted in his films, most of which they have never seen, it is Lee's treatment of black people—and particularly of black men— that should be the most controversial element.

Ranging from Samuel L. Jackson's crackhead thug in *Jungle Fever* to Delroy Lindo's malefic drug dealer in *Clockers,* Lee has not hesitated once to portray certain members of the black community as mesmerizingly unappealing figures. And when they have not been monsters, they have often been clowns (the preposterous black fraternity members in *School Daze,* Wesley Snipes's coy ass bandit in *Jungle Fever,* the boombox-toting lunkhead in *Do the Right Thing,* Lee's one-dimensional pussy hound in *She's Gotta Have It*). While certain white critics have gotten all hot and bothered about the alleged anti-Semitic portrayals of the jazz club owners in *Mo' Better Blues*, hardly anyone has noticed how regularly, and mischievously, Lee has used his films to criticize or at least satirize members of his own ethnic group. It's as if white America has said: It's okay to cast your fellow African-Americans in an unflattering light, because you're black and that's your turf, but for God's sake, leave our ethnic groups alone. In other words, only us drunken Micks can make films about us drunken Micks; only us racist Italians can make movies about us racist Italians.

As a matter of fact, one of the things that is most remarkable about Lee's films is how expertly, how meticulously, how accurately he portrays white people. Name a film where a Yuppie schmuck has been brought to life with more panache than Tim Robbins in *Jungle Fever*. Tell me that Vincent D'Onofrio and his henchmen in that candy shop aren't the spitting images of the boys from Bensonhurst. Or that Danny Aiello and Harvey Keitel don't fit the bill as the Racists with Hearts of Gold in *Do the Right Thing* and *Clockers*. For a clearer idea of Lee's achievement, try to imagine a major white director making a movie about people from Bedford-Stuyvesant that comes within ten miles of the target. Jim Jarmusch? Oliver Stone? Brian De Palma? The Man of Wood?

"What people don't realize is that when you're a minority you know *everything* about the majority culture, because you're bombarded with that every single day," Lee patiently explains while looking out the window at Brooklyn Hospital. "So I think that Hispanics, Asians, and African Americans know everything about white culture, because that's all we see. That's always on television, radio, and the newspapers. The reverse is not the same."

Referring to *Crooklyn*, his valentine to his own family, in which a group of black children are seen singing "I Woke up in Love This Morning" along with The Partridge Family, Lee says, "Black kids at that same time watched *The Partridge Family* and *The Brady Bunch*. I hated *The Partridge Family*, but my brother and sisters loved it. I got outvoted."

Since he's so good at it, I ask Lee if he could make an entire movie about white people. I suggested that after the less-than-blockbuster box office take for the sappy *Crooklyn*, the dark, depressing but very compelling *Clockers*, and *Girl 6*, an underrated, often amusing film about a young black actress who gets tired of being asked to show her breasts and instead takes a job as a telephone sex operator, it might be a good idea to pull an *Age of Innocence* and make a movie completely outside the range of his normal experience.

But Lee doesn't take the suggestion in the spirit it was intended.

"It would have to be a good story," he snaps. "But I'm not going to do that to validate myself or to show that I'm not a racist. I get asked that all the time. 'When are you going to do a film with white people in it?' "

It just so happens that Lee has had plans to make one for quite some time. The project, *Reliable Sources*, postponed for now, features a script by Joe Eszterhas and deals with a reporter involved in a hostage situation.

"I think the majority of those characters are white," he says.

I warn the director to make sure Eszterhas does not sell him one of his famous recycled scripts: *Jade* as a remake of *Basic Instinct*, *The Music Box* as a retread of *Jagged Edge*. If Lee has problems with white people now, there's no telling how he'll feel after working with Joe Eszterhas.

Lee's problems raising cash for his long-planned Jackie Robinson bio-pic in the wake of the cost overruns on *Malcolm X*, and the far-from-thrilling responses to *Crooklyn*, *Clockers*, and *Girl 6*, are no doubt a big part of why he has just finished making a quickie film for $2.8 million. *Get on the Bus* deals with fifteen black men trekking from Los Angeles to Washington in October 1995 to attend the Million Man March. Funded by African-American men such as Wesley Snipes and Danny Glover, it stars Ossie Davis, Isaiah Washington, Richard Belzer, Randy Quaid, and a host of others, all of whom worked for scale. The cast includes a gay couple, a policeman, and a father and son who are shackled together by court order. The obvious question: What kind of movie can you make for $2.8 million?

"A very good one," Lee explains. "You just don't have a lot of the toys. You know, you don't stay at the best hotels—all that stuff that really has nothing to do with filmmaking. All the money has to be on the screen."

Although at first glance *Get on the Bus* seems like a "typical" Spike Lee project, it actually bears little resemblance to his other films. *She's Gotta Have It* was an arty comedy. *School Daze*, absent its maudlin ending, was an outright hoot. *Do the Right Thing* was a realistic film suffused with numerous surrealistic elements. *Mo' Better Blues* was the black *Benny Goodman Story*. *Malcolm X* was half gangster story, half solemn epic. *Crooklyn* was an African-American Hallmark greeting card. *Clockers* was a brooding, intense murder mystery. *Girl 6* was a thoughtful, spicy melodrama. Yes, Lee uses the same directing techniques over and over again, and yes, he relies on the same cadre of performers. But thematically, and in terms of overall mood, no two of these movies are alike. More important still, in his determination to show that African-American society is not a monolith, Lee makes some films about poor people, some films about middle-class people, some films about the famous and successful, some films about dismal failures.

Yet somehow, nobody seems to notice this. I ask Lee if it bothers him that his nine very different films are generally thought of as variations on the same theme.

"It doesn't bother me," Lee says. "I know that people try to pigeonhole artists because of films like *Do the Right Thing* and *Malcolm X* and *Jungle Fever*. There are a lot of people, well not a lot of people, but some people who think that my number-one interest in doing films is dealing with racial issues in this country. That's very important to me, but that is not the totality of the types of films, the types of stories that I want to make." He adds, "I don't really think I make any one type of film."

Noting that Quentin Tarantino appears briefly in *Girl 6*, I ask Lee if he envies Tarantino and his protégé Robert Rodriguez the cultural canonizaton they have earned while making movies that are basically about how much they like other movies. By this I mean: If *Pulp Fiction*, *Reservoir Dogs*, *El Mariachi*, *Desperado*, and *From Dusk Till Dawn* have a message, it went over my head. But again, Lee senses a trap and takes umbrage.

"Who says that I only like message films?" he asks. "Why do you even ask me that question? Because I like a film and it's not a message movie, and *that's* something to note. That the only films I like, my taste has to do with films with a message? I went to see *The Rock*, and I enjoyed that. Yes, I do like movies that don't necessarily have a message to them. Spike Lee goes to the movies sometimes just for entertainment. I've never said that every film has to have a message in it."

That's good, because now we can segue into a chat about one of Lee's passions: basketball. Spike Lee has made ten films since his debut in 1986, and almost got himself, well, lynched, three years ago when his courtside taunting of Indiana Pacers superstar Reggie Miller triggered a 25-point fourth-quarter explosion in a playoff game that very nearly cost the Knicks a trip to the NBA finals. Yet to date this self-confessed hoops addict has never made a film about basketball. Would he like to make a film about the subject?

"I would *love* to."

"And what would it be?" I ask.

"Hey, it'd be better than *Eddie*," Lee smiles impishly. "It'd be better than *Celtic Pride*."

Well, yeah, that's a given. But couldn't he be a bit more specific?

"I don't know, because I don't have the story yet."

"Could you make a movie about Dennis Rodman? Has it crossed your mind?"

"No."

"Why not?"

"Because it's not interesting to do a movie about Dennis Rodman."

"Why not?" I ask. "He's an interesting man."

"Many people are interesting," Lee replies, "but that doesn't warrant a movie."

"He's a *very* interesting man," I press on, but Lee is clearly not interested.

"Dennis Rodman you could do a five-minute feature on," he says. In fact, he suspects that if he ever does make a movie about basketball, it will not be about the pros but about college hoops. The pros are just too, well, good.

"What's more dramatic than the actual sport?" he asks. "People watch that stuff on television for free. You can't duplicate what's real in the NBA."

Spike Lee movies, whether comedies like *School Daze*, brooding dramas like *Clockers*, or sprawling epics like *Malcolm X*, all share certain characteristics. They always have mesmerizing opening credits. They always have great soundtracks. They always have terrific dialogue. They always veer back and forth between bleak realism and sentimentality, most recently in *Clockers* where a young drug dealer is seen returning to his apartment, where he ensconces himself in the living room and plays with a massive collection of model trains. And they usually have one or two electrifyingly funny scenes: the ghetto-blaster duel in *Do the Right Thing*, the string of African-American pickup lines in *She's Gotta Have It*, the "Zulu dick" conversation in *Jungle Fever*. To that list, you can add just about the entire script of *School Daze*, but most particularly Ossie Davis's fire-and-brimstone speech to his football team on Homecoming Day—after which they go out and lose 55-7. Black *Rudy*, it ain't.

On the negative side, Lee's films are long, talky, and usually have multiple endings. His heavy-handed sermonizing, his gnawing fear that the audience has still not gotten the point, has led to clumsy proselytizing at the end of *Do the Right Thing*, *Malcolm X*, *Jungle Fever*, and *School Daze*, which make those Red Army operas look subtle by comparison.

Lee has a hard time advancing his plots with images; everything is done through humongous gabfests. In some of his films, the cameraman seems to wander off for long naps, leaving his equipment running on automatic pilot. In this sense, the director he most resembles is not Woody Allen—another short, bespectacled, narcissistic New Yorker with Knicks courtside seats whose acting leaves something to be desired—but Eric Rohmer, the master of the film as one meandering conversation. Indeed, one of the most noticeable features of Lee's films is his affection for arty techniques—blackouts, weird camera angles, characters constantly talking to the camera—that French people adore. He has probably done as much as any American director to make Godardian film-school techniques part of the mainstream. Which, after taunting Reggie Miller into that 25-point explosion, is probably his single greatest crime against humanity.

But one thing that rescues Lee's films from their pacing problems and his reluctance to wrap things up is his ability to coax great, great performances out of his cast. In fact, it is a testimony to the farcical nature of the Academy Awards that nonentities like Marisa Tomei and Brad Pitt are strewn with honors while the work of Samuel L. Jackson (*Jungle Fever*), Delroy Lindo (*Clockers*), and Denzel Washington (*Malcolm X*) is ignored. I ask Lee if the actors in question ever expect to be singled out for their work.

"I don't think they do," he replies. "I mean it would be nice, but it's not something that they're going to put a whole lot of faith in, because they just know what the realities are."

And what are those realities?

"African-American talent is looked over."

At the risk of offending one of the nation's most talented African Americans, I bring up the ending thing in Lee's movies. To my mind, not one of Spike Lee's movies ends when it should or the way it should. Frequently, as in *Malcolm X* and *Do the Right*

Thing, there is a cinematic ending, then some earnest but unnecessary blather tacked onto the end, Oliver Stone style. *School Daze* and *Jungle Fever* have weird, surreal, arbitrary endings, while *Crooklyn* and *Mo' Better Blues* end, and then end . . . and then end some more. A friend of mine says that the Hughes Brothers once suggested that Spike Lee needs to go to Film Ending School. I could not agree more. Speaking as a mildly pretentious, wishy-washy, suburban white person, I can say that nothing Spike Lee has ever said about white people has offended me in the least, not even his request to be interviewed by black journalists because he is tired of being subjected to hatchet jobs by mean-spirited white people like me. Frankly, I can see no difference between Lee's attempts to handpick sympathetic African-American interviewers and white movie stars' insistence that *Vanity Fair* and *Premiere* dispatch the usual blow-job brigade. But his desultory camera work and inability to wrap up his films really gets on my nerves. In late–20th-century America, these, not allegations of covert racism, are the things that bother white people like me. What a society.

But when I bring up this finale problem in the context of *Mo' Better Blues,* Lee insists that the film cannot end on a downbeat note, with Denzel Washington's washed-up trumpet player staggering out into the rain. Instead, he feels that the film must end with the older, wiser musician teaching his son how to play the instrument, but then allowing him to cut his lesson short and go out and play ball. In Lee's view, this shows that the character has grown. Glumly, I realize that I'm not going to get anywhere by suggesting that Lee's film finales leave something to be desired. So I simply drop the subject by noting that anyone who would force his child to play the trumpet is by definition a monster incapable of personal growth. Lee seems amused. I ask if he ever pays any attention to outside criticism of his work.

"Depends who's giving the criticism," he replies. "There are people I respect, and I listen to them; other people I don't listen to. I have an inner circle of friends, people who are very honest with me, people I respect who are filmmakers. If something doesn't work, and they tell me it's not working, then I better check it out because there might be something to that."

In the current revival of *Showboat* that is playing on Broadway, Harold Prince tries to underscore the plight of black people in the late 19th century by having Old Black Joe constantly reappear onstage to sing snippets of the lugubrious "Old Man River." This is precisely the sort of thing that Spike Lee does not do: One of the great features of his films is his ability to portray African Americans as joyous and fun loving in the face of adversity. Even the generally dour *Malcolm X* includes some joyful dance scenes, plus a truly wonderful moment when Lee and Denzel Washington go strutting through the streets of Boston, garishly attired in their absurd zoot suits.

"Oh, we had a lot of fun doing that," recalls Lee. "Putting on those clothes was fun."

Fun is usually left out when white people make films about other cultures. When well-meaning white people get involved in this process, they think it's their job to show how awful black life is. As Lee says of Clint Eastwood's *Bird*, "I liked the music. But, you know, I just had a problem with how he shot the movie. It was very dark, and every scene was raining."

Federico Fellini was once asked what he did on his vacations. Fellini said his idea of the perfect vacation was to make a movie. For him, all the fund-raising, publicity business was work, but the actual process of film-making was fun. I ask Lee if he shares Fellini's attitude. He does not.

"To me, making movies—which I love—is still hard work," he replies. "It's not a vacation, I'm sorry."

"Is it harder work than stuff like this, giving interviews?"

"That's harder," Lee replies. "Press junkets where you do fifty interviews a day and everybody's asking the same question."

"Did you ever interview yourself?" I ask.

"No," he replies.

"Can you think of a question you'd like to be asked?"

Lee ponders the question for a minute.

"No."

"So you can see how hard it is."

"It's not hard. It's just that people are lazy. They don't take time to do their research, so they just ask the same questions."

I now ask Spike Lee a whole series of questions I am sure he has not been asked. I ask him if he would give Mickey Rourke, the man who at least indirectly blamed him for the Rodney King riots, a job. I really want to prove that I am not a lazy reporter, and have actually done my research.

"He was great in *Diner*, but that was a long time ago," Lee replies. "But if there was a part for him, I wouldn't hold that against him."

But what about those nasty accusations?

"Mickey Rourke is not a social scientist," Lee answers dryly. "You have to consider the source."

We proceed. In answer to my assorted, thematically incongruous questions, Lee will *not* be making a film about sixties activist H. Rap Brown, will *not* be making a film about Dennis Rodman or Richie Parker, will *not* be making a film about how awful Peter, Paul & Mary were. In answer to the question, "Has the idea of making a movie about Sammy Davis Jr. crossed your mind?" Lee gets a bit peeved. Hey, who wouldn't?

"Why do you keep asking me questions about what movie to make? Why do you keep suggesting films for me to make?"

"Because they're movies that I would like to see you make," I fire back. "That's all."

Sadly, Lee has no interest in making them. He thinks that H. Rap Brown's life would make a good story, but not for him. He feels the same way about Sammy Davis Jr. In other words: *Yes, I can, but no I won't.*

"Would you like to do an action film?" I ask.

"It would have to be a good script. It would have to have substance to it. It couldn't just be car crashes and special effects."

"So you're never going to get to the point like some of these guys who start out making great films and then they just go and work for the studios putting out product?"

"I hope not," he says, clearly tired of the interview.

I hope not, too.

Note: Since this article appeared in 1996, Albert Belle has moved from the Cleveland Indians to the Chicago White Sox to the Baltimore Orioles. He is still a dickhead.

Note: Since this article appeared in 1996, Spike Lee has continued to make thought-provoking, overly long motion pictures such as He Got Game, *and has continued to make a complete fool of himself at New York Knicks basketball games. After Indiana Pacers superstar Reggie Miller responded to Lee's taunting by burying a buzzer-beating three-pointer that effectively ended the Knicks' season on May 10, 1998, I would have thought the New York players would have taken him aside and kicked his scrawny ass.*

But no such luck.

MODEL ROLES

In recent years, an impressive number of fashion models have successfully made the transition from the runway to the silver screen. Following the path blazed by such notables as Lauren Hutton, Marisa Berenson, and Cybill Shepherd, models like Kim Basinger, Andie MacDowell, Rene Russo, Elle Macpherson, and Liv Tyler have successfully bridged the yawning chasm that separates Seventh Avenue from Rodeo Drive and become glamorous, sought-after movie stars in their own right. They are to be commended for their skill, their drive, their passion, their craft, but most important of all, for their unswerving commitment to bringing the rest of us fine motion pictures like *Outbreak*, *Buddy*, *Groundhog Day*, *Tin Cup*, and, of course, *Nine 1/2 Weeks*.

And yet, there is a dark side to this story, for not every model who attempts to gild her lily in Hollywood finds the streets lined with gold. Films such as *Necessary Roughness* have not made bouncy Kathy Ireland a household name. Iman, whose star once burned oh, so bright, is now banished to such trivial flotsam and jetsam as *House Party 2* and *Star Trek VI*. Grace Jones is but a dim, albeit bad, memory; Paulina Porizkova's career completely went into the tank after a couple of substandard films; Carol Alt is now better remembered for the rats-up-the-stockings *Spy* magazine cover than for movies like *My First Forty Years*; and Brooke Shields—still trying to live down the Vesuvian disaster of *Brenda Starr*—now plays second-banana in Broadway musicals, gets cameo roles in small, horrible movies like *Freaked*, and is forced to shill for her own, critically panned TV show. At this stage in her career, it is not clear what future awaits Elizabeth Hurley, but based on the evidence to date—*El Largo Invierno, Der Skipper, El Largo Invierno, Beyond Bedlam, El Largo Invierno*, and *Passenger 57*—the auguries are not auspicious. Most tragic of all, after Cindy Crawford's dismal debut in *Fair Game*, it is not at all certain that the comely supermodel will ever have a movie career worth discussing. Well, not worth discussing politely.

Dismayed at the worrisome casualty rate among models-turned-actresses, I rented more than a dozen films starring famous models, seeking to determine why they had failed where others had succeeded. Had the actresses in question simply bombed because they lacked the requisite skills necessary to thrive in Hollywood? Or were they the hapless victims of astoundingly poor scripts? Would it have made a difference if Iman had been in *Star Trek III* instead of *Star Trek VI*? *Revenge of the Nerds III* instead of *House Party 2*? And is there any wisdom that young prospects such as Amber Valleta, Shalom Harlow, Linda Evangelista, Christy Turlington, and Naomi Campbell can salvage from the wreckage of these acting careers?

The answer is surprisingly straightforward. With the exception of Grace Jones and Carol Alt, each of whom is a hopelessly bad actress, most of the other young women could have achieved the same level of success as their more renowned colleagues had they been more selective about their material. On the basis of their performances in movies as varied as *Endless Love, The Blue Lagoon, Anna, Her Alibi, Fair Game, House Party 2*, and *Necessary Roughness*, it is fair to say that Brooke Shields, Paulina Porizkova, Cindy Crawford, Iman, and Kathy Ireland are not criminally bad actresses, and given time, love, understanding, acting classes, and therapy, could have been at least as good as Jerry Hall. What prevented this quintet of radiant females from reaching this plateau can be summed up this way:

1. They appeared in far too many films where words like "And Randy Quaid as Elijah Skuggs" appeared in the opening credits.

2. They appeared in far too many films directed by Doug & George, Stan Dragoti, and Yurek Bogayevicz rather than Franco Zeffirelli.

3. When they did appear in films directed by Franco Zeffirelli, they tended to be ones that were even worse than the films directed by Doug & George, Stan Dragoti, and Yurek Bogayevicz.

4. They consistently ignored the abundant forensic evidence that appearing in a film starring *both* Scott Bakula and Sinbad would not advance their careers.

5. Not until it was far too late did they realize that costarring with Sally Kirkland in a movie about a washed-up, mentally ill, not especially nice Czech actress is not the way to become the next Elizabeth Taylor or even the last Elizabeth Hurley.

First, let's get Carol Alt and Grace Jones out of the way. Back in 1984, Jones appeared as a post–Cro-Magnon gladiatrix in *Conan the Destroyer*, the second film in the series that launched Arnold Schwarzenegger's career. Semi-naked, sporting some sort of furry tail, and at one point appearing with a set of gigantic pigtails bulging out from her skull to achieve that elusive perky Mongol affect, Jones looked for all the world like the equipment manager in an all-girl Megadeth. Let us say this on the record: If you are in a movie which includes the line "It is written in the scrolls of Scellus that a woman-child born with a certain mark must make a perilous journey," and that also includes the credit

Music Composed & Conducted
by
Basil Poledouris

and that costars Wilt Chamberlain, your career is probably going nowhere fast. But when your acting is so bad that Arnold Schwarzenegger and Wilt Chamberlain actually start to resemble George C. Scott and Alec Guinness by comparison, where halfway through the film the audience starts asking itself, "Gee, why didn't they cast Tina Turner or Sandahl Bergman in Grace's part?" your career is in really big trouble. The awful truth is: In *Conan the Destroyer*, Grace Jones is best thought of as a black Brigitte Nielsen. This is only slightly better than being the white Grace Jones.

Carol Alt's career is in many ways more disturbing than Jones's, because Alt actually landed a couple of starring roles. The most memorable of these was *A Family Matter*, in which Alt played the *consigliere* to a mob family headed by Eli Wallach. Which is not unlike casting Jim Carrey as King Lear. In the film, a young girl sees her crooner dad get whacked by an Irish hitman played by Eric Roberts, who does look sort of Italian, but does not look at all Irish. Shortly before the murder, her dad had been seen singing "That's Amore," so the assassination may have had some vague ethno-cultural justification.

Because of poor eyesight and a poor script, Alt does not realize until many years later that Roberts murdered her dad. In fact, she does not realize it until the day she gets married to Roberts, when she receives a mysterious wedding gift consisting of a gun and a tape recording congratulating her on marrying her dad's killer.

This sort of mid-nuptial practical joke is apparently an old Sicilian tradition.

There are several problems with this film. One, Eric Roberts is in it. Two, it is so cheap that when someone shoots a gun directly at a man's testicles, the bullet comes out the middle of his back. Three, Eric Roberts is in it. Four, Carol Alt is just a little bit too perky to play a mafia *consigliere*. Five, Eric Roberts is in it. Six, and most important of all, it includes a scene where a mobbed-up midget lounge lizard sings "Volare" to a bewildered crowd. This is one of the most famous telltale signs that a movie is in big trouble. Attention, Chrissie, Elle, Liv, Naomi, Christy, Allison, Linda, or anyone else reading this story: If you're a beautiful model trying to decide what script to sign up for, bear this in mind: *If the proposed film includes a scene where a mobbed-up midget sings "Volare," hold out for something like* Twister.

The movies starring Iman, Brooke Shields, Paulina Porizkova, Kathy Ireland, and Cindy Crawford are littered with similar warning signs. Consider the case of *Necessary Roughness*, in which Kathy Ireland plays a place-kicker for a pathetic college football team called the Texas State Armadillos. The film, directed by Stan Dragoti and starring Scott Bakula and Sinbad, comes with a video box reading: "They just might be the biggest bunch of losers that ever became winners." One gag involves a football getting lodged in a guy's helmet. Another involves a place kick to the genitals. Also, Harley Jane Kozak is in the film. Not good.

Another big mistake models make is allowing themselves to be typecast by appearing in the same role more than once. In *Anna*, Paulina Porizkova plays a lovable young Czech whose English is so bad that no one can understand her. In *Her Alibi*, Porizkova plays a lovable young Rumanian whose English is so bad that no one can understand her. Clearly, this is a dead-end street: There really isn't much of a market in the United States for films about a lovable young Bulgarian, Croat, or Hungarian who can't speak English, so once you've run through all these downscale Central European roles, you're headed straight for the ashbin of history.

But again, as with Jones and Alt, the telltale signs were there from the beginning. If you are making your debut in a film where Sally Kirkland is seen pulling on her pantyhose while she is having a nervous breakdown because nobody thinks she can act anymore, you are not laying a sound foundation for a long career in motion pictures.

Nor am I saying this out of unkindness to Sally Kirkland. From what I can tell, *Anna* is probably the best movie about a washed-up, mentally ill, thoroughly hateful Czech movie star ever made. But movies like that don't make much of an impact at the box office. Believe it or not, for a movie to succeed, someone in the film has to be at least mildly believable. This is one of the big problems with *Endless Love*. Released in 1981, this horrendous Franco Zeffirelli film features Brooke Shields as a fifteen-year-old girl who is being harpooned by her seventeen-year-old boyfriend on a nightly basis. Because she is doing this while lying in front of the living-room fireplace in the middle of the night, her parents eventually find out. They discuss the ramifications of the situation at length. Dad wonders if she's too young to be getting harpooned every night. And if she's getting harpooned by the right guy.

Other pedagogical questions ultimately arise. Should Brooke be taking more drugs? Which ones? Wouldn't it be better if Brooke spent less time screwing this guy and more time taking acting lessons? Eventually, Dad puts his foot down and tells loverboy that he can't come into the house anymore. Romeo quickly makes sure no one can come into the house anymore by burning it to the ground. He gets sentenced to five years' probation, with the provision that he enter a psychiatric program that deals with young men twisted enough to fall in love with someone who looks like she would both date Michael Jackson and marry Andre Agassi.

The youth tries to go straight, but eventually meets up with Brooke's mom, who tries to seduce him. All right, let's stop beating around the bush: This family is dysfunctional. Then, on his way to a rendezvous with Brooke in—where else?—Burlington,

Vermont, he runs into Brooke's dad, who accidentally gets run over by a taxi cab while making faces at him. When Mr. Firebug finally does encounter Brooke again, she tries to convince him that their relationship has become so convoluted and macabre that it might be better if they started playing the field, or at least waited until Dad's safely nestled in the ground. But he persists, and she finally says okay.

MORAL: If you insist on appearing in movies about a pyromaniac who your mom is in love with and who contributes to your own dad's premature death, don't be surprised if you end up getting bit parts in a revival of *Grease*, or in films about mutants that feature soundtracks by the Butthole Surfers and star Randy Quaid as Elijah Skuggs.

Let us now put Brooke behind us. To my mind, the most beautiful model of them all is Iman, yet for some reason, her career on the big screen has never clicked. Why? In part because she is so beautiful that she makes everyone else in the film look ugly. Which is not that hard to do when your costars are Leonard Nimoy and Martin Lawrence. But there are other problems. In *Star Trek VI*, Iman plays a futuristic jailbird with a Franco-Russo-Jamaican-Somali accent, trapped in a neo-prehistoric Arctic gulag, who has a miraculous ability to turn herself into a hideous monster or William Shatner at the drop of a hat. Eventually, Shatner gets sick of her and punches her out. In *House Party 2*, Iman plays a crooked record promoter with an exotic accent who gets punched out by Queen Latifah. Frankly, I think an argument can be made that the moviegoing public is not interested in seeing one of the most beautiful women in the world get punched out by William Shatner or Queen Latifah. Like Paulina Porizkova, Iman seems to have allowed herself to become hopelessly typecast, in this case as the beautiful, mysterious, polylingual tramp that everyone wants to put on the canvas. This is just no way to build a career.

Finally, we come to the curious case of Cindy Crawford. Crawford was savaged last year when *Fair Game* was released, and it must be admitted that much of the criticism was warranted. But my problem was not with Crawford's performance—a whole lot better than anything we've ever seen from Carol Alt—but with the part she chose to play. Call me a purist, call me a stodgy old curmudgeon, call me a pedant, but Cindy Crawford is just not cut out to play a lawyer who happens to be an expert in federal maritime law. This is where Kim Basinger has demonstrated so much more savvy in choosing her roles. Kim Basinger looks like the kind of gal who would date Mickey Rourke (*9 1/2 Weeks*). She looks like the kind of gal who would go on a pointless crime spree with a complete loser (*The Getaway*). She looks like the kind of person who could be from another planet (*My Stepmother Is an Alien*) and be unlucky enough to marry Dan Aykroyd. True, all of these movies were terrible. But they were terrible in a positive, career-boosting way. Kim didn't get punched out by Queen Latifah. She didn't have to turn into William Shatner. And she certainly didn't try to pass herself off as an expert in federal maritime law.

This is why Elle Macpherson deserves such kudos for her sterling work in *Sirens*. Playing second fiddle to Hugh Grant, Sam Neill, and Tara Fitzgerald, Macpherson completely stole the show as a mysterious bisexual living with a grumpy painter and three other women in the Australian outback. Seducing anything that moved, Macpherson demonstrated a genuine comic deftness in this underrated motion picture, but also made a big impression because she was not asked to carry the ball for the entire length of the film. Of all the supermodels who have recently made the transition from the rag trade to Hollywood, Macpherson's career is the one that bears the closest watching.

As for all the others, the jury is still out. Will Alison Elliot's work in *The Spitfire Grill* turn her into the next Halle Berry or the next Jerry Hall? And will Angie Everhart's work in *Bordello of Blood* lead to roles in films like *Get Shorty* and *In the Line of Fire* or to a career in films like *Bordello of Even More Blood*? To answer that question, let's reiterate a few important points about this increasingly popular career path. If you're a gorgeous model like Christy Turlington, Kate Moss, or Niki Taylor and are contemplating a second career in acting, try to keep these ideas in mind:

- Avoid mafia movies starring Eli Wallach and Burt Young. You won't look Sicilian, you'll mispronounce the word "cannoli," and you'll have to spend the entire movie walking around in flats so as not to embarrass these hammy dwarves.

- Ask right up front if the soundtrack for your next picture will feature the Butthole Surfers. If it does, don't make a scene, but quietly, politely ask if John Williams or Bruce Springsteen might not be a better choice.

- If the film in question features guest appearances by anyone with a name like Tony! Toni! Toné!, politely decline the invitation.

- Last but not least, if you are going to be cast as a lawyer, make it a long-legged attorney who specializes in probate, tax shelters, or real estate closings. That federal-maritime-law thing is like chum in the water to critics.

THE MIRROR HAS TWO FACES, ONE WORSE THAN THE OTHER

Barbra Streisand's new film, *The Mirror Has Two Faces*, is a romantic comedy that was directed, produced, partially written, and scored by the star herself. As such, it is the scariest thing since the Ebola virus, the Second Battle of the Marne, or Streisand's last film. Based on a French movie—never a good sign—about an ugly duckling who finally wins the man she loves by shedding a ton of ballast and getting her hair frizzed out, *The Mirror Has Two Faces* is an intensely autobiographical film. Again—never a good sign.

In a series of rare television appearances in the United States, Streisand has repeatedly complained that she grew up thinking she was ugly because her mother never told her that she was pretty. (Julia Roberts, one presumes, had exactly the opposite experience.) From this we can learn one thing: Whatever other crimes Streisand Senior may one day have to answer for, bald-faced lying is not one of them.

Streisand also pointed out that while some people say she lacks conventional beauty, one critic had likened her face to that of an Egyptian princess. This is true, but in all likelihood the princess had been dead for four thousand years.

I do not want to waste the reader's time by going on and on about Barbra Streisand's lifelong inability to come to terms with her train-wreck physiognomy. Suffice it to say Streisand is long past the point in her career where she can boldly cast herself opposite younger costars like Jeff Bridges without drawing unflattering comparisons. Like her contemporary, Woody Allen, another Brooklyn-born egomaniac who goes for the young stuff, Streisand has simply got to stop kissing younger, good-looking men in full close-up. This has gone beyond cradle robbing. This is getting awfully close to child abuse.

However, as I said earlier, I do not want to spend this entire review sneering at Streisand's obsession with a beauty she obviously does not possess. A more constructive approach is to ask whether *The Mirror Has Two Faces*, in and of itself, is a rewarding film experience. After all, it is a romantic comedy, and it does feature a talented cast: Jeff Bridges, Lauren Bacall, George Segal, Brenda Vaccaro, Mimi Rogers. And, oh yes, Pierce Brosnan. So even if it is just another vehicle for Barbra Streisand's monstrous self-worship, surely it must contain some memorable scenes, a few good jokes.

To ascertain whether or not this was true, I decided to sit through the film and mark down the number of times I laughed. If I only laughed a couple of times, it would prove that the film was a hopelessly outdated dinosaur that could not possibly appeal to anyone with a nineties sensibility and therefore sucked. If, on the other hand, I did laugh a fair number of times, it would prove that the comedic infrastructure of the movie was perfectly fine, and that its only failing lay in the main casting. This would prove that even if Streisand the Movie Star was a hatchet-faced crone, Streisand the Producer, Director, Screenwriter, and Composer was still a force to be reckoned with.

The opening sequences of the movie produced nary a titter.

Bridges, playing a shy mathematics professor at one of America's most prestigious universities, decides that his previous relationships have all been sabotaged by too much emphasis on sex. Therefore, he takes out an ad in a newspaper seeking a nonsexual relationship with a bright woman. Eventually, he hooks up with Streisand, a dumpy, frumpy, putatively thirtysomething English professor who also teaches at one of America's most respected universities, and who promptly falls in love with him. No laughs here.

When Lauren Bacall, playing Streisand's horrid mother, finds out about her new boyfriend, she asks, "Is this The One?" Streisand fires back: "Mother, stop asking if this is The One. It's like you're picking out a lobster." Then, when Bridges agrees to come over for dinner and asks if he should bring anything for Babs's mother, Streisand replies, "Yes, a wooden stake and a crucifix." At this point, I realized that the movie was forty-five minutes old and I had not laughed a single time.

Forty-five minutes turned into sixty, then ninety, and as the film lumbered toward its denouement, I realized with guilty, *schadenfreudic* pleasure that it just might be possible to sit through this entire film without laughing once. When Babs's and Jeff's low-rent city hall marriage and awkward first night together produced nary a chuckle I realized that Streisand was now seriously threatening Chevy Chase's record for Romantic Comedy with Fewest Jokes.

When Bridges's and Streisand's disastrous night in bed elicited nary a chuckle, I knew that we were in the home stretch. I had not laughed when Bridges spits toothpaste onto the bathroom mirror, had not cracked a smile when Streisand puts on some mellow jazz to get her hubby "in the mood," had not even tittered when The Babster and Brenda Vaccaro trade jokes about salad dressing. One hundred minutes into the film and I had not come close to laughing. This was Dan Aykroyd Territory we were heading into.

Then, just a few moments before the film ended, Bridges

caught me with a right hook out of nowhere. After their dud conjugal tryst, Bridges has flown off to Europe for a speaking tour and Babs has spent the summer at the gym, peeling off the pork. When he returns, she is decked out like a sultry vamp, but Bridges finds the effect somewhat, well, repellent. But then the hunted becomes the hunter. Bridges shows up at her apartment early one morning (not funny), wrestles with the doorman (not funny), and wakes all the neighbors (not funny).

Finally, Babs rushes outside. I checked my watch. The movie couldn't have had more than two minutes to go: 120 seconds to immortality! And then it happened. Catching me completely off guard, Bridges looked directly at his costar's implausible face and said, "God, you're beautiful."

That's when I started laughing.

That's when I started laughing really hard.

Why, I laughed so hard, I cried.

THE KIDNAPPERS ARE ALL RIGHT

Around Christmastime of 1993, Kevin Costner appeared in a movie about an amiable kidnapper who also happened to be a murderer. *A Perfect World* was not your typical Yuletide fare. Making a clean break with the admirable, well-scrubbed, Middle American Big Boys Next Door he had played in the past, Costner herein starred as a white-trash jailbird who busts out of prison, abducts a small boy, guns down his own accomplice, and then takes the child on a violent rampage across Dixie until wizened law officer Clint Eastwood tracks him down. Costner's character is so unhinged that after one sequence in which he threatens to kill a man who has taken him in for the evening and supplied him with a damned fine meal and impeccable lodging, the precocious abductee sees no alternative but to get hold of the gun and shoot him right in the guts.

In crossing the line into the shadowy netherworld of justifiable manslaughter, the gun-toting tyke was clearly speaking for most

Middle Americans, who generally don't warm up much to this kidnapping stuff. Which is not terribly surprising, given that most Middle American moviegoers either have or still are children, and generally prefer to see kids in a pristine, cuddly, un-kidnapped condition.

On the surface, the very notion of making a film whose central character is a violent lowlife kidnapper seems unbelievably moronic. But when we look at the recent history of American filmmaking, we can see that the decision to cast Kevin Costner in this morally ambivalent role did have a certain marketing logic to it. In 1992, Neil Jordan broke into the big time by directing and scripting an offbeat little number called *The Crying Game*. This film starred Stephen Rea as a congenial member of the Irish Republican Army who helps capture a British soldier, befriends him, listens to his amusing anecdotes, and then flees the site of his murder, defects from the IRA, and falls in love with the dead man's girlfriend, who turns out to be a rather well-hung man. In other words, Jordan was asking his audience to enthusiastically sympathize with one of God's rarest creations: the likable terrorist.

A few months after *The Crying Game* appeared, Brian De Palma released a film called *Carlito's Way*. This action-packed tale, set largely in the gloomy South Bronx, invited the audience to commiserate with a forty-something heroin dealer and murderer who has recently been released from prison because of a minor legal technicality, and who is now trying to raise $75,000 so he can launch a completely legitimate car dealership somewhere in the tropics. In other words, the audience was being asked to sympathize with another of God's rarest creations: the likable heroin dealer.

More recently, Robert De Niro directed *A Bronx Tale*, an odious film about a mobster with a heart of gold; somebody directed *Bad Girls*, a movie about role-model prostitutes; and Jordan came out with *Interview with the Vampire*, a movie about a likable if confused sucker of human blood. Just like *A Perfect World*, *The Crying Game*, and *Carlito's Way*, each of these films invited audiences to sympathize—nay, identify—with an array of morally deformed protagonists given to extravagant gestures of antisocial behavior.

At this point, many—perhaps most—readers are going to throw up their hands in exasperation and say, "All right, buster: So what's your goddamn point?" My goddamn point is this: Hollywood is not making films about congenial kidnappers, likable heroin dealers, and charming terrorists because of some massive oversight, some hideous lapse of taste, some inexplicable faux pas. Hollywood is making films of this nature because it has run the numbers and determined that there is a market for these movies. To put a fine point on it, Hollywood, by applying the peerless methodological techniques pioneered by Pat Robertson and Newt Gingrich, has determined that roughly 43 percent of the people living in the United States today are evil, and most of them are Democrats. In a nation of 250 million people, that translates into a potential audience of roughly 107,500,000 ticket-buyers. Most important of all, Hollywood has established, beyond the shadow of a doubt, that evil people consume more popcorn per capita than any other segment of the population. And that's not factoring in the enormous retail potential in overseas markets like Thailand and France, where *everyone* is basically evil.

Viewed in this context, it is much easier to understand why the seemingly benighted powers that be in Hollywood would hand Clint Eastwood a reasonably large amount of money to direct a film about a trigger-happy convict who blazes a trail of violence across the rural South in the company of a small boy he has abducted from a woman who was about to be raped by his even-more-trigger-happy partner, whom the likable kidnapper eventually has to shoot, if only to outfit the film with the most tenuous moral compass imaginable.

The way Hollywood has things sized up, the public is starting to develop a taste for these maverick protagonists. They'd turned out en masse for a movie about an IRA terrorist who falls in love with a woman who has a big cock. The usual claque of De Palma buffs seemed to enjoy a bloodcurdling movie about a personable heroin dealer. Bobby De Niro won numerous plaudits for his film about a chivalrous mafioso. And *Interview with the Vampire* was a film that all sorts of dysfunctional, hopelessly amoral people could identify with.

This being the case, it is not hard to understand why Luc Besson, director of *La Femme Nikita*, would try to push the envelope a trifle further with his phantasmagorically unappetizing film *The Professional*. This Franco-American morass of ethical ambiguities stars a goofy knucklehead named Jean Reno as a congenial, milk-guzzling hitman who befriends, and ultimately, falls in love with a twelve-year-old tartlet whose entire family has been wiped out by renegade DEA agents headed by a demonic Gary Oldman. (Oldman even seems to have lent Reno the blindman's sunglasses he wore in *Bram Stoker's Dracula*, perhaps in the desperate hope that they would deflect attention away from the fact that the lactophilic Reno's English is even worse than Dracula's.)

The feisty nymphet, who often appears in fetching hot pants throughout the film, begs Reno to teach her the tricks of the assassin's trade that he himself has learned at the hands of Danny Aiello, uncharacteristically cast as a loathsome meatball. Particularly memorable is the scene where Reno takes the child up onto the roof of a Manhattan skyscraper where she can practice her newly acquired Lee Harvey Oswaldian techniques by shooting a high-powered rifle at a jogging politician who looks suspiciously like Bill Clinton. Luckily, the gun was loaded with blanks.

Jesse Helms must have loved this film.

Clearly, in presenting social pariah, revolting vermin, or well-meaning vampires as heroic figures in a string of movies, Hollywood has tapped into some primal longing lodged deep in the dark recesses of the collective psyche of the American people. Therefore, as a service to these primal longers, I have compiled a list of morally repugnant movies featuring charismatic scumbags as sympathetic protagonists. Hopefully, this anthology of films can be used as the basis for a doctoral dissertation, a low-budget BBC special, a French film festival exploring primal longings lodged deep in the dark recesses of the collective American psyche, or yet another unreadable book by Michael Medved.

A Prayer for the Dying. Mickey Rourke plays a guilt-ridden IRA terrorist who comes to London to escape from his deeply conflicted past. Not to be confused with *The Crying Game*, where Stephen Rea plays a guilt-ridden IRA terrorist who comes to London to escape from his deeply conflicted past. In other words, *A Prayer for the Dying* is a movie about *a likable assassin.*

Bad Girls. Also known as *Bad Actresses*, *Whores on Horses*, and *Fools on Mules*. Andie MacDowell, Madeleine Stowe, Drew Barrymore, and Mary Stuart Masterson abandon dead-end jobs as prostitutes to enter the lumber business. Stowe spends much of the movie speaking in Spanish, apparently saying, "Call my agent and tell him to get me out of this movie." In short, *Bad Girls* is a movie about *prostitutes with hearts of gold, but brains of lead.*

A Bronx Tale. Early in this film about an Italian-American kid growing up on the mean streets of the Bronx in the early 1960s, mob chieftain Chazz Palminteri gets on everybody's bad side by killing a man in a dispute over a parking space. But as the film progresses, the audience realizes that Sonny isn't such a bad guy after all. He's a snappy dresser, he has enlightened attitudes about dating black girls, and he's always more than ready to lend his nifty red convertible to his young protégé. By the time he finally gets gunned down by the son of the man he killed in the parking dispute, the audience has come to love and respect this quirky *capo di tutti Bronx caputi.* In short, *A Bronx Tale* is a movie about *a likable mobster.*

Carlito's Way. Although he is a heroin dealer and a murderer, and thus would seem to be a not-very-nice person, Carlito comes across as a fairly gregarious sort, largely because Sean Penn is in the same movie. Also, in a clever scripting ploy, establishing once again why Brian De Palma is one of the most gifted directors in the history of motion pictures, the audience is *told* that Carlito is a heroin dealer, but never actually *sees* him selling heroin to twelve-year-olds. And while the audience is *told* that Carlito has killed a lot of people in the past, he assures Penelope Ann Miller—an actress so bad that she deserves to be one of his victims—that all the people he killed were "bad guys." *So that's okay.*

What's more, the audience never actually sees most of the people Carlito has killed. The only people the audience sees him gun down are two Hispanic criminals early in the film, and then an Italian-American gangster, and then another Italian-American gangster, and then another Italian-American gangster. And, oh yeah, he does help Sean Penn murder a mobster who's bobbing around in the East River waiting to be rescued and yes, okay, okay, he does take the bullets out of Penn's gun so he'll be defenseless when the mob comes gunning for him in his hospital bed after they screwed up by sticking a knife in his chest but not sticking it in deep enough. So, fine, technically speaking, the audience *does* see Carlito participate directly in eight homicides, but it never sees him doing anything really unpleasant—like sending someone a jar with a penis and a pair of testicles inside it like Jack Nicholson does in *Hoffa*. Carlito may be evil, but he isn't gross. Which is what gives this film about a *likable mass murderer* its special cachet.

Dangerous Games. Harvey Keitel plays the troubled director of a low-budget movie about spouse abuse, whose own marriage disintegrates when he chooses the day of his father-in-law's funeral as the ideal moment to tell his wife that he's been screwing Madonna—the last thing any woman wants to hear on the day she's burying her father. In short, the central character in *Dangerous Games* is a *likable director of creepy, sadomasochistic films, not totally unlike Abel Ferrara, the director of Dangerous Games.*

Eight Men Out. Charlie Sheen, John Cusack, Christopher Lloyd, Michael Rooker, David Strathairn, and a cast of eight star in John Sayles's 1988 costume drama about the 1919 Chicago White Sox, a bunch of disgruntled baseball players who accepted a bribe from known gangsters to take a dive in the World Series, and, by doing so, came very close to destroying America's faith in its national pastime, the most perfect sport ever devised by mankind. In short, *Eight Men Out* is a movie about *likable crooked athletes*.

Geronimo: An American Legend. Although he was known to rape, pillage, rape, mutilate, rape, burn, and rape; had a reputation as a person who would kill anything that moved; wasn't much liked, even by his own people; and ended his life as a pathetic drunk, this politically correct 1993 film portrays the dreaded Apache renegade as a pretty swell guy, a Lancelot of the Arroyos, if you will. In short, *Geronimo* is a movie about a *likable bloodthirsty savage*.

The Godfather Part III. In this star-studded film, directed by one of the greatest Italian-American directors ever to come out of New York University Film School, Al Pacino plays a congenial mobster who vainly attempts to erase the stigma of his murderous past. Not to be confused with *Carlito's Way*, a film directed by one of the greatest Italian-American directors ever to come out of New York University's film school, in which Al Pacino plays a congenial mobster who vainly attempts to erase the stigma of his murderous past. In short, it is a film about a *likable capo di tutti capi*.

GoodFellas. In this 1990 film, directed by one of the greatest Italian-American directors ever to come out of New York University's film school, Ray Liotta plays a charismatic mafioso who agrees to testify against his own confederates in exchange for a chance to go into the Federal Witness Protection program. Not to be confused with *My Blue Heaven*, the 1990 film in which Steve Martin plays a charismatic mafioso who agrees to testify against his own confederates in exchange for a chance to go into the Federal Witness Protection program, which is also a film about *a likable snitch*.

Hoffa. Danny DeVito's odious paean to the mobbed-up union boss Jimmy Hoffa, now widely believed to reside beneath the goalposts at Giants Stadium in the swamps of northern New Jersey, was not a box office gusher. The day I saw it, the only other people in the theater were seven fat men in dark suits who all had cellular phones and beepers, and who did not seem to be in the communications business. How to explain the public's dislike of *Hoffa*? One of the film's many shortcomings was DeVito's disastrous decision to include a scene where an overly enterprising newspaper editor is sent a package containing a set of male genitals pickled in formaldehyde, ostensibly as a warning to stop being so overly enterprising. After this scene, it was probably very hard for most audience members to emphathize with the problems of Jimmy Hoffa, despite a fine performance by Jack Nicholson. Or put it this way: It's a safe bet that 50 percent of the people in the audience felt that this scene cut a bit too close to the bone. In short, *Hoffa* is a movie about *a likable racketeer.*

Light Sleeper. This is a movie that literally must be seen to be believed. Willem Dafoe plays a middle-aged drug dealer who wants to get into another line of work because the pressures from his unorthodox profession are starting to get to him, because there really isn't much of a future for middle-aged drug dealers, and because he hates working nights. Also, his employer, Susan Sarandon, doesn't pay benefits. Most significantly, after decades of dealing downers and ludes—whatever they are—Dafoe is starting to feel pangs of conscience about his career.

"I'll sell you a gram and some downers," he tells a steady customer at one point in this typical Paul Schrader mess, "but I am not going to put you in the emergency room."

That most elusive of cultural archetypes—the Drug Dealer Who Cares—Dafoe talks with Sarandon about taking some sound-editing courses and perhaps getting into the music business—the very best place to escape from dangerous drugs—but his dreams are crushed when he ends up murdering a client who pushed his ex-wife, a lapsed cokehead played by Dana Delany, off a balcony.

"I am able to change; I can be a good person," Dafoe confides to his diary at one juncture. His diary doesn't seem to believe him. The crowning moment in this barmy yuckfest is the scene where Dafoe tells Delany—even more convincing as a cokehead than she was as a dominatrix in her recent *Exit to Eden* incarnation (I was *so* scared)—that he's changed his way of living and completely cleaned up his act since they'd broken up a few years before. That is, he doesn't *do* drugs anymore; he merely *sells* them. In short, *Light Sleeper* is a movie that invites the audience to sympathize with the plight of a *likable drug dealer*.

The Lover. In this lugubrious 1992 adaptation of Marguerite Duras's touching autobiography, which she has been rewriting as a play, a novel, or a screenplay nonstop for the past forty years, Tony Leung plays a ne'er-do-well Chinese playboy who pounces on a fetching morsel of Franco-Viet jailbait—Maggie herself, I assume—and gives her the gift that keeps on giving: his unsheathed manhood. In short, this is a movie about a *likable statutory rapist*.

Mean Streets. The always appealing Harvey Keitel and the ever-so-charming Robert De Niro star as doomed small-time hoods who can't seem to catch a break on the tough streets of Little Italy back in 1973, in part because Keitel has fallen in love with his epileptic cousin, and rigorous Sicilian-American social mores condemn such sordid liaisons. In short, this film, directed by one of the greatest Italian-American directors ever to come out of New York University Film School, is a movie about *likable mooks*.

Midnight Express. In Alan Parker's harrowing 1978 film, scripted by Oliver Stone, the now deceased Brad Davis plays a twenty-something American suburban punk who is sentenced to life imprisonment in a Turkish prison after he unwisely attempts to smuggle several kilos of hashish out of the country and into the United States. In short, this is a movie about a *likable drug smuggler*.

The Pope of Greenwich Village. Mickey Rourke and Eric Roberts star as doomed, small-time hoods who can't catch a break on the tough streets of Little Italy back in 1984. The movie has one truly rewarding sequence in which Roberts gets his thumb sliced off by a Mob enforcer (in light of his hyperbolic acting style, his tongue would have been a better choice), and also contains an unforgettable moment when Daryl Hannah, playing an aerobically oriented creature of one sort or another, tells Rourke: "Why are you always one inch away from being a good person?" Daryl, as usual, is a bit confused. In short, this is a movie about *likable dirtballs*.

The Professional. Awful, but not nearly as bad as it should have been, in part because neither Dana Delany nor Penelope Ann Miller is in it. Besson took some of the harsh edges off his hitman character by depicting him as a milk-guzzling simpleton who only kills people who are worse than himself, who really doesn't understand that what he does for a living is bad, and who lovingly nurses an exotic houseplant throughout the motion picture. Many—perhaps most—people viewing this film for the first time have erroneously assumed that the houseplant merely symbolizes the assassin's childlike desire to *put down some permanent roots of his own.* But this is too narrow a reading of Besson's subtle cinematic and metaphorical vocabulary. In fact, the killer's assiduous devotion to the mysteries of the botanic universe actually symbolizes his heartfelt desire to *turn over a new leaf.*

One question remains. Why, after the public failed to respond to a movie about a likable kidnapper, would Hollywood make a movie about a likable hit man with a prepubescent sidekick? For starters, we should not rule out the possibility that a perky twelve-year-old hitchild decked out in hot pants would inevitably cast a spell over the largely male, dysfunctional audiences that gallop off to see such fare the very night such films are released. And, as noted above, neither Penelope Ann Miller nor Dana Delany was in the movie. In short, *The Professional* is a movie about *a likable Franco-Belgian, lactophilic hit man.*

Reservoir Dogs. In Quentin Tarantino's ebulliently sadistic 1992 directorial debut, the always appealing Harvey Keitel plays an easygoing gangster who provides welcome comic relief from the exploits of Michael Madsen, a lunatic who slices off a policeman's ear with a straight razor while dancing to a crummy pop tune that was popular back in the 1970s. In short, this is a movie about *likable gangsters.*

The Silence of the Lambs. The enormous popularity of Jonathan Demme's 1991 film is a perfect expression of the American public's mixed feelings about cannibalism. As far as I can tell, no one in this country was especially broken up by the news that mass murderer Jeffrey Dahmer had gotten his head cracked wide open by a fellow inmate who thought he was an emissary of God in a Wisconsin prison bathroom last November. But when Demme's movie was released, the American moviegoing public seemed to feel that Hannibal Lecter was a pretty suave fellow, an intellectually stimulating sort of chap who didn't really deserve the appalling treatment that had been meted out to him by the callous, insensitive, untrustworthy prison authorities in *The Silence of the Lambs*. In short, this is a movie that seeks, and actually succeeds in eliciting, compassion for *a likable cannibal*.

Three of Hearts. In this 1993 ball of fluff, Billy Baldwin plays a charismatic stud who makes his living by screwing rich Park Avenue matrons whose husbands cannot get it up. In short, this is a film about a *likable gigolo*.

True Romance. Christian Slater steals $500,000 worth of cocaine from the Detroit Mob, then has trouble marketing it on the streets of Los Angeles because he, unlike the Cosa Nostra, does not have the correct merchandising infrastructure in place. In short, this is another movie about a *likable drug dealer*.

Wilder Napalm. This peculiar film, released to almost universal silence in 1993, stars Dennis Quaid and Arliss Howard as feuding fraternal firebugs with telekinetic arsonous powers whose adult lives are destroyed by their unresolved feelings about a childhood "prank" which cost a man his life after they set his cabin on fire. The movie concludes with a scene where the now rehabilitated Quaid, at long last reconciled with his brother, does a guest stint on *The David Letterman Show*. In other words, arson is okay if you get to meet Paul Schaffer. Or so we are to conclude from this repugnant film about *likable pyromaniacs*.

Purists may object that this list is incomplete without such classics as *M*, a film about a likable infanticide, *The Informer*, a film about a likable stool pigeon, *The Eagle Has Landed*, a movie about a likable Nazi, *Bonnie and Clyde*, a movie about likable bank robbers, *Nuts*, a film about a likable whore, *Pretty Woman*, a movie about a much more likable whore, *Natural Born Killers*, a film about likable serial killers, *Tequila Sunrise*, a film about a likable drug dealer, and *Pulp Fiction*, a film about virtually all of the above. The purists, as always, are right. But I don't want to write another word about Barbra Streisand, Oliver Stone, or Quentin Tarantino, ever. And besides, whores *are* likable. So let me conclude this essay with a few words about 1993's smash hit, *Mrs. Doubtfire*, the film in which Robin Williams dresses up as a daft English nanny in an ill-conceived attempt to stay close to his estranged children.

The varied responses of the American viewing public to this film vividly illustrates the yawning chasm that divides those who enjoy movies that lionize somewhat unnerving protagonists from those who find such films completely repulsive. When I screened this movie for my two children, aged seven and ten, they were repelled by Williams's appearance in drag, particularly the sequences where he struggles in and out of that queen-sized brassiere. They found the cross-dressing Williams to be lewd, leering, predatory, hideous, frightening, revolting, and creepy.

On the other hand, they really liked *Hoffa*.

Note: Since this article appeared, Hollywood has made Boogie Nights, *a film about a likable porn star,* Grosse Pointe Blank, *a film about a likable hit man, and my personal favorite* The Jackal, *which pits a nasty terrorist (Bruce Willis) against a likable terrorist (Richard Gere).*

BIG WIGS

Thomas Jefferson is arguably the single most important person that the United States has ever produced. Author of the Declaration of Independence and third president of the country that he basically founded with a little help from his friends. The man responsible for the purchase of vast tracts of the midwestern United States from a cash-strapped Napoleon Bonaparte, Jefferson was by turns an author, an architect, a statesman, a farmer, a philosopher, a politician, and a revolutionary. He was a star of the same magnitude as Washington, Lincoln, and FDR. That's why his face is on Mount Rushmore. That's why Barbra Streisand goes around telling people that she's *re*-reading her Jefferson. Given the man's Olympian stature, his admirers can breathe a sigh of relief that James Ivory and Ismail Merchant did not decide to cast Emilio Estevez or Steven Seagal in the lead role for their new film, *Jefferson in Paris*. Like it or not, they could have done worse than Nick Nolte.

But not much worse.

Look at it this way: If a pair of artsy filmmakers two centuries hence decided to make a movie about the life of Nick Nolte, it's unlikely that they'd choose a brilliant, sophisticated, violin-playing intellectual from Virginia to play the part. People would laugh their film right off the screen. That's what I did when I saw *Jefferson in Paris*. I laughed. In fact, I laughed a whole lot. No, I was not laughing at Nick Nolte. Nick Nolte has done exemplary work in films as varied as *Down and Out in Beverly Hills*, *Q&A*, *48HRS.*, *The Prince of Tides*, and *Cape Fear*. He's a good actor, one of America's best. But he's a good actor in the same way that Bob Hoskins is a good actor. If you like your actors big and rugged and oafish, Nick and Bob are your boys. But if you prefer actors who look like they might be able to spell the word "Montesquieu," you'd better look elsewhere.

Why then did Merchant and Ivory choose to get Nolte all dolled up in pantaloons and a wig and have him embarrass himself in this ludicrous film? The closest I can figure is this: They wanted to trash Thomas Jefferson, the historical icon, by transforming one of America's true intellectual lions into a clumsy doofus. Watch a tongue-tied Thomas Jefferson make a fool of himself in front of a bunch of cunning French intellectuals. Watch klutzy Thomas Jefferson break his hand while tripping over a pile of logs. Watch pussy bandit Thomas Jefferson get it on with one of his slaves.

The impression created by *Jefferson in Paris* is that Jefferson was a fake, a hypocrite, a philanderer, and a rube. When first seen on the screen, Jefferson has just arrived in Paris in 1783, where he will serve as the infant United States' ambassador to France until 1788, one year before the French Revolution. Belabored shots of *sans-culottes*, street urchins, and housewives clamoring for bread drive home the point that all is not gay in Paree, that heads will soon roll. Sadly, the film ends in 1788, a year before the French got the guillotine into high gear. Thus, any hopes for actual action in a Merchant and Ivory film go up in smoke.

While the French are clamoring for bread and freedom, Jefferson is seen hanging out with a bunch of fops and hangers-on at

King Louis XVI's court, cultivating a romance with an Italian countess (Greta Scacchi) who is trapped in a marriage of convenience with a homosexual painter played with belligerent campiness by Simon Callow. Jefferson is madly in love with the countess of Scacchi, but cannot resist having a bit of fun on the side with a perky slave named Sally Hemmings (Thandie Newton), whom he soon impregnates. This is the closest that the impressionistic *Jefferson in Paris* ever comes to a theme: that Jefferson, who fought so valiantly to secure freedom for his fellow Americans, was himself a hypocritical slave owner and slave abuser.

There is no way to defend Jefferson's status as a slave owner, other than to offer the obvious excuse that he was a creature of his times, and of his region, the South. But the legend of his affair with Sally Hemmings is just that—a legend—spawned by his political enemies during his first term as president (1801–1805). By presenting this legend as historical fact in their ponderous costume drama, Merchant and Ivory have done exactly what Oliver Stone did in *JFK*: transformed tabloid gossip into gospel truth.

Personally, I don't care about the filmmakers' taking liberty with the truth. Filmmakers have only one obligation to the public: to make movies that people can stay awake through. If Merchant and Ivory had made such a movie, I wouldn't have cared if they had Thomas Jefferson sodomizing the goldfish. They have not. They have made a dreary, tedious, condescending film that, given its sexual subplot, is quite amazingly passionless. A partial list of the things that are wrong with this film would include the following:

1. The movie starts with a flashback, the most hackneyed storytelling device of all.

2. The movie constantly uses voice-overs, the second-most hackneyed storytelling device of all.

3. Greta Scacchi never takes off her clothes.

4. Wigs, wigs, wigs!

5. Harpsichords, harpsichords, harpsichords!

6. Thandie Newton never takes off her clothes.

7. Pantaloons, pantaloons, pantaloons!

8. The movie uses flashbacks within flashbacks.

9. The movie opens with James Earl Jones, a hack who has become the black Charlton Heston.

10. Fops, fops, fops!

But in the end, the biggest failing of all is the casting of Nick Nolte as Jefferson. To get the full flavor of this absurd casting decision, try to imagine Sean Connery as Oscar Wilde, Michael Caine as Dante Gabriel Rossetti, or Emma Thompson as Michael Caine. Better yet, don't.

YOU CAN'T ALWAYS GET
WHAT YOU WANT

Tell me if this situation sounds familiar: You're lying in bed with a bad cold or a broken ankle or cholera or an allergic reaction to Prozac and what you'd really like to do is just sit back and watch a nice film to take your mind off your unspeakable agony. Seeing that you're totally incapacitated and may even be pretty close to death, and seeing that your local video store doesn't have a delivery service, you're forced to send your spouse or your roommate or your little sister or, God forbid, your mother down to the store to rent you a film.

Neither your mom nor your kid sister, nor, for that matter, your significant other nor your roommate is as plugged into the whole video scene as you are, so if you want them to come back with the right film you're going to have to supply them with very specific instructions about the movie you want to watch. Unfortunately, your mind is wandering because of that gimpy ankle or cholera or cold medication, and every contemporary movie title sounds exactly like every other contemporary movie title: *Fatal Attraction, Basic Instinct, Final Analysis, Lethal Weapon, Fatal Instinct.* So you can't remember the name of the movie. This being the case, the best you can do is to say: "Bring me back that movie starring that short white guy who can't act worth spit who accidentally takes a wrong turn off the freeway and ends up getting totally fucked over for the next two hours." (If you're talking to your little sister, and she's under ten, don't use the word *fuck*.)

Having issued this directive, you settle back on your bed of pain, anxiously waiting for your errand person to return with the film *Judgment Night*, which stars Emilio Estevez as a vertically challenged schmuck who takes a wrong turn on the freeway and ends up in a neighborhood where neither he nor anyone else of his general blanched pigmentation belongs—with the possible exception of Denis Leary. Twenty minutes later, Mom or Sis or your significant other strolls into your bedroom, flicks on the TV, pops the videocassette into the VCR, and goes downstairs to pay the latest MCI bill. You prop yourself up on your pillows, dig your hand into a gaping barrel of M&Ms, settle your feet into a nice comfy position, and then look on in horror, confusion, and utter disbelief as the opening credits to *Doc Hollywood* appear on the screen.

"This isn't the movie I asked for!" you bellow downstairs to the offending party. "This is a movie about a short, white schmuck who takes a wrong turn on the freeway and ends up in a whole lot of shit in some redneck Podunk in South Carolina! I wanted the movie about the short, white schmuck who takes a wrong turn on the freeway and ends up in a whole lot of shit in a frightening, black, urban ghetto!"

Mom, Sis, or your significant other apologizes, rewinds the cassette, stuffs it back inside the box, and traipses off to the video store. Twenty minutes later, he or she returns, sticks a new video into the VCR, and again disappears downstairs to pay that long-overdue MCI bill. Once again, you go through the pillow-priming, leg-propping, M&Ms-gorging routine, and are all set for a nice afternoon's relaxation when suddenly the credits for *Bonfire of the Vanities* appear on the screen.

"This isn't the movie I wanted!" you shriek downstairs at your incompetent sister, lover, housemate, or mother. "This is a movie about a fabulously wealthy white schmuck who makes a wrong turn on the freeway and ends up in a whole lot of shit in an ethnically indeterminate ghetto in the much-maligned South Bronx district of New York City! I wanted the movie about a not-so-fabulously wealthy white schmuck who makes a wrong turn on the freeway and ends up in a whole lot of shit in a truly frightening, black, urban ghetto outside of Chicago!"

By this point, Mom, Sis, or your significant other is getting kind of ticked off at your attitude—cholera or no cholera. They've followed your instructions to the letter by trooping down to the video store and asking for the movie you've described, but every time they come back with a movie almost perfectly matching your description you say it's the wrong one. But, because they love you, care about you, and want you to be happy in this, the darkest hour before the dawn, they climb back into the Mazda or the Jeep Cherokee and head over to Blockbuster to get what you sincerely hope will be *Judgment Night*, whose title you still can't remember.

Twenty minutes later, Mom, Sis, or your significant other comes back into the room and pops the cassette into the VCR. This time, you should have no reason to complain. The video that now appears on the screen chronicles the adventures of a very schmucky white man who takes a wrong turn on the freeway and ends up in a whole lot of trouble in a terrifying black ghetto. But the schmuck is played by Kevin Kline, himself no schmuck, instead of Emilio Estevez, an actor born to play a vast series of schmucks. And the movie is not *Judgment Night*, but *Grand Canyon*.

Life isn't turning out the way you planned, is it?

There are two problems in getting other people to rent videos for you in today's world. One is that all movies sound the same. The other is that all movies *are* the same. Unless you are the sort of person who has an encylopedic knowledge of film—and is there really any mileage in growing up to be Roger Ebert?—you're not going to be able to remember which movie you really want to see, so you'll never be able to get the person you're living with to rent the right movie for you. You'll always have to do it yourself. Which is going to be a big problem if you ever break your leg or come down with cholera.

This is particularly true once a video has gotten a little bit of age on it: Was *Body Double* the movie where Kathleen Turner was really hot? Or was that *Body Heat*? Was *City of Joy* the inane movie where Patrick Swayze plays a charismatic figure who helps bring peace to a crime-ridden slum? Or was that *City of Hope*? Did Clint Eastwood play the disoriented bodyguard in *The Bodyguard*? Or was that *In the Line of Fire*? Did Harvey Keitel take off his clothes so we could all get a load of his gargantuan schlong in *The Piano*? Or was that in *Bad Lieutenant*? And while we're on the subject of the infuriatingly ubiquitous Harvmeister, did Keitel play a crooked cop in *Bad Lieutenant*? Or was that *Rising Sun*? Or was that him playing an honest cop in *Thelma and Louise*? And what's the name of that movie where Mary Stuart Masterson was really, really, *really* annoying?

Benny & Joon?

Fried Green Tomatoes?

Bad Girls?

Some movie stars confuse the issue by deliberately making movies that all sound the same. A case in point is Steven Seagal, star of *On Deadly Ground, Hard to Kill, Under Siege, Not Too Smart.* Imagine going to the video store and asking the clerk, "Could you tell me the name of the movie where Steven Seagal plays a tall, sadistic psychopath with a pony tail?" The clerk would be sure to say: "Sure—first aisle on the left, right next to the movie where Sylvester Stallone plays a super-patriotic moron on steroids."

Gee, thanks.

It certainly doesn't help matters that video stores always seem to stock a copycat movie that sounds exactly like the movie you actually want to see, and that they start stocking the copycat film just weeks after the movie you really want to see finally gets released on video. Every time somebody like Francis Ford Coppola releases a *Bram Stoker's Dracula*, somebody named Roger Corman releases a film called *Dracula Rising*. For every *Body of Evidence* there are three *Body Chemistry*'s (though, considering Madonna's acting, this may actually be a good thing). Every time we get a *Hoffa*, we also get a tidal wave of movies with names like *Hit the Dutchman*, *Teamster Boss*, and *Ruby*. Most of these movies star Danny Aiello—or worse.

Hollywood also confuses the issue by releasing hordes of movies with identical-sounding names. You send someone to the video store for *Homicide* and they come back with *Homicidal Impulse*. You ask someone to pick up *Three of Hearts* and they come back with *Cheating Hearts*, *Cross My Heart*, or *Hearts & Souls*. You ask your sister to pick up *Cyborg Cop* and she comes back with *RoboCop 2* or *Cyborg* or *Cop and a Half*. You're really looking forward to watching *Crossing Delancey* and instead you wind up with *Crossing the Bridge*. The movie you want is *Singles;* the movie she brings back is *Single White Female*.

There's also the little matter of *nepotistic information overload dissonance*, a situation that prevails when there are too many tapes in the store featuring members of the Baldwin, Quaid, Siemaszko, or Carradine families that you've never heard of, and that their own siblings may have never heard of. An additional complication in shopping at video stores when you really don't know what you're doing is that you have to wade through an alarmingly large number of movies starring somebody named Jason.

The thing that really confuses the issue for the home rental market is that Hollywood only knows how to make a handful of movies, so inevitably these movies all resemble one another. You send your roommate out to rent the movie where a woman who's already in love with another guy goes to the gambling capital of the United States and agrees to sleep with a guy who used to be a big star in the seventies in exchange for a truckload of money that will wipe out all of her significant other's money problems. Your roommate comes back with *Indecent Proposal*. You wanted *Honeymoon in Vegas*.

Or you wanted the smash-hit comedy featuring one of America's most radiantly self-infatuated black performers. You're expecting your errand person to come back with *Coming to America*, starring Eddie Murphy. She comes home with *Made in America*, starring Whoopi Goldberg. When you ask for the outrageous comedy about a goofy American who gets mistaken for British royalty, you're all set to spend a rollicking evening with John Goodman and Peter O'Toole in *King Ralph*. Instead, you get treated to Rick Moranis and Eric Idle in *Splitting Heirs*.

You think this situation only exists in the world of mainstream, commercial movies? Think again. Think Hindu. You tell your boyfriend to stop by the video store and pick up that charming movie about Indians who are having trouble adjusting to their new life in North America. You're expecting him to come back with *Mississippi Masala*, which stars Denzel Washington. Instead, he comes back with *Masala*, which doesn't star anybody.

The same situation prevails in the world of Merchant Ivory. Imagine sending someone out for the film where Emma Thompson plays a sourpuss, or where Helena Bonham Carter plays a Victorian neurotic, or where Anthony Hopkins plays a repressed Brit. It's like asking for the movie where Maggie Smith plays somebody who's got a few screws loose.

To understand how widespread this problem of video rental confusion has become, simply consider a highly praised, much-honored film like *Philadelphia*, whose genesis probably came about something like this:

Jonathan Demme goes to the film studio to take a meeting.

Jonathan: I'd like to make a movie about AIDS.

Studio Head: I'm sorry, Jonathan, but we don't make movies about AIDS here. You may not have noticed this, but this studio has been in existence for seventy-five years, and we have never,

ever made a movie about AIDS. Lou Gehrig's Disease, yes; MS, certainly; but AIDS, no. It's not something we're particularly proud of, but there you have it. Now, do you have any cannibal projects on the back burner or anything?

Jonathan: No. And, quite seriously, I think it's time that Hollywood made a movie about AIDS. An important movie. A movie that shows that we care.

Studio Head: But we don't care. That's what I'm trying to get through to you. If we cared, we would have already made a movie about AIDS. We would have made ten of them. And one of them would have starred an actor who is actually gay. But we haven't. So we don't. Are you getting all this, Jonathan? Now, could we get back to that cannibal thing?

Eventually, after many unsuccessful meetings, Demme meets a producer who says that he'll take on the project, but only as long as Demme can shoehorn the film into a highly traditional format. The producer tells Demme to write the script in the traditional Cops-on-the-Take format, where the good cop has AIDS. Demme says he doesn't think that will work. The producer then suggests the Serial Killer format, where every one of the killer's victims has AIDS and the police suspect that a psychopathic hemophiliac may be on the loose. Demme says that this approach lacks sensitivity. The producer then suggests the Sibling Buddy Film where two brothers, one with AIDS, set out on a voyage of self-discovery that either leads them to Las Vegas or El Salvador, where they find out that deep down inside they really have an awful lot in common. Except that only one of them has AIDS. Demme rejects this suggestion, too.

Just when it seems that the roadblocks preventing Demme from ever realizing his laudable project are too great and too numerous to be overcome, the producer comes up with an inspired idea. Why not use the old tried-and-true, if-it-ain't-broke-don't-fix-it young-lawyers-with-big-problems format as the scaffold from which to hang the AIDS story that makes up *Philadelphia*? That way gay people will buy tickets to see a film about AIDS, whereas middle Americans will buy tickets to see a movie about lawyers. Seeing that middle Americans are all lawyers anyway.

Demme asks for more information. The producer happily supplies it. Remember a couple of years ago when Rob Reiner made *A Few Good Men*? Now, here was an engrossing courtroom drama about a wise-ass young lawyer played by Tom Cruise who doesn't care about anything other than his own career until the day he is asked to take a case that he has no chance of winning, which will pit two earnest young men who are being railroaded by the authorities against a mean-spirited old bastard (Jack Nicholson) who smokes big, big cigars.

Demme goes off and makes his movie, which gets lots of press attention, and wins personal kudos for the director, not to mention a Best Actor award for Tom Hanks on Oscar night. On the surface, *Philadelphia* is, of course, a movie about prejudice, insensitivity, injustice, and the ravages of AIDS. But at its core, *Philadelphia* is a traditional courtroom drama centering on a wise-ass young lawyer played by Denzel Washington who doesn't care about anything other than his career until the day he is asked to take a case that he has no chance of winning that pits a young man who is being railroaded by the authorities against a mean-spirited old bastard (Jason Robards) who smokes big, big cigars. In short, *Philadelphia* is *A Few Good Gay Men*.

This has got to be terribly confusing for someone who's not used to going to the video store every night and who's only doing it as a personal favor. You tell your mom or sis or your significant other to rent you that engrossing film where Tom Cruise plays a hot-shot Ivy League graduate who gets himself into all kinds of trouble once he starts the practice of law. She brings back *A Few Good Men*, in which Cruise graduates from Harvard. You wanted *The Firm*, in which Cruise plays a hot-shot Ivy League graduate who gets himself into all kinds of trouble once he starts the practice of law—also after graduating from Harvard. Or maybe Mom misheard you, and thought you said that you wanted the film where Tom Hanks plays a hot-shot Ivy League graduate who gets himself into all kinds of trouble once he starts the practice of law. That was in *Philadelphia*, where he plays a lawyer who graduated from Penn. All told in 1994, four films about Ivy Leaguers with problems were nominated for Academy Awards (*The Firm, Six Degrees of Separation, Philadelphia, Dave*), not counting *In The Name of the Father*, where Emma Thompson plays a hot-shot lawyer who gets herself into all sorts of trouble and who almost certainly graduated from Oxford or Cambridge, the English equivalent of the Ivy League. Once again, no movies about struggling young lawyers from North Carolina A&T or Central Connecticut State this season.

Is there any way to avoid this kind of confusion when dispatching a loved one, confidant, or menial to fetch an entertaining video that involves young lawyers with big problems? Yes, by asking for the film where Keanu Reeves plays a young lawyer with big problems. This occurred in *Bram Stoker's Dracula*, where Reeves plays a hot-shot law school graduate who gets himself into all kinds of trouble once he starts the practice of law, primarily because his first major assignment is to visit Transylvania and persuade Count Dracula to sign some important documents pertaining to esoteric real estate transactions conducted in the Greater London area. "Get me that film where Keanu Reeves plays a lawyer," is all you'll need to tell your girlfriend, and she'll be back in a jiffy with Francis Ford Coppola's mesmerizing weirdathon. Conversely, if you say, "Get me that film where Keanu Reeves plays a moron," you could be sending her back out to the store every night for the next three weeks till she gets the right one.*

One thing that people who rent a lot of movies forget is that for many people, a video store is a deadly combination of a minefield and a sepulcher. It's a minefield because the unsophisticated

---

*Since this article appeared in 1994, Keanu Reeves has appeared in *The Devil's Advocate*, a second film where he plays yet another young lawyer with big problems. So just ignore this whole section.

video store patron can't tell *A Stranger Among Us* apart from *Strangers* or *When He's Not a Stranger* or *When A Stranger Calls*, just as he has no way of distinguishing *Only the Strong* from *Only the Lonely*, or *Sudden Impact* from *Point of Impact*. Nor will he have any way of distinguishing *Mr. Mom* from *Mr. Nanny* or *Mrs. Doubtfire* from *Mr. Wonderful*, any more than he could tell the difference between *Mr. Saturday Night* and *Saturday Night Fever*. And he will certainly lack the cinema-going expertise to distinguish *The Good Mother* from *The Good Father*, or *The Good Son* from *GoodFellas*. (Hint: Macaulay Culkin is an even more revolting screen presence than Joe Pesci.)

But a video store is also a sepulcher of sorts because no other business that you can think of devotes 70 percent of its retail space to products that are stone dead. The average appliance store does not devote 70 percent of its shelf space to twelve-year-old televisions and discontinued refrigerators. The average bakery does not reserve 70 percent of its shelf space for ten-year-old loaves of bread and twelve-year-old English muffins. But the average video store does devote an amazing portion of its shelf space to films by Henry Winkler, John Ritter, and Sally Kirkland—the cinematic equivalents of twelve-year-old loaves of bread, and, in Sally's case, with quite a bit of mold on them. Like a cemetery, the average video store is teeming with long-dead, long-forgotten corpses. *Here lies Robby Benson. Here lies Anson Williams. Here lie those two guys named Corey.* And, as is the case with a cemetery, you really don't want to be walking around there at night, when the corpses have been known to come out of their coffins and commit unspeakable crimes.

So the next time you send Mom or Sis or your significant other out to the video store to rent you a film, consider their predicament. They really don't have the kind of savvy that you have in hacking through the artistic undergrowth with the machete of good taste that you always carry around with you, so if you ask them to rent *Judgment Night*, don't be surprised if they come back with *Night and the City*, *The Night We Never Met*, *Night on Earth*, or *Night and Day*, all of which will be sitting right next to each other in the More or Less Recent Rentals section. Similarly, if you ask for *Benny & Joon*, don't be surprised if you get stuck with *Henry and June*; if you ask for *Mo' Better Blues*, don't be surprised if you end up with *Mo' Money*; and if you ask for *Mad Dog and Glory*, don't be surprised if your errand person comes back with *Hope and Glory* or *Man Bites Dog* or even just plain *Glory*. Hollywood only uses eighty-seven words in its titles and none of them have more than two syllables. I mean, *Gone with the Wind*?

Are there any useful tips that a videophile with a broken leg or cholera can use when persuading someone else to rent a film for him? Yes, and here they are:

1. When requesting a recent Woody Allen movie, never say things like, "Get me the one where Alan Alda plays a schmuck." This narrows things down about as much as saying, "Get me the one where Dianne Wiest plays a neurotic" or "Rent the one where Mia Farrow plays a numbskull." Be specific. Say things like, "Get me Woody's black-and-white paean to Franz Kafka and Fritz Lang that stars Madonna and Lily Tomlin, and really bites the big one."

2. Never say things like, "Rent me the movie about the heart-warming adventures of unsuccessful retailers in downtown Baltimore." You do that and you'll wind up with *Tin Men*, when what you really want is *Avalon*.

3. Never, ever say things like, "Rent me the film about the guy who has to resort to all sorts of elaborate security mechanisms to protect his family from a psychopath who wants to fuck his wife." If you want to rent *Unlawful Entry*, say so. Otherwise, you're going to end up with *Cape Fear*.

4. If you're renting a film that Quentin Tarantino scripted or directed, be very specific about the kind of cop mutilation

you want to see. If you don't specify that you want the film where a cop gets his ear cut off (*Reservoir Dogs*), you could get stuck with the film where an ex-cop gets his hand sliced to ribbons and drenched in carbolic acid (*True Romance*). Wouldn't that be a letdown?

5. When renting movies where Melanie Griffith plays a spunky bimbo who tries to pass herself off as someone that she is not (a Nazi, a member of the Lubavitcher Hassidim, an intelligent person), specify whether the language she has trouble speaking in the film is German (*Shining Through*), Yiddish (*A Stranger Among Us*), or English (*Working Girl*).

6. Try as hard as humanly possible to avoid having a broken leg or cholera or an allergic reaction to Prozac. And if you do come down with a malady that confines you to your bedroom for an extended period of time, forget about sending your mom or your significant other or your little sister down to the video store. Watch Showtime or something. In the long run, you'll expend a lot less mental energy this way. Remember: A video store is no place for an amateur.

Halfway through the life-affirming, Southern Gothic, small-budget, female buddy film *Fried Green Tomatoes*, the impish Dixie peach, Mary Stuart Masterson, hits upon the gastronomically suspect but matrimonially efficacious stratagem of concealing her best friend's wife-beating, Ku Klux Klan husband's carcass in a large vat of barbecue mix at her unpretentious dining establishment. The film, told largely in flashback, is set in rural Alabama in the 1930s, at a time when the Klan was making life miserable for blacks and, to a lesser extent, Catholics and Jews, and when Klan-bears like Mr. Barbecue were also making life unbearable for their hapless WASP wives.

Be this as it may, there is nothing in the annals of 20th-century Alabamian written or oral history to suggest that wife-beating Klan members were routinely, or in fact, *ever* mixed in with some piquant barbecue sauce and served for lunch in local eateries back in this era. This would seem to suggest that the characters in *Fried Green Tomatoes* did not get the idea of hiding the wife-beater's battered corpse in the barbecue sauce from their own experiences inside the movie, but from the person who wrote the screenplay, who obviously did not get the idea from studying early 20th-century, rural-Alabamian packing, jarring, or cooking traditions. No, *she* probably got the idea from watching *Eating Raoul*, a 1982, small-budget, non–life-affirming black comedy in which the body of the eponymous Raoul, a Chicano lowlife, is chopped into tiny strips and served at a formal dinner—precisely because the cooks could think of no better place to hide the body.

I am not suggesting that the idea of hiding the body in the barbecue sauce in *Fried Green Tomatoes* came *directly* or *exclusively* from *Eating Raoul*. The screenwriter may have also been influenced by the popular 1970s musical *Sweeney Todd*, or by *Sweeney Todd: The Demon Barber of Fleet Street*, the 1936 black-and-white film that inspired the play. Or she may have been influenced by *The Cook, the Thief, His Wife & Her Lover*, the 1989 artsy-craftsy affair centering around a trendy restaurant and the people who inadvertently make their way into its cuisine. Or, she may have drawn her inspiration from *Motel Hell*, the 1980 black comedy in which Rory Calhoun plays a sort of sausage-packing Norman Bates. For that matter, the screenwriter may also have been influenced by *The Tenderness of the Wolves*, the 1973 German film in which a homosexual vampire with an entrepreneurial bent first lures young men to his apartment in post-World War I Berlin, seduces them, and excises huge chunks from their necks—effectively removing them from the gay, post-war German nightlife scene forever—and then packages their remains as tasty cutlets, which he sells to local merchants desperate for prime beef at a time of massive meat shortages everywhere.

Whatever the truth of the matter, it is safe to say that the cannibalism motif in *Fried Green Tomatoes*, which is set in rural Alabama in the 1930s, almost certainly derives from a low-budget black comedy set in Los Angeles in the early 1980s, or from a medium-budget 1970s German, neo-expressionist horror film set in Berlin in the 1920s, or from an inexpensive 1936 black-and-white

British film set in London in the 1800s, or from a very inexpensive slasher film set in the unidentified American boondocks in the late 1970s. This is yet another example of the motion picture industry's amazing ability to cannibalize itself, even when making a film about cannibalism.

Of course, as is so often the case with my theories, I could be completely wrong.*

Almost since Hollywood began making motion pictures, innocent people have been getting devoured in them, but this is, to my knowledge, the first time that anyone has ever attempted to write a comprehensive essay about what the Germans call *das essenfilm*, what the French call *le cinebouffe*, and what the Italians refer to as *film mangiare*: films in which people get eaten. Yet our goal here is not to discuss *every* movie in which people have been eaten— there are far, far too many to even contemplate such an under-taking—but to at least consider every *genre* of movie in which people get eaten. Thus, we will be looking at movies featuring cannibalism (*Alive, Eating Raoul, Suddenly Last Summer, Night of the Living Dead, Soylent Green, The Silence of the Lambs, The Cook, the Thief, His Wife & Her Lover, Fried Green Tomatoes*), unexpected aquatic dining (*Piranha, Leviathan, Thunderball, Orca, Jaws, Jaws 2, Jaws 3-D, Jaws the Revenge*), reptilian buffet (*Alligator, Live and Let Die*), insects that manifest a penchant for human flesh (*The Naked Jungle*), man-munching mammals (*Grizzly, Cujo*), peckish rodents who develop a taste for *pithecanthropus erectus* (*Willard, Ben*), as well as smorgasbord films in which humans are eaten, or at least gnawed on, by a wide range of predators: humans, dogs, wolves, bears, saber-toothed tigers, Adrienne Barbeau (*Quest for Fire, Cannibal Women in the Avocado Jungle of Death*). Hopefully, by looking

---

*In fact, the idea comes directly out of Fannie Flagg's 1987 novel, *Fried Green Tomatoes at the Whistlestop Café*. So once again, an ingenious theory gets shot right to hell.

carefully at films such as these we will all learn a little bit more about the world around us, and perhaps even a little bit more about ourselves. Though frankly, I kind of doubt it.

In discussing films in which people get eaten, it is important to distinguish between works in which:

1. People get eaten primarily for nutritional reasons;

2. People get eaten primarily for legitimate ritualistic or religious reasons;

3. People get eaten just for the hell of it.

It is also important to distinguish between films in which the eating of human flesh is a minor, incidental element (*Fried Green Tomatoes*) and films which are basically about human cuisine and not much else (*Alive, Jaws, Piranha, Motel Hell, Little Shop of Horrors, Soylent Green*). For example, *The Last of the Mohicans* includes a scene in which Mugwa, the sadistic faux Mohawk (he is secretly a Huron), rips the heart out of a British officer and is just about ready to jam it down his gullet when the camera meekly wanders off to see what the more refined Madeleine Stowe is up to at the time. The scene clearly establishes that Mugwa is a primeval brute, a feckless traitor, and at least a part-time cannibal, and thus not a guy to be messed with. But *The Last of the Mohicans* is not *primarily* a film about eating human flesh. *The Last of the Mohicans* is primarily a film about hacking, cleaving, hewing, flaying, impaling, and roasting human flesh. It is vital that we make this distinction.

A far different sort of film is *Jaws the Revenge (This time . . . It's personal)*. Much like its predecessors, this fourth installment of the popular series is about a big fish that likes to eat people so that it can become an even bigger fish. However, unlike *The Last of the Mohicans*, which also deals with such issues as love, grace under pressure, the inevitable cultural fallout from a head-on collision between a highly developed, market-driven European civilization and a Paleolithic, socialistic culture, the indispensable role of a volunteer militia in a free society, and no taxation without representation, *Jaws the Revenge* deals almost exclusively with a large shark that likes to eat people. It has, as it were, no subtext.

The same distinction can be made between *Quest for Fire* and *Alive*. Although both films are protein-oriented, in the sense that the people who get devoured in them do not get eaten for personal reasons but because those who eat them can't find anything else to nibble on, *Quest for Fire* is basically a film about a valiant group of prehistoric men desperately seeking to master the element of fire in order to survive. The cannibalism stuff is just a sidelight. Otherwise, the film would have been called *Quest for Chucksteak*.

Alive, on the other hand, is almost entirely a film about enlightened cannibalism. In this life-affirming, small-budget, South American Gothic buddy film, a group of young Uruguayan rugby players, having survived an airplane crash, an avalanche, and Vincent Spano, must eat one another in order to survive. Although the film deals in a tangential fashion with certain other themes—man's inhumanity to man, the need for a more cohesive relationship between Uruguayan and Chilean civil aviation authorities, the importance of always carrying extra radio batteries and large bars of chocolate on one's person during long rides across desolate mountain ranges—the film is fundamentally about cannibalism, a subject foreshadowed early in the story when one of the characters breaks open a bottle of red wine, which, of course, is only served with red meat.

Lamentably, most films in which people get eaten do not deal with larger themes and do not feature characters who would forego eating human flesh if they had any other choice. In most films, ruthless creatures chow down on human beings for one simple reason: Because there's nobody in the immediate vicinity who is big enough and bad enough to stop them. It is impossible to believe that the mammoth white shark in the original *Jaws* only gobbles up pretty coeds and helpless little kids because *there's nothing else in the whole Atlantic Ocean to eat.* No, he eats coeds and helpless little kids because he's an ornery son-of-a-bitch who likes to get in people's faces, and while he's in them, to eat them. While a certain revenge motif comes into play in *Jaws 3-D* and *Jaws the Revenge,* we are still basically talking about sharks that eat people just to annoy everybody. There's no reason they couldn't eat marlin or bluefish or red snapper or medical waste like all the other sharks. But then again, *they're not like all the other sharks, are they?*

Another subset of "people-eating" movies includes films in which people get eaten by creatures that get put up to it by other humans. The most obvious example is *Willard,* which deals with a dysfunctional youngster who breeds his own army of rats and then turns them loose on his neighbors. There is no reason to believe that the rats would ever have ruined the big party that Ernest Borgnine was holding had the decision been left up to them; rats don't like parties. They were pressured into doing it by the dysfunctional youth.

Humans are also to blame for the tragedies that befall their fellows in *Piranha, Leviathan, The Killer Shrews, The Little Shop of Horrors, Empire of the Ants, Alligator,* and *Orca: The Killer Whale,* all of which deal with man-eating monsters created by humans, usually scientists. In *Alligator,* a parody of *Jaws* scripted by John Sayles, a baby alligator flushed down the toilet grows to humongous proportions thanks to toxins dumped into the sewage system by an unscrupulous chemical company. The result? A bunch of people played by actors you never heard of get eaten. The same thing happens in *Empire of the Ants* and *The Killer Shrews.* In *Orca,* a killer whale minding its own business is transmogrified into a killer-diller whale by Richard Harris, an unscrupulous fisherman. The result? The whale wantonly kills its mate. Then Keenan Wynn gets eaten, and young Bo Derek gets half eaten. (Charlotte Rampling, playing an anorexic marine biologist who befriends Harris, apparently escapes a similar fate because there's not enough meat on her to interest any self-respecting killer whale.)

In *Leviathan*, a monster spawned by an unscrupulous defunct country that used to be called the Union of Soviet Socialist Republics grows to humongous proportions thanks to some chemicals planted in the vodka. The result? Richard Crenna gets eaten. In *Piranha*, another parody of *Jaws* scripted by John Sayles, a school of killer fish grow to humongous proportions thanks to some chemicals spilled into the water by an unscrupulous country called the United States of America. The result? Keenan Wynn gets eaten again. And in *Devil Dog: The Hound of Hell* a German shepherd grows to humongous proportions thanks to an unscrupulous group of Satanists who don't dump any chemicals in the water system, but who look like they would if given half a chance. The result? Well, Richard Crenna *almost* gets eaten.

Coincidence, you say?

In discussing films in which the consumer becomes the consumed, it is imperative that we distinguish between films in which the people who get eaten deserve to get eaten and films in which they do not. Based on our exhaustive sample of thirty-three motion pictures in which people are devoured, we found ninety-three cases in which the movie told the audience enough about the person being eaten to make a determination of whether the individual deserved his cruel fate. In the overwhelming majority of cases (seventy-two), the people being consumed—swimmers, surfers, lovers, vacationers, plumbers, Uruguayan rugby players—did not deserve to be eaten and were unfortunate victims of circumstances. Of the twenty-one other victims, eighteen indisputably deserved to be eaten, and three were toss-ups. For example, the wife-beating Ku Klux Klanner in *Fried Green Tomatoes* certainly got exactly what he deserved, as did the balding asshole in *Night of the Living Dead* who wanted everyone to remain "hidden" (in the basement where it's *safe*), as did Vincent Spano and Keenan Wynn, for reasons too obvious to discuss, in *Alive, Orca,* and *Piranha*.

Less open-and-shut cases are the roving pederast in *Suddenly Last Summer*, who didn't deserve to be eaten, but who should certainly have chosen a better neighborhood in which to be picking up small boys; the duplicitous British major in *The Last of the Mohicans*, who didn't deserve to have his heart eaten, but certainly deserved to have his throat slit; and Lorraine Gary's youngest son in *Jaws the Revenge*, who deserved to have his arm torn off for having her as a mother, but who probably didn't deserve to have his entire body ripped to shreds just because he had Roy Scheider for a father.

Within the admittedly disequilibrating genre of people-eating movies, it is nonetheless possible to discern the difference between films that are merely tasteless (PG), and films that are really gross (PG-13). For example, it is important to make a distinction between films in which people get eaten after a modicum of preparation (dressing, garnishing, seasoning, cooking) and films where people get eaten raw. Whatever their other failings, *Eating Raoul* and *Fried Green Tomatoes* handle the subject of cannibalism delicately, so that even if you freeze-frame the film on your VCR you still really can't tell that the food being eaten comes from a human being; in both cases it looks like something you might order at any roadside Greek diner. In *Quest for Fire*, on the other hand, the slabs of human flesh that the cavemen munch are clearly human limbs that have merely been parboiled over an open flame and eaten *steak tartare* fashion. Similarly, in *Alive*, the stranded rugby players simply tear off little portions of beef by using a penknife, and then stuff the human flesh right into their mouths. This is really disgusting, and I can't believe in the long run that it's going to help Ethan Hawke's career to have done it. Gnawing on morsels of flesh torn off the backs of corpses played by obscure Hispanic actors or Vincent Spano is the sort of thing you're supposed to do at the *end* of your career. Just ask Rory Calhoun.

As noted above, it is also important to distinguish between these very dissimilar cinematic properties:

1. Films in which animals have a legitimate right to eat their human prey because they are themselves hungry and will die without some immediate means of sustenance;

2. Films in which animals eat human beings because they've gone completely bonkers and can't be held responsible for their actions;

3. Films in which the animal has some sort of a personal vendetta against the person he plans to eat;

4. Films in which animals eat people just to show off.

In the first category are such movies as *Piranha* and *Alligator*, where the man-eaters, through no fault of their own, have grown to gargantuan proportions and simply must eat or die. In these films, the audience feels a certain grudging sympathy toward the monsters, because the monsters didn't ask to be transformed into man-eaters and therefore can't really be blamed for their gastronomic transgressions. Thus, even after the school of razor-toothed butchers has ripped a bunch of little kids and a cute camp counselor to pieces in *Piranha*, one does not feel any special antipathy toward the murderous fish. They were only doing their job.

The same is true in Stephen King's *Cujo*, which is set in Maine, where people don't get out often enough, and even when they do, they're still in Maine. As is Stephen King. In *Cujo*, a previously cuddly St. Bernard with no prior history of substituting raw human flesh for Alpo is suddenly driven straight out of his mind by a vampire bat that impudently bites his snout. Admittedly, Cujo does put Dee Wallace and her little kid through all kinds of hell for an entire weekend, and does end up eating his master, his master's drinking buddy, and a careless cop. But the audience never feels any special animus toward Cujo as he gnaws his way toward Nantucket because it isn't the psycho-pooch's fault that he's acting this way, and besides, Dee was screwing the local stud behind her husband's back, so she probably had it coming. In a very real sense, Cujo himself is a victim.

Victim is not a word that can be applied to any of the sharks in the four *Jaws* movies that have been made to date. Any way you cut it, these great whites are a gang of heartless sadists who deserve whatever they get. (That's right: Fuck you, Greenpeace!) Whereas the man-eating monsters in *Alligator, Orca, Cujo, Leviathan,* and *Piranha* look like simple, garden-variety predators that are going about their business devouring everything in sight, the sharks in the *Jaws* movies actually seem to be *enjoying* their meal. In the original *Jaws,* the great white appears to be chuckling as he forces a perplexed Robert Shaw down his feedbox. In *Jaws 3-D,* the great white seems to be taunting the tourists trapped below sea level in Sea World's brand-new see-through facility. In *Jaws 2,* the shark devours a helicopter, and in *Jaws the Revenge,* the shark actually destroys an entire airplane, raising the possibility that in *Jaws 5* we might get to see a shark swallow the *QE II* or the Concorde. These are sharks that you really don't want to be fucking around with.

One of the questions that poses itself in an essay of this sort is this: If you had to pick a creature to be eaten by, which one would it be? Great white shark? Soldier ant? Alligator? Grizzly bear? Rabid dog? Piranha? Norwegian rat? Killer whale? Psychiatrist? Well, let's do it by a process of elimination, based on the illuminating information provided to us in these movies. Right off the bat, soldier ants get the hook; based on what takes place in the 1954 Charlton Heston vehicle, *The Naked Jungle,* it's safe to say that the ants work slowly—guaranteeing that your death will be long and hideous—and they also tend to crawl up your clothing and go right for the eyes. Thus, you would have to lie there, screaming in abject horror, as the little devils nibbled their way right through your iris, your retina, and your cornea, and then into your brain before you died.

Who needs that?

For similar reasons, rats are out. Unlike sharks and killer whales, which basically kill you off in a couple of heaping mouthfuls, rats tend to play with their food—a nibble here, a nibble there—and even if there are a whole bunch of them on hand for the festivities, you're still looking right down the barrel at a lingering, excruciating, nauseating kind of death. It's also important to remember that rats are kind of gross; if you do have to be eaten to death by some creature, you'd probably prefer it to be a shark or a whale because that reads a lot better in the newspaper, partially because of that whole romance-of-the-sea business. Compare the following obituary headlines, as they might appear in your local newspaper:

WESTCHESTER MAN EATEN BY GREAT WHITE SHARK

or

SANTA MONICA MAN EATEN BY KILLER WHALE

and

LOCAL MAN EATEN BY RATS

If you are still seriously considering exiting this world by having your carcass feasted upon by famished rodents, first take a gander at *Willard* and see what they did to Ernest Borgnine. If that doesn't change your mind, nothing will.

On the surface, 'gators, crocs, grizzly bears, piranha, sharks, and killer whales all seem like reasonably good alternatives if you absolutely, positively have to leave this planet by being eaten to death. Yes, they're better than rats and soldier ants, but when you take a closer peek at how these heartless predators operate, I think you'll see that they are all in their own little ways profoundly inadequate. 'Gators, crocs, piranha, and killer whales all tend to eat every last mouthful of their victims, so once they are through with you there won't be anything left for your family to bury. Sharks and grizzly bears tend to screw around with their food, ripping a human being in half and maybe eating the head and torso but allowing the ankles and fibula to wash up on the shore where some distraught parent has to identify the remains ("Yes, that's Timmy, I'd know that femur anywhere.") and then bury them in a shoe box. If the funereal niceties mean anything to you at all, I'd take a rain check on most of these creatures.

That leaves humans and dogs, and I honestly believe that if you're backed into a corner on this food imbroglio and have to choose between dogs and men, you should go with Fido & Co. every time. I'm not saying this merely because of the innate dread we all feel vis-à-vis the subject of cannibalism. No, I'm saying this because of the despicable behavior of known cannibals *after* they've had their fill. "A census taker once tried to test me," Hannibal Lecter gloats to pert FBI trainee Jodie Foster in *The Silence of the Lambs*. "I ate his liver with some fava beans and a nice Chianti."

This is the kind of cynical remark that you and your survivors would be up against long after you're gone. When a shark or a rat or a school of killer piranha eat you, there's no way they can come back to gloat about it, but a cannibal can hang around making wisecracks about you for decades because of our lax judicial system which refuses to send these vermin to the electric chair. Personally, this would really piss me off. I'd rather get eaten by a shark or a grizzly bear and get the whole damn thing over with.

For this reason, I'd suggest that if you absolutely, positively have to choose the creature that is going to eat you, I'd go with a big, husky dog like Cujo. Although the frothing, saliva-drenched St. Bernard is pretty horrible to look at, and does tear massive, bloody chunks out of the thighs, abdomens, and upper torsos of the people he attacks, it doesn't take him long to polish off his victims and, more important, he doesn't eat the entire body— meaning that you can still have a decent burial, and perhaps even a viewing. If you're a Roman Catholic like me, that whole wake thing is pretty important, and—provided Cujo doesn't start munching on the face—a good mortician might have enough left to set up an open-casket viewing, which, again, is pretty important to me as a Roman Catholic. All things considered, I'd rather be partially eaten by a rabid St. Bernard than swallowed whole by a killer whale or torn into fish chum by a ravenous great white shark.

I hope all this has been helpful.

TOY STORY

In the new, putatively heartwarming film *Jingle All the Way*, proto-Teuton Arnold Schwarzenegger plays a Type A mattress salesman who spends Christmas Eve careening around Minneapolis—one of America's least photogenic cities—desperately trying to find a popular plastic toy called Turbo Man in order to brighten his son's yuletide. Alas, Schwarznegger has waited so long to do his Christmas shopping that all the toys are sold out. He must therefore gain access to other stems of the merchandising pipeline if his son is not to succumb to heartbreak, depression, drug abuse, or suicide (here, I'm surmising). From this ingenious premise cascades the copious humor of this unrelentingly swell, anything but standard-issue, never-seen-anything-like-this-before, just-peachy film.

The day that *Jingle All the Way* opened in New York, I decided to spend the afternoon buying toys for my ten-year-old son. Although it was not yet Christmas, my son was laid up in bed with a bout of pneumonia, and thus furnished me with a perfect seasonal foil for my consumer extravaganza. Just to make the outing a bit more interesting, I decided to limit my purchases to merchandise with a movie tie-in. The object was to see which, if any, movie merchandise would warm the cockles of my bronchially ravaged son's heart.

Upon arriving at the capacious Toys 'R' Us in Manhattan's legendary Herald Square, I loaded up on monsters from *Independence Day*, plastic basketball players from *Space Jam*, and expensive spacecraft from *Star Wars*. But as I made my way through the aisles of the toy store, past the adorable puppies from *101 Dalmatians*, I realized that a trip to an emporium such as this was also fraught with bittersweet memories. For there in the deepest recesses of the shop lay dusty, graying, unwanted merchandise from movies of bygone years: The Ghost of Bad Movies Past, if you will.

There sat Leonardo and Donatello, the legendary Teenage Mutant Ninja Turtles, who had once ruled the silver screen. Four years ago, they were as popular and hard to find on Christmas Eve as the Turbo Men of *Jingle All the Way*. Now they lay there completely unwanted, paying mute testimony to the vanity of human, and perhaps even amphibian, wishes. Sadly, Vanilla Ice action figures were nowhere in sight.

The Turtles were not the only toys that had been banished to the establishment's nether regions. Not far away languished a whole slew of once-popular action figures from the *Batman* films— now no longer hot, no longer cool. And a few yards up the aisle, in a musty corner that few patrons would ever visit, hung Dennis Quaid and the rest of the overpriced action figures from the ill-fated *Dragonheart*.

As I inspected these sad little relics of a film that had clearly not become the merchandising juggernaut it was expected to be, I fantasized about wiser merchandising decisions the studios could have made. For example, a line of *Braveheart* figurines with detachable limbs and removable entrails would have gone down very well in my house. Ditto a complete set of *Trainspotting* inaction figures: *Hey, kids! Check out these nifty Scottish heroin addicts! Collect the entire set!* And for the girls, let's not forget that upscale line of My Little Emma Thompson dolls.

At one point I was interrupted by a Toys 'R' Us salesman who asked if he could be of any assistance. I said that my kid had a kind of macabre streak so I wondered if the store carried any *Reservoir Dogs* merchandise: perhaps a cop with a detachable ear or a Tim Roth figurine who bled to death when you tickled his tummy. The clerk assured me that no such merchandise existed, the same answer he provided when I asked about Barbra Streisand figurines with retractable noses from *The Mirror Has Two Faces*.

When I had finished my shopping, I rushed home, laden down with packages, anxious to bathe my son in joy. Sadly, my purchases did not have the intended effect.

"Why'd you buy this?" Gord said, coughing, when I presented him with his Ninja Turtle doll. "He doesn't do anything."

"This is kind of dull," my son wheezed as I presented him with a basketball figure from *Space Jam*.

"He doesn't really move a lot," my son rasped, crestfallen, when I presented him with his very own Hew (with Boulder-Launching Catapult) from *Dragonheart*. "And you can't really play with him with any of your other toys."

"Why not?" I inquired.

"Because he's not famous like Darth Vader or Batman," my son explained. "The other toys won't know who he is."

Were there any toys that did drive away the furrow from my pulmonarily afflicted son's brow? Yes, he really liked the *Star Wars Millennium Falcon* space station, which at $35 was by far the most expensive of my purchases. Why, I inquired, did he like a toy tied in with a twenty-year-old movie so much more than the Batman action figure I'd purchased?

"Batman always wins, so it's boring," he explained. "In *Star Wars*, the good guys lose a lot of the time so you get to blow them up. Also, the space station costs more."

Finally, I pulled out a lovable $22 Dalmatian puppy I intended to give as a present to his twelve-year-old sister. When you pulled on a chain around its neck, the puppy wagged its head. It was really quite remarkably cute.

"Do you think she'll like it?" I asked.

"She'll say that she likes it to keep you happy," my son replied. "But it's kind of corny. It might make a nice souvenir, but nobody over five would enjoy it."

That night, I presented my daughter with the cuddly puppy. She promptly wrapped it up and gave it as a birthday present to one of her friends. Looking back on the events of the day, I was really happy that I hadn't had to stagger around the streets of downtown Minneapolis on a frigid December night just to round up all this crap for my children. They didn't appreciate it; they weren't impressed; and to be perfectly honest, I don't blame the little bastards for their lack of enthusiasm. Let's not kid ourselves: Any father who brings home action figures from a dud Dennis Quaid movie and expects his children to be grateful deserves all the abuse he gets.

THE DRILLING FIELDS

Several months back, a good friend phoned and said that I absolutely must rent a new video entitled *Captives* starring Julie Ormond as a dentist doing pro bono work on Tim Roth's recidivist teeth in a London prison. As this sounded like exactly my kind of movie, I immediately repaired to my local video store and asked the proprietress, "Do you have that new film about a dentist?" To which she replied, with an equanimity so blithe I still find it disconcerting, "Which one?"

At that instant, I realized that I was living through one of the most unique eras in all human history, that rare, precious, and beautiful moment, perhaps never to be repeated, when better video stores everywhere would be offering not one, but two just-released films about dentists. With the virtually simultaneous appearance of *Captives* and *The Dentist*, an HBO production dealing with a troubled practitioner of the orthodontic trade, the dental profession for the first time in decades—nay, perhaps the first time in its history—had reached the point where the movie industry was finally sitting up and taking notice of its deceptive allure.

True, dentists still did not find themselves in the same ballpark as the medical profession, about whose exploits films keep appearing in staggering profusion, nor even in the same league as architects, whose craft—for no good reason—was recently canonized in a half-dozen films during one three-year period. Nevertheless, with the release of *Captives* and *The Dentist*, it could be safely argued that the dental profession was finally showing up on the cultural radar screen, after years of submersion in the briny depths.

And yet, despite the euphoria that dentists everywhere must have felt when word got out that such esteemed thespians as Julie Ormond and Corbin Bernsen would soon be appearing in dental roles, the release of the two films has not been an unqualified triumph for the field. In *Captives*, Ormond commits the one unforgivable sin cited in the dental catechism—falling in love with a patient who has bad teeth—and ends up conspiring with her patient to smuggle contraband into the prison. And in *The Dentist*, Bernsen plays a sadistic general practitioner so obsessed with his wife's infidelity that he subjects her to the most hideous oral surgical torture ever filmed, mutilating her lovely face beyond recognition. And this after killing his dental technician, an esteemed colleague, an IRS auditor, and even his pool man.

Thus, at the very instant that the dental profession seemed poised to enjoy its greatest cinematic triumph, victory was snatched away by the lurid and repellent elements in these two films. Just when dentists seemed ready to take their place in the sun, after too long an eclipse of Planet Periodontia by heart surgeons, trauma specialists, and even osteopaths, Hollywood saw fit to release not one but two films depicting dentists as dangerous sociopaths. And so, a profession riddled by low self-esteem, chronic drug abuse, and a terrifyingly high suicide rate once again found itself the brunt of a cruel joke.

"I couldn't sleep the night I saw *The Dentist*," says Dr. Peter Zegarelli, who happens to be my dentist in Tarrytown, N.Y. "It was one of the most disgusting pictures I've ever seen. Why do people make these things?"

As someone who has always had great respect for dentists, and most particularly for the unfailingly professional Dr. Zegarelli, I too am perplexed and infuriated by the unsavory portrayal of dentists in these two recently released films. I too would have preferred something more upbeat, perhaps a dental version of *Sling Blade* or *Shine—Forrest Gum*, if you will. And yet, one need only glance at the profession's long, unhappy celluloid history to see that this fresh serving of cinematic abuse was simply par for the course.

Ask the average person to name a movie about doctors and he'll probably cite something powerful and upbeat, like *Dr. Zhivago*. Ask the average person to name a movie about dentists, and he'll almost certainly cite *Marathon Man*, in which a completely over-the-top Laurence Olivier plays a fiendish Nazi who uses macabre dental techniques to extract information from bug-eyed Dustin Hoffman, the archetypal reluctant patient. Anyone who has seen the film will agree that Olivier's hair-raising performance is not fair to dentists. But what is most horrifying is that it may not even be fair to Nazis.

And yet, if truth be told, the negative image of dentists in motion pictures does not begin with *Marathon Man*. Almost from the industry's birth, the dental profession has been the object of derision, ridicule, and contempt, not to mention revulsion and fear. The legendary Erich von Stroheim kicked things off with his 1925 epic *Greed*, which focuses on a do-it-yourself dentist named McTeague, whose life is destroyed by a miserly wife and meddlesome bureaucrats who strip him of his livelihood because he got his degree at the University of Conestoga rather than at a real dental school.

With its grim portrayal of Wild West dental techniques, coupled with a telling scene in which McTeague smooches his future wife while she is under anesthesia, *Greed* introduces the two themes that will characterize dental films for the rest of the century. One, dentists are butchers. Two, dentists are always looking to cop a feel.

Dentists fare no better in the controversial 1932 short *The Dentist*, starring W. C. Fields. As was the case in *Greed*, Fields *qua* dentist is a complete hatchet man, mouthing inanities like, "Hand me that 404 circular buzz saw, will you?" But he is also a full-blown lecher. As he drills into a female patient's mouth, she gyrates so lasciviously—actually wrapping her legs around him—that she appears to be having an orgasm. The film caused a bit of a furor when it was released, due to outrage from dentists all across America who quite understandably objected to being portrayed as sex-crazed boobs. Alas, sixty-three years later, with the release of *Captives*, the only thing that's changed is that the sex-crazed dentist *has* boobs.

1933 saw the release of *One Sunday Afternoon*, in which Gary Cooper played a dentist tormented by the thought that he has married the wrong woman. Thus, within the space of a single year, Hollywood released one movie with a lunatic playing a dentist and a second with one of the screen's all-time nincompoops playing a self-loathing dentist. This did nothing to upgrade the image of dentistry in general. And it established a pattern that would be repeated on three other occasions, when Hollywood, after years of completely ignoring the profession, would inexplicably release two anti-dental films within scant months of each other. Coincidence, you say? Or conspiracy?

Things did not improve for dentists in the years to come. In his 1934 thriller *The Man Who Knew Too Much*, Alfred Hitchcock introduced a creepy, bespectacled dentist who was clearly in the employ of some malignant, fascist Central European government hellbent on crippling democracy. Working out of a rundown London suburb, in an office signposted by an illuminated set of choppers, the dentist first extracts a molar from a man whose tooth does not need to be extracted, then is easily overpowered by his next patient, who now masquerades as a practicing dental surgeon in order to extract vital information about his kidnapped daughter's whereabouts from the dentist's chum, the shadowy Peter Lorre. In filming this scene, Hitchcock clearly sought to devise a powerful symbol for the parlous state of British dentistry in this century. That is, in a country where the local dentist is an incompetent Nazi who hangs out with people like Peter Lorre, is it really all that surprising that the Brits are so reluctant to come in for regular checkups?

The forties were a golden age of Bad Dentist movies. In 1941 came *The Strawberry Blonde*, a remake of *One Sunday Afternoon*, starring James Cagney as a mail-order dentist who eventually goes to jail for fraud. The story, told in a series of flashbacks, gradually builds up to the climactic moment in which Cagney gets to avenge himself on the man who stole his girlfriend and railroaded him into a two-year stretch in the hoosegow. Needless to say, his vengeance is spectacularly incisive in nature.

One question that this amusing but badly flawed motion picture does not answer is why any well-heeled individual in his right mind would agree to have his teeth worked on by a man who got his dental credentials through the mail while serving a prison sentence for a crime that the patient himself had committed. Particularly after stealing the dentist's girl. Not until 1996's *The Dentist*, in which an IRS agent agrees not to prosecute Corbin Bernsen for tax fraud in exchange for free dental care will the public again be exposed to a patient with such stupefyingly poor judgment.

1941 also witnessed the release of *Footsteps in the Dark*, one of the strangest Errol Flynn movies of them all. Looking terribly out of character in a suit and tie, Flynn plays an investment banker who secretly writes mysteries under a pseudonym. Inadvertently embroiled in a murder case in which he ultimately becomes the prime suspect, Flynn locks horns with Ralph Bellamy, a murderous dentist who has concocted a complex scam with a dithering showgirl he subsequently kills off.

Notable for an unforgettable scene in which Bellamy and his

patient Flynn exchange pleasantries while smoking cigarettes in the clinic itself, this film, like its predecessors, gives voice to the public's deepest fears about the profession: These guys all seem to suffer from low self-esteem, are always on the prowl for fresh talent, and will do anything for a fast buck. Worse yet, they smoke.

In 1944, the famous director Preston Sturges made his one truly bad movie, *The Great Moment*, which chronicles the life and times of Dr. William T. G. Morton, the man who invented dental anesthesia. With Joel McCrea, the Steve Guttenberg of his time, badly miscast as a studious dental pioneer, the movie is replete with botched operations, terrified patients, highly unethical dental practices, and unbearable slapstick. Looking about as comfortable amidst his mountain of medical research textbooks as Keanu Reeves would look with the concordance to the *Complete Works of Moliere*, McCrea is a tragic, albeit shitheaded, figure who ends his career in disgrace. Once again, low self-esteem runs rampant, as witnessed by the scene where McCrea's fiancée tearfully explains to her mother that her intended hopes to become a dentist.

"Oh, and he seemed like such a nice young man," says Mother.

Again, in 1948, there were not one but two movies dominated by a dental theme. In *One Sunday Afternoon*, the third version of the vindictive dentist film first released in 1933, the flatulent Dennis Morgan reprises the Cooper-Cagney role in a film most notable because it is a musical. Needless to say, the music is very bad, as only befits a profession whose operating theater ambiance will eventually come to be intimately identified with Kenny G, Chuck Mangione, and the appalling John Tesh. Thus, in one fell swoop, this prophetic retread film achieved the unlikely hat trick of being both years behind and decades ahead of its time, while also sucking in the present.

That very same year, Bob Hope appeared as a hapless dentist in the oater comedy *The Paleface*. Early in the film, Hope is seen using a hammer on his patients while reading dentistry technique from a manual. When his patient tries to explain that he is drilling into the wrong tooth, Hope snaps: "Please, no clues, you'll spoil all the fun." As with virtually every other movie in the genre, Painless Potter is clearly a lecherous individual plagued by crippling self-revulsion. Enlivened by a great scene where Jane Russell, a holster strapped round her undies, guns down a couple of ornery varmints, *The Paleface* also includes a scene where Hope actually kisses an Indian, though not on the lips. This eerie sequence seems to suggest that forty-five years before the making of *Philadelphia*, Hollywood was on the verge of confronting the issue of onscreen homosexual activity, even if it was only in a harmless, semi-aboriginal setting. But then the studios must have gotten cold feet and pulled back.

My heavens, what a great opportunity lost!

For whatever the reason, the 1950s were a surprisingly dental-deficient era in motion pictures. Things changed abruptly in 1960 with the appearance of *Bells Are Ringing*, in which Dean Martin plays an aspiring playwright who falls in love with the woman who runs his answering service. Through the machinations of this *femme fatale*, Martin becomes involved with a singing dentist who secretly dreams of writing musicals. As is only to be expected, Dr. Joe Kitchell is an absolutely terrible dentist with horrendous taste in music. Once again, the same dominant themes take center stage: bad dentistry, low self-esteem, execrable music.

The 1960s continued lugubriously with Roger Corman's *Little Shop of Horrors*, featuring a sadistic dentist and his masochistic patient, Jack Nicholson. Dentists fared no better in such bottom-shelf offerings as *Dentist in the Chair* (wacky crime-fighting dental students), *Get on With It* (wacky dentist inventors), *The Secret Partner* (blackmailing dentist), *The Shakiest Gun in the West* (wacky Don Knotts in a deadly remake of *The Paleface*), and *Cactus Flower*, where Walter Matthau plays the jowliest dentist of them all.

Indeed, the next time that the public would be exposed to dental expertise of any note was in John Schlesinger's watershed film *Marathon Man*, released in 1976. What makes *Marathon Man* so fascinating is that it is, to my knowledge, the only film in the entire canon of dental cinema in which the dentist does not suffer from low self-esteem. Yes, Laurence Olivier plays a sadistic Nazi hiding out in South America. Yes, he is a fiendish killer. And yes, Olivier's character is a practitioner of some of the most unconventional dental procedures imaginable. But nothing in his performance suggests in even the slightest way that he suffers from any doubts about his own worth as a person or a dentist. That's one thing you have to give the Third Reich: They really knew how to make their employees feel good about themselves.

Perhaps owing to the dark shadow cast over the profession by Olivier's nauseating antics, dentistry did not resurface in any meaningful way until 1985, when Joe Mantegna played a mobbed-up dentist in *Compromising Positions*. This intermittently entertaining film, starring Susan Sarandon as a nosy housewife/reporter investigating the dentist's murder, opens with some fascinating shots inside her mouth, with Mantegna asking if she's been using unwaxed dental floss and the Water Pik. This is, as far as I can determine, the first time that flossing is ever mentioned in a film about dentists. *And doesn't that say a lot about Hollywood's idiot culture?*

Compromising Positions is permeated with the archetypal issues that have dominated dental films from the very start. According to one character, the murdered Bruce Fleckstein was "not just a dentist; he was a periodontist, he was a hotshot gum expert." According to Sarandon, he was "the Don Juan of dentists." In other words, once again, we find ourselves face to face with an ass bandit cursed by low self-esteem. The ubiquitous Edward Herrmann, playing Sarandon's husband, frames the whole self-esteem question nicely when he says, "God, I'd love to kill a dentist." Hey, who wouldn't?

The film has many fine touches: impressive diagnostics, solid drill work, several highly realistic patient-doctor exchanges. But in the end, it is the same old story: Self-loathing dentist comes to a macabre end, gutted with his own equipment. Sadly for the profession, it turns out that Bruce was taking pornographic pictures of his patients and selling them to the mob. Sarandon's big tip-off occurs when she visits Bruce's widow (the murderess) and is immediately greeted by a dog who goes right for her lap, digging straight into her crotch. I do not want to even try to imagine what horrible dental experiences the filmmakers suffered through that would prompt them to devise such a withering denunciation of the dental profession. Especially if the dog was in the room during the root canal.

Though dentists appear in supporting roles in movies as varied as *Brazil*, *Houseguest*, *Serial Mom*, *Reuben*, *Reuben*, the Rick Moranis remake of *Little Shop of Horrors*, and Pedro Aldomovar's *What Have I Done to Deserve This?* (which features a pedophile dentist who wants to adopt the female lead's teenaged boy), none of those films need concern us here. In this study, we are primarily interested in films that deal with dentistry in some substantive way, not as an incidental plot point. And films of this nature, where dentists absolutely command the spotlight, do not surface again until 1996, when both *Captives* and *The Dentist* appear.

But, as previously noted, what at first seemed like a cause for jubilation among dentists has ultimately proven to be a crushing disappointment. The very fact that the fetching Julie Ormond would even consider having an affair with a convicted murderer with bad teeth demonstrates, once again, the chronically low self-esteem that seems to bedevil the profession. And even though *Captives* contains an edifying amount of dental footage, with Ormond clearly having diligently prepared for the role, the film cannot be considered an unqualified artistic success. Because it is set in a London prison, and is therefore teeming with riffraff cursed with very bad teeth, it is almost impossible to understand any of the dialogue that does not pertain to good hygiene. What's more, the plot is a bit far-fetched. No dentist, no matter how self-loathing, who looks as good as Julie Ormond, is going to voluntarily stick her tongue inside Tim Roth's mouth. It's not just a question of hygiene. It's not even a question of sex. It's a question of dental aesthetics. You might stick your fingers inside Tim Roth's mouth, or even your nipples. But your own tongue? I can't think of any dentist who would do that.

This brings us to *The Dentist*, one of the most uncompromisingly revolting motion pictures I have ever seen. As the film opens, suburban dentist Corbin Bernsen is clearly coming apart at the seams, fatally wounded by his wife's affair with the pool man. He now sets out on a barbaric spree, gleefully drilling into his patients' gums, strangling his assistant with pantyhose stripped from a sedated female, murdering his colleague, using a weird quasi-medieval torture instrument to mutilate a hapless IRS agent, and finally extracting all of his wife's teeth before literally cutting her tongue out.

"You don't know what it's like—the discipline, the long hours, and the lack of respect in a world that goes on ignoring dental hygiene," Bernsen declares in one of his numerous jeremiads against the American public. He has a point; we don't, and for this he has earned our compassion. But when he tells a young girl he will kill her unless she promises to brush three times a day and never eat candy, he steps across the line and becomes the stuff of our collective worst nightmare: the dentist who takes his work far too seriously.

As the foregoing makes clear, dentists have never fared well on the silver screen. In fact, in a recently released movie called *Good Luck*, Hollywood's contempt extends even further down into the orally hygienic undergrowth, with Gregory Hines playing a paraplegic dental technician determined to win a white-water raft race with a blind football player as his partner. Needless to say, the film is irredeemably stupid, and casts the entire world of dentistry in an even more frivolous light.

All in all, I was feeling pretty bad about the subject of dentistry by the time I'd finished watching all these films. As a lifetime proponent of the theory that motion pictures address the American public's deepest fears, giving cinematic expression to our darkest, most hidden neuroses, it troubled me that every single movie dealing with dentists should portray them as buffoons, sadists, sex addicts, or outright charlatans.

Then, one afternoon, when I was visiting Piermont Pictures Video in suburban New York, I had a tremendously uplifting experience. Ric Pantele, the proprietor of the best video store I have ever been in, told me that Daniel Day-Lewis had once appeared in a little-known film called *Eversmile New Jersey*, which actually portrayed dentists in a positive light. And, as is always the case with this amazing little store, he had it in stock.

I rushed home to watch it, and can truly say that the next hour and a half was a revelation. *Eversmile New Jersey* deals with an evangelical Irish dentist traveling around the world on a motorcycle, spreading the word of dental consciousness. Filmed on location in South America, this dental-hygienic *Easy Rider* follows Dr. Fergus O'Connell as he wanders around the Argentine countryside, preaching the dental gospel from his fully equipped dental chopper.

Wielding his toothbrush like a scimitar, O'Connell encourages peasants to avail themselves of his expertise, declaring, "Cavities have no mercy on cowards" and "There can be no pity for bacteria and their accomplices." Inevitably, his unconventional dental approach brings him into conflict with the reactionary forces of the Argentine dental establishment, who naturally denigrate nomadic dentists, and may—the movie is not clear on this point—reserve their deepest scorn for Irish practitioners from New Jersey. This leads to the confiscation of O'Connell's passport and a sort of nervous breakdown. But in the end, as opposed to almost every other dental film I know, the hero emerges triumphant, with his dignity intact. What's more, he gets the girl.

I am not going to argue that *Eversmile New Jersey* is a great motion picture. It has far too much pennywhistle music, a bit too much footage of proper flossing procedure, a few too many arty scenes of hooker gas station attendants dressed like angels. Yet, in its respect for the practice of dentistry itself, and in its portrayal of a dentist who does not suffer from low self-esteem, it goes a long way toward redressing the imbalance caused by the leering dentalphobia of most other films in this genre.

Tragically, only those people who live close to a store with nineteen thousand videos in stock is ever likely to see this film. Everyone else out in the hinterland is doomed to go on seeing bad dentist movies forever. That's the main reason I don't live in the hinterland. If the American Dental Association had any sense, it would make millions of copies of this exceptional film and distribute them throughout dentists' offices all across America. But no, Bible Belters would probably start complaining about the hooker dressed like an angel and the sex in the shower and the fat bitch who likes to seduce roving dentists by luring them to her own private oral surgery. So forget I even suggested it. If dentists want to improve their public standing, they can't expect Hollywood to do it for them. And they certainly shouldn't hold their breath waiting for help from me. All things considered, I think essays like this just make things worse.

A FOREIGN AFFAIR

Several months ago, I suffered through *Godzilla*, the film in which the French government sets off a nuclear explosion somewhere in the South Pacific thereby making it impossible for a genetically mutated Matthew Broderick to ever act again. The same week, I gritted my teeth through *Deep Impact*, the film in which half the population of the East Coast of the United States is wiped out by a tidal wave engineered by unscrupulous hair stylists determined to make sure that the heavily banged Kewpie Doll played by Tea Leoni is really dead. Finally, a few weeks later, I sat through *Armageddon*, the film in which Bruce Willis and a bunch of unemployed oil drillers accept a temporary job on an asteroid hurtling toward Planet Earth because the Texas economy is on the ropes, the benefits in Outer Space are better, and Liv Tyler's pouting makes them anxious to leave this solar system.

Each of these movies was implacably stupid. More stupid than the usual drivel I had to watch as part of my job. In fact, the extreme discomfort I experienced watching this troika of moronic, vastly overhyped, utterly dimwitted, recrudescently American films made by complete simpletons caused me to long for an earlier, innocent time, a time before I became a film critic, a time when I would never dream of ingesting such tripe. Back in those halcyon days of yore, I would while away the days gazing at legendary films crafted by such titans as Federico Fellini, Ingmar Bergman, François Truffaut, and Rainer Werner Fassbinder. Now I whiled away the days gazing at films starring Billy Zane. Whatever had happened to that wide-eyed youth, so full of *brio, panache, joie de vivre, je ne sais quoi*? How had he allowed himself to degenerate into a middle-aged philistine, hanging around half-empty theaters every afternoon watching jerry-rigged flapdoodle like *Godzilla* and *Deep Impact*? What had happened to that personal Golden Age when he only went to see films with tiny yellow subtitles where taciturn Scandinavians played chess with Death? How had he become so lowbrow, so *crass*?

Right then and there I made a crucial decision. After ten years of writing about American movies for publications such as *Movieline*, I'd had it up to here with the repellent effluvia emanating from Hollywood like a bottomless Danube of Dung. From here on out, I was going to make a complete break with my previous movie-going habits. From this point onwards, I was only going to see foreign films, the kind of sensitive, intelligent, well-scripted, beautifully acted motion pictures that were all but extinct in Hollywood. From this moment on, I would only watch movies that spoke to the human heart, not drek like *Lethal Weapon IV* and barnyard hooey like *Doctor Dolittle*. From here to eternity, I would seek out the one, the true, and the beautiful, none of which I was likely to find in movies starring Joe Pesci. From this day onward, I was going first-class all the way.

Things did not get off to such a great start. Although the critics assured me that Pavel Chukrai's *The Thief* would steal my heart, the only thing *The Thief* stole was my money. A ponderous tale of woe set in Russia in 1952, when Josef Stalin still ruled the roost, the film chronicles the misadventures of a young woman named

Katya who falls in love with a charismatic professional thief named Tolyan. Because Katya desperately needs a husband and her adorable six-year-old boy Sanya desperately needs a father, she agrees to masquerade as the thief's wife, making it possible for them to obtain lodging in apartment houses he then pillages. But the thief turns out to be a complete monster, not unlike Josef Stalin, also a bit of a thief himself.

In fact, just to make sure that no one misses the point of the film, Tolyan has a tattoo of Stalin emblazoned on his chest. It quickly becomes obvious that *The Thief*, which involves a good deal of smoking, starvation, subarctic weather, death, unnecessary accordion-playing, and peeing in one's pants, is an indictment of Stalin, the pitiless tyrant who broke his country's heart by stealing everything he could get his hands on. Well, that and killing 65 million people.

Although I enjoy unbelievably depressing movies set in rural Russia in 1952 as much as the next guy, I cannot pretend that *The Thief* was my cup of tea. For starters, there was way too much accordion playing by chain-smoking harpies, which I've always found a bit of a turnoff. Second, I'd already read that Stalin was kind of a prick. Third, the acting was straight out of the silent film era. The *Commie* silent film era. Not to put too fine a point on it, the acting was a bit overwrought. Sure, *The Thief* was a better film than *Godzilla*, in that it posed a large number of serious philosophical questions and didn't star Matthew Broderick, but all in all I can't actually say that I *enjoyed* it. *The Thief* was not in a class with the great foreign films I'd seen as a young man; it was tedious, didactic, maudlin, and, well, grim. I sincerely hoped that my next outing would be more successful.

My next outing was actually less successful. Even though Zhang Yuan's *East Palace, West Palace* is perhaps the finest movie ever made about the plight of sexually ambivalent mainland Chinese park police caught in the throes of a struggle to maintain civic order in an environment invaded by promiscuous young homosexuals, it still basically sucked. In it, a thirty-something, ostensibly straight, park policeman working the mean bushes of Beijing arrests a good-looking young homosexual for soliciting sex with strangers and then spends the entire night interrogating the perp about his sexual predilections. The cop, needless to say, is dressed in a black leather jacket, and needless to say, the young detainee eventually confesses that one of his earliest sexual fantasies was spawned when his mother warned him: "Be good or the policeman will come and get you." Since that time, the young man has gone out of his way not to be good. Tonight could be the big payoff.

Much of what the young man has to say proves disgusting to the policeman. For instance, when he talks about being tortured by an older man who beat him with a belt and put out cigarettes on his chest, he notes: "It was unsettling, but pleasant." In the subtitles, the cop rebukes the young man with the word "despicable," but I think the term he's really looking for is "gross." As the movie progresses, it becomes clear that the Hunan House of Love has many rooms and that this Pekinese party animal has been in all of them.

Happily, the film was not as deadly serious as *The Thief*. For example, the young homosexual tells his captor that the authorities did make several attempts to cure him of his sexual affliction, eventually sending him to a hospital where he was fed food that he liked while watching straight films, but food that he hated while watching gay ones. The therapy did not work, perhaps because Taco Bell was involved. He also recalls that as a youth he fell in love with a girl named "The Bus," because "anyone could get on her." But at some point he decided to get off.

Since I had never before seen a film about the travails of sexually ambivalent mainland Chinese park police plagued by irksomely precocious young gays, I initially found the subject matter quite engrossing. But then when the cop forced his captive to get all dolled up like a hooker, complete with wig, high heels, and lipstick, I felt that the movie was careening into the realm of the obvious. I felt the same way about the obligatory Oedipal flashback where the five-year-old boy is seen sucking his mother's breast.

As the film ends, the cop realizes that he is probably gay, and very possibly the only gay Chinese park policeman on the mainland. Clearly, this could hurt his chances for promotion. He is last seen staring off into the distance, perhaps thinking: "If I'm going to stay in this line of work, I should probably think about moving to San Francisco." The director has probably had the same fleeting thought; the film was banned in China, a joke country if there ever was one.

Dialogue-wise, *East Palace, West Palace* was no great shakes, and from a technical viewpoint it was alarmingly primitive, with a camera that rarely moved, and lots of flashbacks and voice-over, the hallmarks of low-budget, indy cinema. And, as was the case in *The Thief*, there was an awful lot of smoking, though mercifully, no accordion playing.

A footnote: Although I have been a journalist for many years, I am basically a very unobservant person. So it wasn't until a chunky man sat down right next to me in a 200-seat theater that housed only fourteen or fifteen patrons that I realized that this was the first time I have ever attended a gay film. I had come to Manhattan's artsy Quad Theater expecting to see a foreign film, which usually draws a lot of old men in Greek fishermen's hats and unattractive middle-aged women carrying PBS tote bags who sometimes have to leave early because they need to get home and feed their cats, but this crowd consisted entirely of gay men who had, I suspected, come here to see a *gay*, as opposed to a *foreign*, film. So when the guy sat down right next to me in a theater filled with rows upon rows of empty seats, the bulb finally lit up.

"I'm sorry," I explained politely. "I'm just a critic."

Discreetly, he moved away.

I was sure that things were going to improve dramatically when I went to see Benoit Jacquot's *Seventh Heaven*, but here again my hopes were smashed to smithereens. *Seventh Heaven* deals with a woman who cannot have orgasms because her father died when she was only six years old and she's been unhappy ever since. Inevitably, Mathilde becomes a shoplifter to cope with her pain. One day she is caught stealing in a department store, faints, and is remanded to the custody of a mysterious hypnotist who seems to have some informal relationship with this decidedly unorthodox retail establishment. The hypnotist waltzes Mathilde off to lunch and asks her to describe the layout of her apartment. Based on her responses, he decides that she is sleeping with the bed facing in the wrong direction. In not so many words, he tells her to go home and feng shui her apartment, then return for some more hypnosis sessions, during which he feels her up while she's suspended in a deep trance, then overcharges her.

Right on the spot, Mathilde experiences her first orgasm. But when she later has a second orgasm while making love with her husband, Nico, he becomes suspicious and starts following her, convinced that she is sleeping with her hypnotist. Now, *Nico's* the one who can't have any orgasms. So he visits his own overcharging hypnotist, but the hypnotist is a dud, and things go downhill from there. Clearly, this marriage needs a lot of work.

By this point, I was starting to have second thoughts about my decision to jettison American films just because they were unbelievably dumb and starred people like Matthew Broderick. At several points in this stilted, incoherent, pretentious film, where people spend a lot of time sitting around in cafes smoking, discussing the big issues, I kept hoping that a tidal wave or an asteroid the size of Texas or a mutant reptile would burst in and pep things up a bit. I also wished the audiences were a bit more animated.

Yes, one thing that was really starting to piss me off about my film-going adventures was the comatose demeanor of the patrons. Though I'd rented a number of French, Japanese, German, and Chinese films in the past few years, I hadn't gone to the theater to see a foreign film since *Il Postino* was released in 1995.

I'd completely forgotten that for foreign-film buffs, attending these screenings was a nigh-on religious experience, where everyone sat transfixed, exhibiting no visible reaction to what was transpiring on the screen, even when the dialogue was completely ridiculous. I had forgotten that in the rarefied world of foreign films, the events transpiring on the screen were supposed to be treated with a mixture of reverence and awe, and you weren't supposed to laugh when dialogue like this appeared in the subtitles:

Unethical French Hypnotist. "You'll feel better when you've eaten."

French Kleptomaniac Who Can't Have Orgasms. "I'm not hungry."

Unethical French Hypnotist. "Neither am I. Let's go."

And this exchange:

Sleazy French Hypnotist. "Have you ever had an orgasm?"

French, Sex-Starved Klepto-Kitten. "No."

Sleazy French Hypnotist. "Waiter, some blank paper, please."

I, on the other hand, could not keep myself from laughing at such transcendent malarkey. And when I laughed, I could see that I was annoying the other patrons. These were serious film-goers, *aficionados* to a man. Or woman. No place for chuckling here, *mon vieux*.

My subsequent film-going experiences reinforced my mounting fear that I had bitten off more than I could chew. First I went to see *Western*, a road movie directed by one Manuel Poirier and set in Brittany. Although the critics assured me that this charming tale of two ne'er-do-wells searching for love in rural France would win my heart, it actually made me want to strangle somebody. To me, the essential component of a great road movie is a *road* like the one in *Rain Man* or *The Color of Money* or *Thelma and Louise*. For a road movie to work, the characters have to cover hundreds and even thousands of miles, with the very immensity of the voyage serving as a cartographic symbol of the vast emotional distance the characters have traveled. The characters can't just hitchhike fifteen kilometers farther down a country road in Brittany, a region roughly the size of my back yard. When the characters in a road movie set out down that long, lonesome highway, it's absolutely imperative that the long, lonesome highway be *long*.

There were a few other things that annoyed me about *Western*. One, there was way too much smoking. Two, the soundtrack sounded like an evil synthesis of Jim Croce and the Gipsy Kings. And don't even get me started on the accordions. Three, the director had the characters sit around the table endlessly discussing the meaning of life so the cameraman could take the next half-hour off for *cassoulet*. Once again, I found myself wishing that an asteroid or a tidal wave would suddenly sweep through Brittany and give these self-centered bohos a good kick in the pants, or, better still, kill them dead. Where the hell was Godzilla when you really needed him?

But it wasn't until I saw *The Saltmen of Tibet* that I fully realized what a fool I'd been to so cavalierly cut myself off from commercial American fare. *The Saltmen of Tibet* is a Swiss/German documentary, written and directed by Ulrike Koch, that follows a group of nomadic herdsmen and their 160-yak caravan as they trek to the sacred Himalayan lakes to gather raw salt for their assorted saline needs. Much of the conversation involves yaks.

"The other three have gone to look for the yak herd," observes one typically laconic nomadic tribesman.

"What are we to do with this poor little yak?" asks another.

For the first time since I'd embarked on my self-imposed exile from American films, I found myself fantasizing about how good Uma Thurman probably looked in that black leather cat suit. Sure, I'd heard that *The Avengers* bit the big one, that Ralph Fiennes was completely adrift in the role of John Steed, that Sean Connery ate all of the scenery that wasn't nailed down and quite a bit of the scenery that was, and that Uma, as usual, couldn't act her way out of a paper bag. But I'd just paid $8.50 to watch a movie about a dying yak and the noble yak herders who would long mourn its passing. So who was I to be choosy? Frankly, Uma was looking better and better with each passing minute.

For the sake of my own well-being, I was forced to take a few days off and think things through. In the end, I had to admit to myself that this whole foreign film thing was one huge scam. Long ago, when giants ruled the earth, foreign films were impressive technical achievements that served as a viable counterpoint to their more explicitly commercial, far less cerebral, American cousins. But most of the movies I'd been watching were cloying, technically retrograde clattertrap. They weren't *foreign movies* in the sense of *Jules and Jim* or *Aguirre: The Wrath of God*. They were, for the most part, mediocre-to-bad, low-budget movies that happened to have been made in a foreign country. There was nothing special about them. There was nothing awe-inspiring about them. They were dull. They were predictable. They sucked.

Any hopes that the Filipino film industry would bail me out were brutally shattered when I dragged myself into the Walter Reade Theater at Lincoln Center for an afternoon screening of *A New Hero* by Bagong Bayani. This 1995 docudrama concerns itself with a Filipino maid working in Singapore who is accused of murdering her best friend and the victim's little boy. A glorified student film, the movie features bad camera work, bad acting, a bad script, and a bad scene where the little boy gets drowned in a bucket of water. To make things worse, much of the dialogue is in Tagalog, with misspelled English subtitles. As usual, the thirty-five film buffs sat there spellbound, as if they were watching the second coming of 8 ½.

It was all too much.

As I staggered into the sunlight, my heart sank. Here I'd gone and told all my friends that I was through with American films, that I'd had it up to here with the rank productions of Jerry Bruckheimer and Joel Silver, that I was going to limit my cinematic fare to exquisitely crafted, intensely moving foreign movies. Inadvertently, I had condemned myself to a steady diet of films about sexually repressed Chinese park cops and lovable yak herders.

I am not the kind of person who readily admits that he has made a mistake. This is largely because I hardly ever make them. But this time, I realized that I had backed myself into a corner. The enormity of my error became clear to me when I lined up for a ticket to see *Gadjo Dilo*, the next film on my list. In this militantly charming motion picture, a young Frenchman attempts to assimilate himself into a Gypsy community in rural France. According to the *San Francisco Chronicle* blurb on the publicity stills, the film was "Wonderful. A bouyant, raw look at Gypsy culture." That was enough to put the fear of God into me. I only needed to look at those stills outside the theater and study the colorfully attired Gypsy women dancing in unison while middle-aged men in natty fedoras sawed away on their ancient violins in the background to recognize that I couldn't walk another step down this particular road, that my pathetic little experiment was over. Sadly, I drifted away from the queue and made my way back home.

For the next few days, I carefully weighed my options. Generally, I see three to four movies a week, yet five days had now passed without my venturing into a theater. Though the newspapers were trumpeting the merits of *Chambermaid on the Titanic*, a thoughtful, heart-warming romance recently imported from France, I no longer had the stomach for heart-warming foreign romances. My spirit had been broken. It was time to admit my mistake. I bathed, shaved, then hauled myself off to a local theater, queued up in what proved to be a very short line, and meekly said, "One ticket for *The Avengers*." Then I went inside.

As I'd expected, the film was atrocious. Ralph Fiennes was horrible. Sean Connery was ridiculous beyond belief. And Uma Thurman, as usual, was absent without leave. But the film was 100 percent yak-free, the dialogue was not in Tagalog, and the soundtrack did not sound like Jim Croce alchemically fused with the Gipsy Kings. Most important, Uma looked terrific in that cat suit.

So I was happy to be back in the saddle. Some men look at a glass and say that it is half-empty. Others say that it is half-filled. That's exactly the way I look at things. Some men look at the current lineup of foreign films and say, *"Viva Gadjo Dilo!"* I look at the current lineup of foreign films and say, *"No más."* Pardon my French.

DON'T TRY THIS AT HOME, PART III (1999)

Seven years ago, responding to its mission as an informal, cultural consumer-protection agency, *Movieline* magazine commissioned me to re-enact a number of inspired scenes from famous movies to see if they would work in real life. The results were profoundly disheartening. Despite my industrious efforts, I was not able to persuade a prostitute to accompany me to a business dinner and pretend to be somebody incredibly sophisticated named Vivian, the way Richard Gere did with Julia Roberts in *Pretty Woman*.

I was similarly unsuccessful in persuading women to swallow numerous unappetizing foodstuffs the way Mickey Rourke did in *9 ½ Weeks*, and had no luck landing a job as head of a prominent psychiatric institution without even coming in for an interview the way Gregory Peck did in *Spellbound*. Based on my exhaustive review of more than a dozen motion pictures, I felt it was safe to say that movies were just incredibly stupid, replete with tantalizing ploys, clever gambits, and ingenious tricks that looked great up on the screen but would never work in the real world.

"Don't Try This at Home" sent shock waves through the film industry. No sooner did it appear in print than the leading lights at the major studios ran for cover, pretending to be genuinely unaware that the plot lines in their films were so studiously implausible. Through the grapevine I learned that directives had immediately come down from on high demanding that directors and script writers start hewing more closely to the fabric of reality, and stop shooting absurd scenes where women fake orgasms in public (*When Harry Met Sally . . .*), open dead-bolt doors with credit cards (*The French Connection*), or obtain highly useful sexual advice from complete strangers (*Annie Hall*).

Yet when I embarked on a follow-up study of this facet of the cinematic arts in 1993, I was chagrined to find that improvement in this area was progressing at a glacial pace, if at all. Unlike Sharon Stone in *Sliver*, my female acquaintances were not prepared to take off their panties in public; hot candle wax did not have a stimulating aphrodisiacal effect when dripped on the genitals as it seemed to have when Madonna pulled this stunt on Willem Dafoe in *Body of Evidence;* and no matter how many times I hurtled headfirst into a tall bookcase, it was impossible to get the structure to collapse on top of me, thus taking my life, the way it clearly did to James Wilby in *Howards End*.

What's more, when I tried to recreate the scene in *White Men Can't Jump* where Woody Harrelson toasts Wesley Snipes in a game of pickup basketball, I got my ass whipped. It's not just the fact that white men can't jump; they can't dribble, they can't rebound, and they can't shoot either. In the end, I came away with the same conclusion I had reached four years earlier: Hollywood remained "a twisted dream factory, spoon-feeding the public a hopelessly skewed, transparently fake vision of reality."

In the five years since "Don't Try This at Home: The Sequel" appeared, I have held my tongue on this subject, hoping, perhaps foolishly, that my second implacable exposé would produce the results that my first attempt had so dismally failed to elicit. And for a while, it seemed that there might be a tiny glimmer of light at the end of the tunnel. Based on my extensive exposure to the industry's finest products in the years 1993–1997, it did appear that some effort had been made to invest popular films with a higher degree of verisimilitude. For example, in *Speed*, Jan De Bont faithfully captured the daily horrors of the modern transportation experience, just as *Kingpins* came pretty close to reproducing the everyday life of the modern Amish male. I also felt that Steven Spielberg had the Nazis pretty well pegged in *Schindler's List*.

But in the past year or so, it has become evident that this Golden Age of Celluloid Credibility is at an end. No matter how you cut it, people like Johnny Depp (*Donnie Brasco*) never get jobs as mobsters, psychiatrists do not take hitmen for clients the way Alan Arkin does in *Grosse Point Blank*, and die-hard Red Sox fans do not give up their tickets to Game 6 of the World Series just so they can be with some fucking girl the way Robin Williams does in *Good Will Hunting*. And in real life, guys who look as ordinary as Dermot Mulroney does in *My Best Friend's Wedding* never get to *choose* between Julia Roberts and Cameron Diaz. They get to choose between Tori Spelling and Illeana Douglas. If they're lucky.

Of course, the foregoing are merely *observations*, not hard-won truths derived from the rigorous scientific analysis that characterized the first two installments of "Don't Try This at Home." And so, if only to give Hollywood the benefit of the doubt, I decided that it was time to plunge once more into the breech and determine, with the aid of the most precise calibrating instruments available to the human intellect, to what degree contemporary films deviate from the established parameters of what laymen and clinicians alike refer to as "reality."

Titanic seemed like a good place to begin.

Whether or not *Titanic* as a whole presents a credible reenactment of the events of April 14–15, 1912, need not concern us here; personally, I didn't find the poor-little-girl-traveling-on-an-ocean-liner-with-gold-digging-mother-forcing-her-into-the-arms-of-cold-hearted-Midas-when-she-really-prefers-down-at-the-heels-scamp storyline any more believable in the King of the World's daft blockbuster than when I first watched Dyan Cannon and Walter Matthau stumble through it in *Out to Sea*. But *Titanic* contains one pivotal scene so glaring in its rupture from reality that I felt honor bound to re-enact it if only to once again warn the public: "Whatever you do, don't try this at home."

This is the scene where Leonardo DiCaprio spends eight minutes in the frigid waters of the North Atlantic blabbing away to Kate Winslet while the life force ebbs out of his spindly body. From the moment I first saw *Titanic* I knew that there was something thermally suspect about this feat of human endurance, if only because Lenny and Kate had already spent almost four minutes partially submerged in the bowels of the listing ocean liner a half-hour before the leviathan finally plunged to its icy doom, yet didn't seem to be any worse for wear. To follow that up with eight minutes fully submerged in 28-degree water was obviously stretching credibility even further. So my very first assignment was to leap into the ominous waters of the Atlantic at roughly the same time of year that the *Titanic* sank and establish:

1. How long I could stay in the water without dying.

2. How chatty I would be under the circumstances.

Here, a word about methodology. Because *Movieline* has a constricted research budget, it was not possible for me to travel 453 miles south of Newfoundland and plunge into the arctic waters where the *Titanic*'s 1,523 passengers met their fate. Instead, I decided to re-create the scene thirty yards off the shore of a New York area beach. It goes without saying that the water, though a tad nippy, would be significantly less icy than the 28-degree waters that engulfed the *Titanic* that tragic night eighty-six years ago.

What's more, I carry quite a few more pounds than the sleek Leonardo DiCaprio, and could rely on my body fat to keep me going longer than he did. It was thus entirely possible that I might last longer in the water than DiCaprio did, suggesting that his seemingly superhuman feat was within the range of possibility.

On the other hand, I have a few more years on me than the young DiCaprio, so it's possible his nervous system would outperform mine. All things considered, I decided that the assorted variables would ultimately cancel themselves out. If I could stay in the water for eight full minutes and say things like, "I don't know about you, but I intend to write a strongly worded letter to the White Star Line," it would effectively refute my critique of James Cameron's seemingly zany plot device and make me seem like a mean-spirited old coot who was simply jealous of the director's enormous success, an ornery curmudgeon who never had anything good to say about anyone, and, in a very real sense, a fucking prick. If, on the other hand, I perished in the Atlantic before the eight minutes had elapsed, it would prove to be my final legacy, the last death-defying escapade of a valiant iconoclast who had given his life in the service of the truth.

Here, I'm going to make a long story short. At 4 P.M on March 31, 1998, with the outside temperature in the low 80s due to a record-setting spring heat wave that almost certainly had something to do with all that nuclear testing they're doing up in outer space, I rambled onto a beach a few miles from my suburban Westchester, N.Y., home and got ready for a quick dip. As soon as my wife had the stopwatch ready, I plunged into the water fully clothed and tried as hard as possible to behave in a recognizably DiCaprian fashion. I reckon I was underwater for about thirty seconds before I felt my nuts starting to turn blue. Because I'm a crusty old gamer, I tried to stay submerged as long as I could, but I only lasted forty-seven seconds. At no point in my ordeal did the thought of repeating DiCaprios's assorted remarks to Kate Winslet occur to me. The only thing I thought about was how blue my nuts were turning and what a stupid way this was to earn a living.

Because I had the option of lifting myself out of the water and retreating to the safety of the beach—an option not available to DiCaprio—it is entirely possible that I simply pussied out and could have lasted another couple of minutes in the water before my nervous system started to shut down. So the question of how long I would have survived is still open to debate. What is not open to debate is this: Once a fully clothed male plunges into the water of the Atlantic in early spring, before the ocean has had time to warm up, he's not going to be thinking about love, honor, grandchildren, or ironic, post-modern epistles to the White Star Line. And he's definitely not going to be very chatty. He's going to turn blue in the face, he's going to swear an awful lot, and the last thing on his mind is going to be women. This is, to my best knowledge, the only situation a heterosexual male can place himself in where women would be the last thing on his mind

In summation, *Titanic* is pure horseshit.

Pure horseshit is precisely what I encountered in my subsequent investigation, which involved *Conspiracy Theory*, a treasure trove of stupefying scenes that will not work in real life. This is the movie where Mel Gibson plays a deranged New York cabbie who is both a menace to public safety and a garrulous conspiracy theory nut. How this would distinguish him from any other New York cab driver I have ever met is anybody's guess. Abducted by a shadowy organization that preys on deranged New York cab drivers, Gibson is bound hand and foot and locked in a basement in the deserted wing of a mental hospital previously occupied by the people who financed this movie.

Julia Roberts, playing the same likable nitwit she played in *The Pelican Brief* and *I Love Trouble*, sneaks into the hospital in search of Gibson, and eventually hears him shouting to her through the heating vents. She then follows the shouts to their source, tries to rescue the dysfunctional cabbie, and basically screws everything up, but that's a whole other story.

From my point of view, the only thing of interest here is the premise that if you are ever bound hand and foot and locked in the basement of the deserted wing of a mental hospital, a fate most movie critics fear, it will be possible for you to escape by shouting through the heating ducts at a beautiful woman who just happens to be out for a morning constitutional because there's not much happening in her career. Well, I tried it in three different buildings, including a local hospital. And it didn't work. It flat out didn't work. So if you're ever trapped and bound hand and foot in the basement of the deserted wing of a mental hospital, just lie there and hold your breath and try to take your mind off your predicament by figuring out brain twizzlers like: Why would a bunch of villains under the command of the typically over-the-top Patrick Stewart take the trouble to bind me hand and foot and lock me in the basement, but not gag me? What kinds of morons are they?

Screenwriters?

Another scene in *Conspiracy Theory* that will not work in real life is the one where Gibson, strapped into a wheelchair with his eyelids taped open, escapes from his captors by madly pedaling the wheelchair down a long corridor and then bouncing down two flights of stairs, all without sustaining serious physical injury. First off, unless you're a person who has spent a substantial amount of time in a wheelchair, you're not going to be able to escape from your captors. That's because they are not in wheelchairs, have fully working appendages, and are armed with guns. Second, as soon as you try careening down a flight of steps in a wheelchair, the device will begin to pitch forward, meaning that you'll land on your head and probably die. While it is possible to descend two flights of stairs in a wheelchair if you grab the railing with one hand and brace yourself against the wall with the other, this will seriously impede your progress and enable your pursuers to catch up with you, even if one has just had the front part of his nose bitten off like Patrick Stewart did. Actually, here I am engaging in pure speculation because while I did climb into a wheelchair and try to descend a flight of stairs, I never actually bit off the tip of anyone's nose and asked him to chase after me. Still, I think the reader will be willing to make allowances for this slight deviation from orthodox movie reenactment techniques because biting off all or part of somebody's nose is kind of gross.

Almost without exception, my attempts to reenact scenes from recent movies met with crushing failure. In *Romy and Michelle's High School Reunion*, the fetching pinheads played by Mira Sorvino and Lisa Kudrow try to pass themselves off as the inventors of Post-it notes but are humiliated when their claim is proven false. I, on the other hand, didn't have any trouble persuading people that I had invented Post-it notes, not only because I know a lot about epoxies and resin substitutes, but because people I know never really believed that I bought my gorgeous house on the money I make writing articles like this, so they were relieved to find out that my principal source of income was derived from a more conventional revenue stream.

Other reenactment attempts met with similar failure. When I called my mom and asked if I could move back in with her and try to "find myself" the way Albert Brooks did with Debbie Reynolds in *Mother*, she said, as always, that I was "a sketch." I should also point out that when Albert Brooks returned home, he found that his mother had kept all of his old trophies, posters, records, and knickknacks—in short, all his old "stuff"—in the garage. But my mom doesn't have a garage, and even if she did it's doubtful that she would have kept my old "stuff" in it. I don't think my mother has even kept any of my baby pictures.

When I asked a couple of my friends if they would re-create the premise of *The Full Monty* and strip for money, they told me to go fuck myself. Not a single one even asked how much money, and, based on what I've seen of their bodies, I was not entirely disappointed by their disinclination to participate in the experiment. And frankly, some of my friends look like they could use the money.

My friends were similarly unenthused when I suggested that a bunch of us get together and reenact the key party scene from *The Ice Storm* where suburban wives agree to sleep with the owners of whatever car keys they pull out of a basket.

"That only works if one of the women looks like Sigourney Weaver," a male friend sagely explained. "But it's a better suggestion than that *Full Monty* idea of yours. Keep trying."

I also didn't have any luck doing the one-handed pushups Demi Moore pulls off in *G.I. Jane*. Nor was I able to learn Portuguese in twenty minutes the way John Travolta did in *Phenomenon*. No, when I went to a Brazilian restaurant and tried to order my meal in the native language of Vasco da Gama after twenty minutes of full immersion in the idiom, the waiter clearly had no idea what the hell I was talking about. At this juncture, purists may complain that in the movie John Travolta inherited prodigious autodidactic skills after being knocked flat on his ass by some supernatural force, and this explains how he was able to learn Portuguese in just twenty minutes. But I think that even after being pulverized by some amazing supernatural entity, a guy like John Travolta would still have gotten a lower score on his SATs than I did, so if I couldn't learn a foreign language in twenty minutes, neither could he.

I had two other restaurant experiences worthy of note. One afternoon, I visited a trendy midtown Manhattan restaurant and ordered the waitress to clear away the silverware so I could ostentatiously eat with my plastic knife and fork just like Jack Nicholson did in *As Good as It Gets*. Unlike Jack, who is reviled by the wait-staff because of his cutlery-based idiosyncrasy, nobody in the restaurant thought my behavior the least bit odd. Instead, the waitress treated me the way she would have treated any other customer, laboriously reciting a list of house specials I had no interest in hearing.

It was more of the same when I invited a friend to lunch at the Times Square Olive Garden and began singing "I Say a Little Prayer for You." If you remember the scene in *My Best Friend's*

Wedding, once Rupert Everett begins singing the abysmal Dionne Warwick hit to Julia Roberts while they are dining in what appears to be a Red Lobster, everyone at the table immediately joins in, and shortly after that everyone in the restaurant participates in a festive rendition of the sappy chestnut.

This was not my experience. No one in the restaurant joined in when I began singing:

> The moment I wake up
> Before I put on my makeup,
> I say a little prayer for you.

Instead, they tried to ignore me. So did my friend. There was no spontaneous eruption of Warwickophilia, no sense that everybody in the restaurant had been waiting thirty years for precisely the right moment to publicly display their affection for the long-forgotten vocal stylings of a woman now best known for her affiliation with telephonic psychiatry. Instead, everybody just kept eating.

"You must do a lot of karaoke," said the waitress when she brought my food. She said this the way people used to say, "You must do a lot of coke."

I also think she thought I was gay.

On that note, I'd like to close out this essay by briefly touching on the subject of homosexuality in the movies. In *In and Out*, Kevin Kline plays a high school teacher scheduled to be married just a few days hence who is unexpectedly "outed" by a former student played by Matt Dillon. Although everyone, including Kline himself, has always assumed that he is straight, everyone, including Kline himself, now begins to suspect that he is, in fact, gay.

To settle this matter once and for all, Kline purchases an instructional audiotape which enables him to determine whether he is gay. The premise is simple: Straight men do not, will not, and cannot dance. Gay men do, will, and can. According to the voice on the tape, "Straight men work. Straight men drink. Straight men have bad backs." But they do not get down and boogie, and they never, ever get funky. Thus, if the person taking the test could successfully listen to "I Will Survive" without getting the urge to shake all or part of his booty, it would prove beyond a shadow of a doubt that he was not gay.

The scene in the movie is actually very amusing. Kline, clad in manly clothing—untucked flannel shirt, blue jeans, work boots—stands in the middle of the room and tries to resist the infectious beat of the aforementioned disco-era Gloria Gaynor hit. But gradually his fingers start a-tapping, his legs start a-thumping, his shoulders start a-swaying, and before you know it, he's a-bouncing right off the walls. The verdict is in: Kline is indisputably gay.

Here, once again, Hollywood had gotten things completely wrong. I have a wife, two kids, a Philadelphia Flyers poster, a Van Halen album, and an almost pathological dislike of Barbra Streisand. So there's no way that I'm gay. But when I put on the flannel shirt, the jeans, and the work shoes, and then cued up "I Will Survive," I immediately started dancing, just like Kevin Kline. I didn't dance well, and I didn't dance for long. But I danced. So putting a scene in a movie suggesting that men who dance are gay is like putting a scene in a movie suggesting that people who talk like John Travolta can learn Portuguese in twenty minutes. And there's another thing: If straight men can't dance, how do you explain John Travolta?

The facts are in and the conclusion is unavoidable: Once again, Hollywood is completely out to lunch. The Navy Seals are not actively recruiting people who look like Demi Moore. MIT is not giving scholarships to its janitors. Nobody in the Irish Republican Army has hair like Brad Pitt or girlfriends named Gwyneth. When all is said and done, motion picture studios continue to hornswoggle suckers by filling their films with immensely entertaining scenes that bear no relationship to events taking place in the real world.

For the third time since 1991, I had undertaken a systematic investigation of this phenomenon, and my take on things now is the same as it was then. *Fagghedaboudit.* Return to your humble farms and villages, attend to your families and 401K plans, and just dismiss from your mind whatever you saw up there on the silver screen. If you try to ride sidesaddle at full-gallop the way Judy Dench does in *Mrs. Brown*, you'll be in traction for six months. If you try to stand on the prow of an ocean liner without holding the railing, you will die. And if you're thinking about going into a lesbian bar to pick up a chick the way Ben Affleck does in *Chasing Amy*, you'd be better off leaping headfirst into the North Atlantic at two in the morning on a frigid night in April. You'll last longer, the reception will be warmer, and you'll definitely have a better chance of meeting the girl of your dreams.

INDEX